CW01500132

Acknowledgements

FIRSTLY, I would like to thank Jane at Pitch for publishing this book, and Duncan Olner for the cover design.

I would also like to thank the following people and organisations who helped in different ways and are listed in the order in which their contributions appear.

The Permanent Secretariat of the Alpine Convention kindly provided permission to reproduce the link to the map of its perimeter.

From Austria, Hans Gruber, head of the city library in Feldkirch, provided loads of invaluable material about the origins of football in his part of the world. Folke Postmeyer, vice-chairman of FC Blau-Weiß Feldkirch, very generously gave me a copy of a book documenting the history of the game in Vorarlberg.

Bettina Hurgitsch and Maria Saegebarth from Zoo Leipzig, Jonas Bittner and Benedikt Knüppe from Erlebnis-Zoo Hannover, Ramon Messinger from Zoo Vienna Schönbrunn, and the Alpenzoo Innsbruck, all provided information about the European Zoo Football Championship.

Dominik Festl, chairman of SSK Werfen's football section, answered my questions about his team and allowed me to use a photograph taken at the club's stadium. FC Bad Gastein's Alwin Wigele took the time to tell me about the incredible achievement of one of his club's youth teams.

Moving to France, Adrien Lucchino provided me with an insight into his footballing activities playing for FC Pays Voironnais as well as being a video analyst for Grenoble Foot 38 and the Haiti women's team.

In Germany, Christoph Saller, formerly a player at 1. FC Garmisch-Partenkirchen, described to me the pressure of taking a last-minute penalty to save his team from relegation.

Florian Nyer, youth leader of SV Kleinwalsertal, was incredibly helpful by providing loads of information about the history of football in his remote valley and the coaching of junior players.

Italian club FC Südtirol kindly provided permission for me to reproduce a photograph taken inside the Stadio Druso in Bolzano. The Archivio storico del Comune di Domodossola helpfully supplied details about the history of the football stadium temporarily used by ASD Virtus Villadossola.

In Liechtenstein, Fredy Wolfinger, president of FC Triesen, generously took the time to speak to me about his club, and the development of women's football in the principality, as well as providing permission to reproduce a photograph taken at the Sportanlage Blumenau. Managers of the youth hostel in Schaan, the Jugendherberge Schaan-Vaduz, kindly provided permission to use a photograph taken on their premises.

A representative of AS Monaco's media department kindly gave permission to use a photograph taken inside the Stade Louis II.

From Switzerland, Thun town councillor Alice Kropf went to a great deal of trouble to tell me about the

YODEL

WHEN YOU'RE WINNING

YODEL

WHEN YOU'RE WINNING

Football and the Alps

ALY MIR

First published by Pitch Publishing, 2025

1

Pitch Publishing
9 Donnington Park,
85 Birdham Road,
Chichester, West Sussex,
PO20 7AJ

www.pitchpublishing.co.uk
info@pitchpublishing.co.uk

© 2025, Aly Mir

A CIP catalogue record is available for this book
from the British Library.

ISBN 978 1 83680 153 5

Typesetting and origination by Pitch Publishing

Printed and bound on FSC® certified paper in line with
our continuing commitment to ethical business practices,
sustainability and the environment.

Printed and bound in India by Replika Press Pvt. Ltd.

Contents

Acknowledgements 7
Introduction 11

1. **Austria: Vorarlberg** 17
   i.   The Strange Case of the Stilts 17
   ii. Going Berserk about Leagues: FC BW
        Feldkirch, 447m/1,467ft. 23
2. **Austria: Tyrol** 30
   i.   Diamonds Aren't Forever: FC Wacker
        Innsbruck, 589m/1,932ft 30
   ii. Three Lynx on a Shirt 38
3. **Austria: Salzburg** 42
   i.   The Sound of Red Bull: FC Red Bull
        Salzburg, 430m/1,411ft 42
   ii. Spreading the Wings 55
4. **Austria: Salzburgerland** 60
   i.   Cold-Water Challenge: FC Bad Gastein,
        1,081m/3,547ft 60
   ii. Under the Castle of Eagles: SSK Werfen,
        524m/1,719ft. 68
5. **France** 72
   i.   Money Doesn't Grow on Trees: Grenoble Foot
        38, 217m/712ft. 73
   ii. Footy and the Chocolate Factory: FC Pays
        Voironnais, 305m/1,001ft 80
6. **Germany: Bavaria** 89
   i.   Knees like Pudding: 1. FC Garmisch-
        Partenkirchen, 704m/2,310ft 90
   ii. From Villa Bader to Bad Villain. 100
7. **Germany and Austria: Junior Football** 103
   i.   Primary Objective 103
   ii. Mini Football in the Little Valley: SV
        Kleinwalsertal, 1,108m/3,635ft 108
   iii. Off the Hook: TSV Fischen, 760m/2,493ft. . . 118

8. Italy 123
  i. Where Am I? FC Südtirol, 261m/856ft. 123
  ii. Patience is a Virtue: ASD Virtus Villadossola,
      281m/922ft 132
9. Liechtenstein: Women's Football 140
  i. Women on the Ball 141
  ii. Football is Female: FC Triesen, 466m/1,529ft . 144
10. Monaco 154
  i. Just Short of Football's Summit: AS Monaco,
     21m/69ft 155
  ii. Coppa delle Alpi 168
11. Slovenia 170
  i. The Gloves are Off: NK Škofja Loka,
     340m/1,115ft 171
  ii. *Poplava*: Football and the Alpine Environment . 182
12. Switzerland: Bernese Oberland 190
  i. From the Cowshed to Highbury: FC Thun,
     569m/1,867ft. 191
  ii. Spirit of Spiez 209
13. Switzerland: Fan Scenes 213
14. Switzerland: Valais 227
  i. Football's Officer Class 227
  ii. The Impossible Stadium: FC Isérables,
      1,030m/3,379ft 231
15. Switzerland: Mountain Village Football 243
  i. Hiking up to Europe's Highest Football Stadium 243
  ii. Can You Hear the Balfrin Sing? FC Gspon,
      1,923m/6,309ft 247
  iii. (Not Quite) As Old as the Hills 257
16. Champions from the Foothills 262
17. Football and Altitude 270
18. Conclusion 279

Appendix: List of Matches Involving Alpine Teams . 282
Bibliography 284

controversies involving ultras and the local authorities in her part of the Bernese Oberland. Kevin Crettenand and Gérard Favre were very helpful showing me around their 'impossible stadium' at FC Isèrables, as well as supplying lots of information about the story of its construction and allowing me to use a photograph taken during one of the team's games. None of this could have happened without Alain Mermoud, director of VS Fruits, pointing me in the direction of that village perched above the Rhône. I am also grateful for the assistance provided by Marcel Blumenthal about the football veterans' tournament in Valais. Helpful information about local football was provided by both the Valais Football Association and the East Switzerland Football Association. FC Gspon kindly gave me permission to reproduce photographs taken at Europe's highest permanent football stadium.

Last but not least, my wife Josie accompanied me on all the trips to the Alps and was particularly helpful with her knowledge of various foreign languages, as well as taking ten of the photographs which appear in the book. I took the others myself.

ALPINE REGION
MATCH LOCATIONS

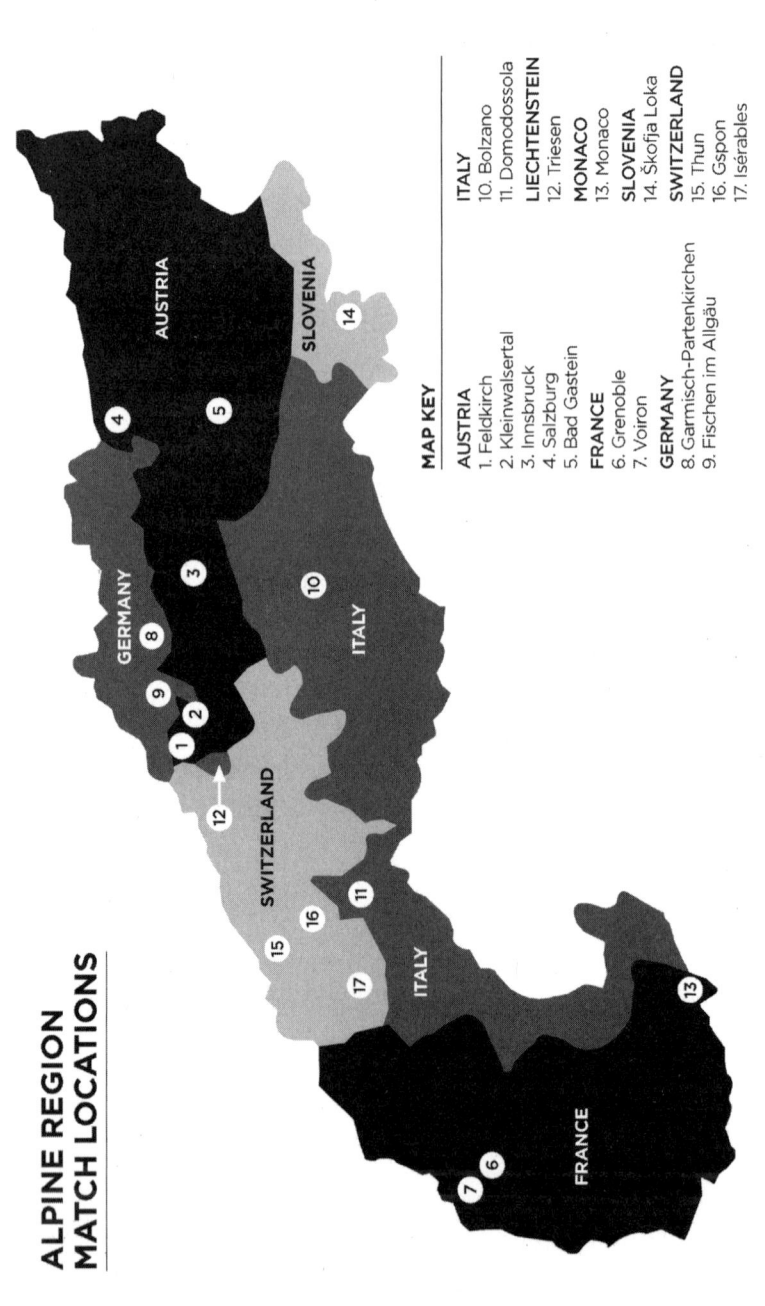

MAP KEY

AUSTRIA
1. Feldkirch
2. Kleinwalsertal
3. Innsbruck
4. Salzburg
5. Bad Gastein

FRANCE
6. Grenoble
7. Voiron

GERMANY
8. Garmisch-Partenkirchen
9. Fischen im Allgäu

ITALY
10. Bolzano
11. Domodossola

LIECHTENSTEIN
12. Triesen

MONACO
13. Monaco

SLOVENIA
14. Škofja Loka

SWITZERLAND
15. Thun
16. Gspon
17. Isérables

Introduction

CHOCOLATE-BOX VILLAGES, picture-postcard lakes or snow-capped mountains are how many people see the Alps, and if asked about sport there, most would think of skiing. Like a lot of stereotypes, they contain an element of truth; however, not everyone in the Alpine region lives in a flower-decked chalet, and as for sport, arguably the biggest in terms of the number of all-year-round participants is football.

The majority of towns and large villages around the Alps have their own football clubs, including some that have made important contributions to the story of the beautiful game, told in the pages that follow.

I stumbled across my first Alpine football match purely by chance during a summer hiking holiday in 2002. Until then, I'd developed an interest in overseas football, but only pursued it through weekend breaks in cities like Rome or Madrid rather than the Alps. However, after a 12-hour ascent and descent of a peak in the Bernese Oberland, my sore feet demanded a rest, so I went to a nearby match to recuperate. Although I'd never heard of the home team, the game turned out to be a six-goal thriller. Over 20 years later, I decided to write about my experiences attending football matches involving Alpine teams, ranging from Champions League down to amateur village level.

Like my first publication, *Ten Big Ears: An Alternative Account of FC Barcelona in Europe*, this book provides a mainly eyewitness account. Such an approach skews the coverage towards what I have seen, featuring snapshots of certain football teams, games, and players that are perhaps not so well known, but frequently provide a more interesting, even quirky, perspective. Counting a one-day veterans' tournament as a single event, a total of 25 fixtures are described from direct personal observation.

What do we mean by Alps? The word comes from the Latin word *Alpe*, possibly derived from *Albus* meaning 'white', alluding to the snow-capped peaks which are the highest in western Europe. These mountains formed over millions of years when tectonic plates collided, followed by glacial erosion and other weathering creating the peaks and valleys visible today.

For centuries, mountain ranges like the Alps were seen as desolate places, blots on the landscape, barriers to travel, and even the abode of fearsome monsters. Things began to change during the 18th and 19th centuries, when Romantic poets and artists celebrated the natural beauty of the mountains. Later, the Alps became appreciated for their clean air and water, as healthy alternatives to the pollution of the cities, and finally as destinations for tourism and recreation.

Technically, the term 'Alps' doesn't refer to the summits or range of mountains, but to high meadows and pastures. Such places first came to the notice of many outsiders as the home of Heidi, the character in the 19th-century children's story written by Joanna Spyri. Strictly speaking, only the three events hosted by FC Gspon in this account were actually played on or adjacent to high pastures and therefore qualify as Alpine. This partly explains why I have subtitled this book *Football and the Alps* rather than *Football in the Alps*. However, for the most part, I have used the term 'Alps' in the way that many people understand it, to describe not just pastures and meadows, or peaks and mountain ranges, but parts of the surrounding region as well. To help decide which villages, towns, cities and football clubs should be included, I have used the official perimeter of the Alpine Convention as my guide. I am grateful to the Permanent Secretariat of the Alpine Convention for permission to include the link in this book.[1]

Formed in the early 1990s, the Alpine Convention is the first international treaty aiming to promote the sustainable development and environmental care of an entire mountain range. The convention's perimeter stretches for a length of approximately 1,200km/745 miles, with a maximum width of about 300km/185 miles, including parts of Austria, France, Germany, Italy, Slovenia and Switzerland, plus all of the principalities of Liechtenstein and Monaco. Occasionally, the text refers to a location being 'within the Alpine region', indicating that a place is inside the convention's perimeter; however, a description like 'near the Alpine region' would mean it's just outside the perimeter.

While on the subject of geography, settlements are frequently described differently in the eight Alpine countries and often called 'municipalities' or 'communes', terms which are not very meaningful in the UK. Instead, I have decided to refer to places with up to and including 500 inhabitants as hamlets; villages contain over 500 and up to 2,500 residents; built-up areas with more than 2,500 people are towns, until passing 100,000 when they become cities.

---

1   Visit tinyurl.com/Yodel01

Football teams from all eight Alpine countries feature in the book in alphabetical order, with the exception of the Austrian valley of Kleinwalsertal which appears alongside Germany because it features in a joint chapter about junior football.

The book does not include all the matches I have seen in the Alps, nor is it intended to provide full coverage or a complete history of the game in all eight countries. Instead, it is designed to be a taster and general overview of the sport in the Alpine region. As well as the men's game, women's, junior, veterans' and mountain village football all receive the eyewitness treatment.

An examination of how freak weather caused devastation at a Slovenian football club is used to look at the hugely important subjects of climate change, sustainability and the sport's impact on the environment.

The book considers the supporter scene, something often ignored in sporting publications, with a town in the Bernese Oberland providing the surprising location for a case study of fan culture.

Also included are descriptions of hiking up to the continent's highest permanent football stadium, as well as walking by the site of the highest matches played in Europe on a glacier. In the book, altitude will usually be shown in both metres and feet (for the benefit of all generations and nationalities). The height of each Alpine club's stadium is shown in the title of the relevant part of the book. All altitudes are measured at pitch level, rather than up in the grandstands, because it is the height the footballers perform at that is of most significance. One chapter in the book is dedicated to the impact of altitude on footballing performance.

Several players born in the Alps have won both of football's top honours: the FIFA World Cup and the

European Cup/UEFA Champions League. Short profiles of these footballers, including eyewitness accounts of times I saw them play, are included in a chapter towards the end of the book.

Above all, *Yodel When You're Winning* is about seeing the beautiful game in beautiful places.

Aly Mir, March 2025

Chapter 1

Austria: Vorarlberg

ALTHOUGH THE majority of Austrian territory is within the Alpine region, some of the most northern and eastern parts are outside, including the country's three largest cities: Vienna, Graz and Linz. The following four chapters feature matches involving clubs based in the Alps, from the states of Vorarlberg, Tyrol and Salzburg.

i. The Strange Case of the Stilts

The precise origins of Austrian football are disputed. Some histories argue that the sport arrived when a match took place in Vienna in 1894, encouraged by English employees of UK businesses operating in the Austrian capital. Other accounts refer to a game played a few months earlier in Graz, organised by a German medical student after acquiring an interest in football while studying in Prague. However, in the spring of 2024, I investigated the claim of a little-known town in Vorarlberg called Feldkirch.

The most western town in Austria, Feldkirch is the second-biggest settlement in the state of Vorarlberg with a population of nearly 35,000. Feldkirch's medieval centre has been beautifully preserved, with its Schattenburg castle containing the local museum and offering fine views of the area.

The name Feldkirch literally translates as 'field church', which is highly appropriate given that the playing field of a Jesuit-run school in part of the town known as Reichenfeld may have been the site of the first football games, not only in Austria but in the entire Alpine region. How a Jesuit school could have hosted the introduction of football to the Alps seems puzzling; but who better to help solve a mystery than the man behind Sherlock Holmes?

Just over a decade before inventing the most famous detective in history, the author Arthur (later Sir Arthur) Conan Doyle arrived in Feldkirch to enrol in a school called the Stella Matutina (Latin for 'Morning Star').

Officially known as the Society of Jesus, the Jesuit Order was set up in the 16th century to promote Roman Catholicism during the Protestant Reformation. Jesuits put particular emphasis on educational and cultural activities; one example being the Stella Matutina founded in Feldkirch in 1856. Having already studied at a Jesuit college in his Scottish homeland, Conan Doyle travelled to Feldkirch in September 1875 as a 16-year-old boy to extend his education and acquire fluency in German.

While the fictional character Sherlock Holmes had no interest in team games, Conan Doyle loved them. His many sporting experiences included playing amateur football in the 1880s for Portsmouth Association Football Club, a predecessor of the famous Pompey.

The Swiss newspaper *St Galler Tagblatt* credits Conan Doyle with being one of the students from the UK who brought football to Feldkirch, 'Sir Arthur Conan Doyle, inventor of the master detective Sherlock Holmes, was also a pupil; one of around 130 students from England, Scotland and Ireland who went to school in Feldkirch. They brought a newfangled sport with them to Vorarlberg: football.'[2]

Hans Gruber, a former pupil at the Stella Matutina who is now head of the local library in Feldkirch, was extremely helpful with my research, telling me, 'There were no games in a league or anything like that, but only internally within the boarding school.'

Philipp Schöbi's 2009 *Der Standard* article, 'Sherlock Holmes an der Stella Matutina' ('Sherlock Holmes at the Stella Matutina'), explains that in November 1875, two months after arriving in Feldkirch, Conan Doyle published several of his poems in a school newspaper that he edited; one of them entitled *A Football Match*. The same article refers to a letter that Conan Doyle wrote to his mother in March 1876, describing the sporting activities he took part in at the school; together with hiking, tobogganing and ice skating, he listed football. Two months later, another letter home detailed his daily routine which involved playing football for an hour at the end of the afternoon. Conan Doyle described those football games as 'wild' and 'uncivilised', partly because the boys had usually been drinking beer and wine beforehand.

An official history of the Vorarlberg Football Association, titled *Vorarlberger Fußballgeschichte*, reports, 'The cradle of the modern game of football is in England, in Vorarlberg it is in Feldkirch … The Jesuit college Stella Matutina, founded in 1856, had an excellent reputation as a private high school and educational institution throughout Europe and also accommodated students from England, the motherland of football. They were allowed to play

---

2 Visit https://tinyurl.com/Yodel02 for the full article.

football next to the institution and some priests are said to have competed with the students in long gowns.'

The town's modern-day football club, FC Blau-Weiß Feldkirch, proudly claims on its website, 'The history of football in Feldkirch is over 140 years old. In 1874, the Stella Matutina private high school, run by Jesuit priests, accommodated students from England who played football in Reichenfeld in their free time.'

However, was this football as we know it? Conan Doyle also referred to a game called *Fußball auf Stelz* ('football on stilts'), also known as *Stelzenspiel* ('stilts game'), which involved the boys moving around on wooden stilts and using them to knock the ball. Highly dangerous, with frequent injuries caused by participants falling off the stilts or being struck by them, the stilts games were played because shortage of space denied them room for a proper football pitch. These stilts games were extremely popular with the pupils, and only banned by the school when suitable space was found in 1877 for a larger playing surface.

By then, Conan Doyle had left Stella Matutina, having ended his one-year spell at the school in June 1876. The young Scotsman's departure from Feldkirch deprives us of further clarification from his letters and memoirs about whether the 'football match' and the 'football on stilts' he referred to were one and the same thing, or two entirely different games that co-existed at the school until the stilts were banned.

Either way, after the ban on 'football on stilts', the pupils devoted themselves to a sport bearing more resemblance to modern football; making 1877 the latest possible starting date for the game in Feldkirch.

However, according to another document, 'Spiel und Sport am Jesuitenkolleg Stella Matutina in Feldkirch'

('Games and Sports at the Jesuit College Stella Matutina in Feldkirch') by Alois Koch, the version of football that took over at the school allowed outfield players to touch the ball with their fists.[3]

For many people, such handling of the ball simply isn't compatible with association football. However, it's worth remembering that the original rules of the game, codified in London at the meeting which established the Football Association in 1863, allowed outfield players to catch the ball, although they couldn't run while holding it; only in 1870 was handling of the ball banned (except for goalkeepers and taking throw-ins).

The Österreichischer Fußball-Bund (Austrian Football Association or ÖFB) was set up in 1904, and three years later the first football club in Vorarlberg appeared in the town of Lustenau. By that time, Vienna had become the centre of Austrian football, with the capital city developing its own professional league which operated separately from the rest of the country.

After ending up on the losing side in the First World War, Austria's Habsburg Empire collapsed and it emerged as a distinct but much smaller country. Despite its reduced size, Austria became one of the world's strongest football nations in the 1930s. Coached by Hugo Meisl, Austria developed a new style of play based more on skilful and clever use of the ball, rather than running or physical strength, earning the title *Das Wunderteam* ('The Miracle Team'). Sadly, Meisl's death in 1937, and the following year's *Anschluss*, which saw

---

3   Alois Koch, 'Spiel und Sport am Jesuitenkolleg Stella Matutina in Feldkirch', published in Schwank, W., (ed.), *Begegnung. Schriftenreihe zur Geschichte der Beziehung zwischen Christentum und Sport*, Volume 4 (Aachen, 2003)

Austria being swallowed up by Nazi Germany, brought an end to the miracle.

The *Anschluss* also led to the closure of the Stella Matutina in 1938, because of Hitler's opposition to the Jesuits, or indeed any group outside his control. After the Third Reich's defeat in the Second World War, Austria regained its independence and the Stella Matutina reopened. From 1966, the Jesuit school had a football team called Kolleg Stella Matutina Feldkirch affiliated to the Vorarlberg Football Association. The team lasted until 1979 when the school finally closed for good.

These days, the building that housed the Stella Matutina at Reichenfeldgasse 9 still stands, but is occupied by a prestigious music school. During my visit to Feldkirch in April 2024, I was pleased to find that much of this imposing building has been preserved, part of the rebranding of Reichenfeld as a cultural quarter. As I walked around on an unusually hot day, the sound of musicians rehearsing inside could be heard through the open windows. The music students regularly perform recitals open to the general public, and as unwitting homage to the schoolboys' drunken football games these occasionally feature works by Johannes Brahms and Franz Liszt.

So, should Feldkirch be regarded as the birthplace of football in Austria, or even the whole Alpine region?

Sherlock Holmes's famous method involved examining all the facts and evidence, then after eliminating the impossible what remains has to be the truth, however improbable it may seem. Using the perimeter of the Alpine Convention to define the Alpine region, Vienna and Graz are just outside, as are Swiss clubs FC St Gallen (formed in 1879) and the now defunct Lausanne Football and Cricket Club (founded in 1860) which are also frequently cited as footballing pioneers. After those four have been ruled out on geographical grounds, Feldkirch is left as a possible candidate. Later chapters of this book will look at the origins of football elsewhere in the Alps, but I have yet to discover another place actually within the Alpine region where the sport started as early as the 1870s.

The remaining point of contention concerns handling of the ball. The boys at Stella Matutina were only seven years, at the very most, behind the Football Association's rule change in 1870 banning handball. With news travelling by snail mail or word of mouth in those days, it seems harsh to deny that they were playing a form of football. To paraphrase Sherlock Holmes, although time is normally of the essence, the game was indeed afoot.

ii. Going Berserk about Leagues: FC BW Feldkirch, 447m/1,467ft

Nearly half a century after students at Stella Matutina first kicked a ball, a local football association was formed in Vorarlberg in 1920, a couple of years after the end of the First World War. Football teams were subsequently established in Feldkirch by three clubs: Sportverein Feldkirch (Feldkirch Sports Club) in 1921; Arbeiter-Turn-Verein Feldkirch (Workers' Gymnastics Club Feldkirch) in 1923; and the Turnerbund Feldkirch (Feldkirch Gymnastics Club) in 1929.

Following the Third Reich's defeat in the Second World War, Vorarlberg became part of the French occupation zone, a situation that lasted from 1945 until 1955. Feldkirch's three football teams decided to merge a few months after the end of the war and set up a new club called FC Blau-Weiß Feldkirch (FC Blue and White

Feldkirch). Named after the team's colours, the club is usually known as FC BW Feldkirch or just BW.

German-speaking football fans often refer to an *Aufzugsverein* ('elevator club'), meaning one that regularly moves up and down through the different divisions; the English equivalent is 'yo-yo', after the toy on a string. BW turned out to be one such team, and having initially participated in the local Landesliga, it bobbed up and down between that tier and the higher Arlbergliga and its replacement the Regionalliga all through the 1950s and 1960s.

Arguably the biggest achievement for Feldkirch footballers came in 1970/71 when a second-placed finish in the Regionalliga meant they nearly won promotion to the Nationalliga (then Austria's top division).

After the formation of the Austrian Bundesliga in 1974, reorganisations of the league structure bumped BW down to the third and then the fourth tier, with the team spending most subsequent seasons competing in either one or the other of those levels.

Getting to grips with the structure of football leagues in foreign countries can often be difficult; not helped by reorganisations, the addition of new tiers, rebrandings and sometimes multiple names for the same division. This book includes my interpretation of the football pyramid for each of the main six Alpine countries; however, in the case of Austria, by the time I reached the seventh-tier Bezirksliga I had nearly gone berserk about leagues! These days, the structure looks like this, with some of the leagues that are mentioned in the next few chapters specifically listed:

1. Austrian Bundesliga
2. 2. Liga

3. Regionalliga (including Eliteliga Vorarlberg and Regionalliga Tirol)
4. State leagues (including Vorarlbergliga, Tiroler Liga and Salzburg Liga)
5. Landesliga
6. Local divisions (including Gebietsliga in Tyrol, 2. Landesliga in Salzburg)
7. Local divisions (including Bezirksliga in Tyrol, 1. Klasse in Salzburg)
8. Local divisions (including 1. Klasse in Tyrol, 2. Klasse in Salzburg)

The BW match I attended during the 2023/24 season was a Vorarlbergliga fixture on the fourth tier of Austrian football.

BW's Waldstadion is located north of the town centre in the suburb of Gisingen. Waldstadion means 'Forest Stadium', but there aren't many trees there these days; instead, the little football ground is situated on the outskirts of Feldkirch next to industrial units and the River Ill, a tributary of the Rhine.

As I arrived at the entrance of the Waldstadion, I met two board members of FC BW Feldkirch: Folke Postmeyer, the vice-chairman, and Wolfgang Strauss, who deals with club administration. After talking to them about my interest in Alpine football and the Stella Matutina's role in bringing the sport to the region, they very kindly gave me a copy of a book called *Vorarlberger Fußballgeschichte* ('Vorarlberg Football History'), a volume so huge it threatened to impede the take-off of my return flight to Gatwick.

Anybody doubting the significance of football in the Alps should take a look at *Vorarlberger Fußballgeschichte*. Published to commemorate the centenary of the Vorarlberger

Fußballverband (Vorarlberg Football Association) in 2020, the book lovingly documents the history of football in the state since those first kickabouts at the Stella Matutina. More than 600 beautifully illustrated pages are filled with league tables, photographs of players and stadiums and newspaper cuttings, making it more like a work of art than a mere sporting history.

Originally built in 1952, the Waldstadion was refurbished in 2005. The football ground consists of a natural grass pitch, surrounded by an athletics track, with an impressive grandstand along one of the sides covered by a new wooden roof. From my seat in the grandstand, the foothills of the Bregenzerwaldgebirge (Bregenz Forest Mountains) faced me, while immediately behind the goal to the right stood the rather less picturesque, but in its own way no less Alpine, Vorarlberg Milch dairy plant.

Kicking off at 5pm on Saturday, 13 April 2024, the match saw BW face Sportverein Frastanz who had travelled from a market town of that name, slightly to the south-east of Feldkirch and also within the Alpine region. With only just over 6,000 inhabitants, the town of Frastanz is much smaller than Feldkirch. Frastanz is best known for its brewery which produces the excellent Frastanzer beer, ironically on sale from the bars in the Waldstadion. According to some accounts, SV Frastanz was formed in 1946, although the club displays the previous year on its badge. For much of its history, SV Frastanz has competed in leagues slightly below BW.

Before the match, BW stood top of the table, with the visitors fifth, after 15 rounds of matches. A few minutes before kick-off, the two teams came out on to the pitch, with BW in light-blue shirts with white sleeves, white shorts and socks, while the visitors wore their usual kit of all green.

The match was refereed by Fabienne Hofer, making it the first men's football match I had seen with a woman as the senior match official. Coming from the town of Höchst in the north-west of Vorarlberg, Hofer had formerly been a midfielder with FFC Vorderland in the top division of Austrian women's football. Hofer combined her playing career with refereeing for several seasons before deciding in 2022 to concentrate on officiating.

Interestingly, this part of the world is ahead of the game when it comes to female referees. Back in the 1930s, a Viennese woman called Edith Klinger became an ÖFB-qualified referee and officiated at both men's and women's games. More recently, Nicole Petignat from neighbouring Switzerland became the first woman to referee a men's club match in UEFA competition when she officiated at the UEFA Cup fixture between AIK Solna and Fylkir in 2003. By comparison, it wasn't until as recently as 2023 that the first English Premier League fixture was refereed by a woman, when Rebecca Welch officiated at a fixture between Fulham and Burnley.

Previewing the game, the BW website described the rivalry between the teams as an '*emotionsgeladenen, brisanten Nachbarschaftsduell*' ('emotionally charged, explosive neighbourhood duel') because of the proximity of the two towns which makes the fixture a local derby.

Unfortunately, the first half turned out to be anything but explosive. The defenders on both sides looked much stronger than the opposing attackers, moves broke down as they entered the final third and any long balls were easily intercepted. A crowd of 633 people attended the game, with most of them occupying seats in the grandstand, including some Frastanz supporters wearing green replica shirts. The two sets of fans sat happily next to each other, but the sedate atmosphere in the stadium, combined with the stalemate on the pitch, made the club's preview seem a wild exaggeration.

Twenty minutes into the second half, the visitors made their first major defensive error, enabling BW's Adrian Hoti to burst through and shoot past the keeper into the corner of the goal. Born in Switzerland, it was the 21-year-old striker's first season at Feldkirch, having previously played for Vaduz and Balzers in Liechtenstein. Hoti milked the applause from the crowd, which seemed fair enough given that he scored his goal at the end by the dairy factory.

Six minutes from time, BW had the chance to secure all the points. Alen Mahmutovic attacked down the left and crossed the ball for David Schnellrieder; however, the striker lived up to part of his surname, acting too hastily and blasting a shot over the crossbar when he had time to show a little more composure, with only the keeper to beat.

Up until then, Frastanz had made hardly any attempts on goal, but BW spurning an easy chance to sew things up seemed to encourage the visitors. With three minutes left, a Frastanz corner led to Attebe Koudou firing a shot which the Feldkirch goalkeeper Jovan Petrovic punched clear. In the first minute of stoppage time, the inevitable happened. Another Frastanz corner was again met by Koudou, but this time the player from the Ivory Coast headed the ball in at the far post for the equaliser. Only then did it become clear from the cheering in the grandstand that about a third of the crowd were from Frastanz.

Having played rather casually for the last 25 minutes, the Feldkirch players were now desperate to regain their lead and the two points that were slipping away. A BW attack ended with a shot hitting the post. Feldkirch's defender Ansumana Njie then appeared to strike a Frastanz player before falling to the ground, pretending that he was the one who had been fouled. The referee flourished a second yellow card for Njie, causing him to be sent off. Another foul a couple of minutes later sparked a mass brawl in the centre of the pitch, with some of the players exchanging punches. Many of the spectators, who until then had stayed calm, immediately shouted encouragement to their players as they piled in. Hofer waited until she had restored order before producing a straight red card for Feldkirch's midfielder Yavuz Bal. According to the ÖFB's website, it was the ninth straight red that Hofer had issued since becoming a referee.

Feldkirch played the final moments with only nine men, and the contest finished in a 1-1 draw. A slow burner, the game picked up considerably in the second half, providing good value for the entrance fee of only €2.50. Overall, I thought Hofer refereed the match well and did her best to allow the game to flow. Two sendings off and a brawl confirmed that the game was indeed an 'explosive neighbourhood duel'. As the BW players trudged off the pitch, still being top of the Vorarlbergliga provided their only consolation.

At the conclusion of the 2023/24 season, BW finished top of the Vorarlbergliga while SV Frastanz came fourth. BW's success earned the team promotion to the Eliteliga Vorarlberg. Some sources describe the Eliteliga Vorarlberg as occupying the third tier of the Austrian football league system offering the opportunity for direct promotion to the 2. Liga. Others claim that the winner of that division merely moves sideways to the Regionalliga West, making it a kind of tier three and a half, while a third version claims that it is on the fourth tier. See what I mean about going berserk about leagues!

Chapter 2

Austria: Tyrol

TO THE east of Vorarlberg, the state of Tyrol possesses some of the most mountainous terrain in Austria, occupying a stretch of land squeezed between Bavaria to the north and Italy to the south. Tyrol is referred to as 'Tirol' by German speakers, but I shall use the English spelling unless writing about the names of football clubs or leagues.

i. Diamonds Aren't Forever: FC Wacker Innsbruck, 589m/1,932ft

Originally a crossing point over the River Inn, Innsbruck's name literally means 'Inn's bridge'. At one time the official seat of the Habsburg Imperial Court before being replaced by Vienna, Innsbruck's Old Town contains a mixture of Baroque and Gothic architecture, with the whole city surrounded by Alpine peaks. Today, Innsbruck is home to about 130,000 people, making it the fifth-largest settlement in Austria. The city is the capital of Tyrol and since 2003 has hosted the Permanent Secretariat of the Alpine Convention.

In sporting terms, Innsbruck is best known for twice hosting the Winter Olympics. Probably the most famous event at these games was Franz Klammer spectacularly winning gold in the men's downhill in 1976, skiing down the slopes of the nearby Patscherkofel at an average speed of over 100km/62mph. Sadly, the city's football club has gone downhill almost as fast on more than one occasion in recent times.

Football arrived in Innsbruck in the first years of the 20th century, although FC Wacker Innsbruck didn't appear on the scene until 1913 or 1914 (the exact date is disputed). The club's name is often shortened to FC Wacker, the word *Wacker* being German for 'brave'. To begin with, the team played friendly matches, but these soon ground to a halt because of the First World War.

After the end of hostilities, a local Tyrol football association was established in 1919, soon followed by FC Wacker playing its first competitive local league games. Following the *Anschluss* of 1938, the Nazis took over the local football associations and reformed the leagues. For the first few years of the Second World War football continued, but it eventually petered out as the Third Reich's military situation deteriorated. In May 1945, American troops entered Innsbruck, although like Feldkirch, the city soon found itself located inside the French occupation zone.

In 1949, the Staatsliga, forerunner of today's Austrian Bundesliga, was formed, enabling teams from all over the country, not just Vienna, to play at the highest level. After FC Wacker resumed competition, a hard climb up the leagues culminated in 1964 when the club secured promotion to the Staatsliga. This success made FC Wacker the first club from Tyrol to reach the top tier of the country's football league pyramid.

In 1970, FC Wacker won Austria's version of the FA Cup, qualifying for UEFA's European Cup Winners' Cup.

After overcoming Albania's Partisan Tirana, FC Wacker came up against mighty Real Madrid in the second round. The little Tyrolean team sensationally beat Real 1-0 at the Bernabéu, but the Spaniards won the second leg 2-0 in front of a packed crowd in Innsbruck to progress on aggregate. Undaunted, FC Wacker ended the 1970/71 season by winning its first Austrian national league championship, dramatically clinching the title in the last game of the season.

At that moment of great success, FC Wacker might have expected to kick on to further glories; instead, the summer of 1971 saw the club engulfed by financial problems. To try and escape these money worries, FC Wacker merged with another club and changed its identity; a pattern of behaviour that would become all too familiar in future years.

In German-speaking countries, it is common for two or more football teams to merge and form a *Spielgemeinschaft* (literally 'game community' often abbreviated to SG) when they are not strong enough to compete separately. FC Wacker did this by hooking up with WSG Wattens, a club from a small town about 13km/8 miles to the east.

The town of Wattens is the home of Swarovski, which provided financial backing for the combined club. Founded in the 1890s by Daniel Swarovski, the company became a famous luxury brand, producing crystal glass and jewellery, including necklaces, bracelets, rings and earrings made from gold, diamonds and other precious materials.

The merged team's official title of Spielgemeinschaft Swarovski Wacker Innsbruck-Spielgemeinschaft FC Wacker Innsbruck-Werksportgemeinschaft Wattens consisted of 105 characters. Mercifully, the team competed under the first part of the joint name and usually abbreviated it to SSW Innsbruck, winning four more Austrian Bundesliga titles before the end of the decade.

In 1986, a new club took over the Bundesliga licence of the Innsbruck team. Known as FC Swarovski Tirol, the club not only had yet another change of name, but its green colours were replaced by blue and white. The club also had a new president, Gernot Langes-Swarovski, the great-grandson of Daniel Swarovski and a big football fan.

FC Swarovski Tirol's first season included a fantastic run in the 1986/87 UEFA Cup, beating Bulgaria's CSKA Sofia, Standard Liège from Belgium, Russian side Spartak Moscow, and Italy's Torino, before losing to Swedish side IFK Göteborg in the semi-final. Gernot Langes-Swarovski then hired the famous coach Ernst Happel and proceeded to win a couple of Austrian Bundesligas in 1988/89 and 1989/90. However, attempts to create a team strong enough to mount a serious challenge on the European stage failed to live up to their early promise, as shown by a heavy 6-0 aggregate defeat by Liverpool in the UEFA Cup. The Swarovski business then decided to reduce its involvement, with Gernot Langes-Swarovski ceasing to be president in 1992. The company remained as a sponsor for the 1992/93 season, when the club was known as FC Wacker Swarovski Innsbruck, before the jewellery business ended its connections altogether.

Further name changes followed, including a spell when the club became known as FC Tirol Innsbruck. Under the last of these titles, the club won three further Austrian Bundesliga championships in 2000, 2001 and 2002. However, it became clear that without the backing of the jewellery company the club had overstretched itself. In order to secure those championships, the club paid out huge sums in wages and accrued debts of over €16m, a figure that was unsustainable with low attendances and revenue. Immediately after the last of those three titles, the club lost its licence to compete in the Austrian Bundesliga and went bankrupt.

In a repeat of 30 years earlier, what was left of the Innsbruck club merged its football team with neighbouring WSG Wattens, using its licence to compete in the third-tier Regionalliga under the name SPG Wattens/Wacker. The magazine *When Saturday Comes* reported in 2003, 'The dramatic collapse of Tirol Innsbruck last year, from Champions League qualifiers to the third division, was probably the most extreme case yet of a club being punished for financial misdemeanours.'[4]

SPG Wattens/Wacker secured promotion from the Regionalliga in 2003. After the dissolution of the partnership with WSG Wattens, the Wattens portion returned to the lower leagues while the independent FC Wacker Tirol went on to win promotion from the second tier to the Austrian Bundesliga in 2004.

Shortly before the game I attended at the start of the 2007/08 season, it had been decided to rename the club as FC Wacker Innsbruck. This added further complications to an already convoluted story, because in 1986 some members of the club had split away when it became FC Swarovski Tirol and set up their own outfit which they had also called FC Wacker Innsbruck, competing in the lower leagues until 1999 when it folded. The old name, FC Wacker Innsbruck, had been chosen as the one favoured by most supporters. Although the new club regards itself as the legitimate successor of the previous club that won a total of ten Austrian Bundesligas, technically it is a

---

4 See tinyurl.com/Yodel03 for the full story.

different organisation and not allowed to claim all of those honours.

On Saturday, 18 August 2007, during a summer holiday in Tyrol, I had the opportunity to see FC Wacker in action. Approaching the stadium, I encountered a few dozen black-clad fans, singing and chanting loudly; it later became clear that they were the ultras of the visiting side Linzer Athletik-Sport-Klub who had travelled 300km/185 miles to attend the game. Located in the northern part of central Austria, the city of Linz stands outside the Alpine region.

Usually known as LASK Linz or LASK, in 1965 the club became the first outside Vienna to win the league and cup double; however, that season proved to be the team's only success in either competition.

Shortly before my visit, the Tivoli-Neu Stadion, home of FC Wacker, had nearly doubled its capacity from about 17,000 to 30,000, achieved by adding an extra tier around three sides of the ground. The improvements were required after Innsbruck's selection as a venue for the 2008 UEFA European Championship, jointly hosted by Austria and Switzerland. Sadly, the stadium was far too big for the club and at the time of my visit only 4,500 people attended the game. My seat along the side provided a clear view of the pitch, with practically all the noise in the stadium coming from the LASK ultras, congregated behind the goal to my left.

Before kick-off, FC Wacker languished second from bottom, while LASK occupied a mid-table position. The home side lined up in a 4-4-2 formation, wearing green shirts and black shorts, while the visitors were arranged in what looked like 4-4-1-1 with black-and-white-striped shirts and white shorts.

Christian Mayrleb played as the LASK centre-forward, with Ivica Vastić in the 'hole' behind him. The game took place towards the start of Vastić's third season with LASK. Still playing well at the age of 37, Vastić had already got two goals from five games that campaign, making him the club's leading scorer.

The first half turned out to be rather uneventful, but fortunately things improved after the break with Mayrleb opening the scoring for LASK just under ten minutes into the second half. Thomas Eder then equalised for FC Wacker shortly after the hour. LASK's noisy fans got their reward deep into stoppage time when Vastić nicked the winner right in front of where they were standing.

A year later, Vastić scored another late goal, this time for Austria against Poland at Euro 2008 in Vienna. Before the game, the Ottakringer Brauerei promised a lifetime supply of free beer to any player who scored for Austria in the group stage; however, according to some reports, the football authorities blocked the boozy prize.

Name changes have occurred repeatedly during the history of FC Wacker Innsbruck and the clubs it is descended from. The club even thought that the latest rebranding could inspire the players, saying on its website, 'The club started the 2007/08 season full of euphoria. The agreement on the founding name created new momentum. Unfortunately, the FC Wacker team didn't pick up on this enthusiasm.' The truth of this became clear when FC Wacker suffered relegation at the end of the campaign.

FC Wacker then spent the next decade acting like an 'elevator club', going through several promotions and relegations between the top two divisions. After FC Wacker suffered another drop to the 2. Liga in 2019, the club's place in the Austrian Bundesliga was taken by its neighbour and former partner WSG Wattens (now known as WSG Tirol). By then, Gernot Langes-Swarovski's daughter Diana had succeeded him as president of WSG Tirol, and at the time of writing the club still competes in the Austrian Bundesliga.

Worse was to come for FC Wacker in 2022, when financial difficulties left its players unpaid. After the footballing authorities denied FC Wacker a licence to compete in the 2. Liga, the club suffered demotion to the fourth-tier Tiroler Liga, its second descent down to the lower leagues in 20 years.

In 2023, Major League Soccer outfit Los Angeles FC announced on its website that it would be investing in FC Wacker as part of a 'long-term partnership with legendary fans and supporters to rebuild this team and return the club to top-level, winning football'.

Previously, organisations and businesses involved in football on the two continents had spread in just one direction: from Europe to North America (such as Red Bull setting up New York Red Bulls and the City Football Group that runs Manchester City launching New York City FC); however, LAFC's investment in Innsbruck is the first time that an MLS club had extended its influence to Europe. Formed in 2014, Los Angeles FC is the richest club in the MLS and nicknamed the Black and Gold. Supporters of Wacker Innsbruck will hope that their latest association with precious metals and materials will prove to be more durable than the previous one.

So far, the partnership seems to be going according to plan. LAFC's investment won the approval of 98 per cent of FC Wacker's club members in a vote at their general meeting. The American investors then announced their aim of the Innsbruck club achieving three promotions in four years, and at the end of the first full season of this partnership (2023/24) FC Wacker was on schedule, finishing top of the Tiroler Liga and winning promotion to the Regionalliga Tirol. However, a potential complication arose in January 2024 when Los Angeles FC also became the majority shareholder in Zürich team Grasshopper Club. Fans in Innsbruck will hope that their team doesn't become a feeder club, losing its best players to the Swiss Super League side. This example of multi-club ownership leads on nicely to the next chapter about Salzburg, but before that we're going to the zoo.

ii. Three Lynx on a Shirt

Having mentioned the Wacker in Innsbruck, it's time to consider the wacky, in the form of a rather unusual football tournament that took place there during the summer of 2023.

Located on the lower slopes of the Nordkette mountain range to the north of the city centre, Innsbruck's Alpenzoo has since opening in 1962 been home to the world's finest collection of Alpine species. Among the creatures that can be seen in the specially designed enclosures built into the steep gradient are brown bears, chamois, golden eagles, ibex, lynx, marmots and moose. About 300,000 people come to the Alpenzoo every year, and I became one of them during my visit to Innsbruck back in 2007. As I strolled around, taking in the sights, sounds and smells of the zoo, I had no idea that 16 years later the people who work there would organise a football tournament! Although I didn't attend the event, only hearing about it later, it's definitely a story worth telling, helped by contributions from three participants who told me about their experiences.

On 17 June 2023, Innsbruck's Alpenzoo hosted the Europameisterschaft im Zoofußball (European Zoo Football

Championship). Held annually since the 1980s, this was the 34th time the tournament had been held, but the first one at Innsbruck. Over 320 players participated in 16 teams: 12 representing German zoos; one from zoo employees in the Swiss city of Basel; a team from Zoo Praha in the Czech Republic; a contingent flying the flag for Zoo Vienna Schönbrunn; with Innsbruck entering a side jointly with yet more Germans from the Grüner Zoo Wuppertal. Innsbruck was the only zoo from the Alpine region to participate. Tournament rules require players to be zookeepers or work in other parts of the zoo, such as offices or ticket booths, and every team has to feature at least one female player.

With hardly any level land on the slopes at the Alpenzoo, the soccer tournament was held at the American Football Zentrum (American Football Centre or AFZ) down in the valley next to the Tivoli-Neu Stadion. Part of the Olympia World complex, the AFZ opened in 2020 and provides the main training venue for the local SWARCO Raiders Tirol American football team. The AFZ training pitch, complete with American football gridiron markings, provided the playing surface for the zoo soccer competition.

The Alpenzoo Innsbruck/Grüner Zoo Wuppertal players appeared in a smart red and white kit, with their shirts sporting an image of a bearded vulture. One of the Alpenzoo's star attractions, this species of bird was successfully reintroduced to the Alps after being hunted to extinction in the region. An important example of the zoo's wildlife conservation work, the hairy-faced scavenger is its main logo. Emblazoned with bearded vultures, the Alpenzoo Innsbruck/Grüner Zoo Wuppertal team finished a very respectable fifth out of 16.[5]

---

5   See tinyurl.com/Yodel04 for the full results.

The best non-German team, the Vienna Schönbrunn Zoo from the Austrian capital, finished just ahead of Alpenzoo Innsbruck/Green Zoo Wuppertal. Founded in 1752, Vienna Schönbrunn Zoo is the oldest operating zoo in the world and I have been lucky enough to visit it on a couple of occasions. The Vienna Schönbrunn Zoo has been taking part in the European Zoo Football Championship since 2005, and zookeeper Ramon Messinger is responsible for its football team. After starting at the zoo in 1996, Ramon took care of various animals, including zebras and ostriches. Since 2005, his main task has been in the elephant range. Ramon said about the tournament in Innsbruck, 'It's a great event that I don't want to miss, even after 18 participations and six wins. Innsbruck's mountain backdrop was special, but the main thing was meeting so many friends who all love being zookeepers and football. I hope that many more tournaments will follow.'

Over the years, the European Zoo Football Championship has been dominated by German teams, and this tournament was no exception, being won by Leipzig Zoo (once famous for the successful breeding of big cats, now known as the 'zoo of the future' with species-appropriate, natural enclosures). Talking later about the Innsbruck tournament, Bettina Hurgitsch, division manager and native Austrian, said, 'The scenery was impressive and winning at the foot of the mountains remains unforgettable.'

Leipzig's triumph was a close-run thing, requiring a penalty shoot-out in the final against Erlebnis-Zoo Hannover (Hannover Adventure Zoo). Jonas Bittner, animal keeper in the Jungle Palace (an Indian-themed area with elephants, tigers and other species), unfortunately missed Hannover's decisive penalty in the shoot-out.

Afterwards, he said, 'It was very special to play in front of such an impressive backdrop. You don't experience something like that every day. We will remember the incredibly exciting final for a long time, even if there is a small downer because of the missed penalty at the end.'

Chapter 3

Austria: Salzburg

THE CITY of Salzburg is located just inside the Alps, with the perimeter of the mountain area skirting its northern suburbs. This chapter takes a look at the biggest football club in the city, arguably the most controversial in the whole Alpine region.

These days, about 155,000 people live in the city of Salzburg; making it the second-largest settlement in the Alps after Grenoble in France. The city is also the capital of the state of Salzburg and a major tourist destination. Large numbers of visitors descend on 'Mozart City' to see the building where the child prodigy was born, or attend the Salzburg Festival which is the biggest annual opera and theatre event in Europe. Other people come because of a certain film released in 1965.

i. The Sound of Red Bull: FC Red Bull Salzburg, 430m/1,411ft

One cold and snowy Friday morning in late November 2024, I boarded a coach in the centre of Salzburg full of tourists eager to see places that featured in *The Sound of Music*. Most of my fellow passengers were American, partly because the von Trapp family of singers that the film is based on had settled in the United States after escaping from the Nazi takeover of Austria in 1938. Lasting for four hours, the tour visited some of the locations from the popular musical dotted in and around the city.

At the start of the tour, the local resident who acted as our guide provided a brief introduction to the city and its history. The guide explained that during medieval times local bishops built the Hohensalzburg Fortress that dominates Salzburg, he then added that the settlement grew in importance because of salt mining. The guide then surprised me by saying that in recent times, 'Red Bull's changed our lives.' Later, after we had seen one of the buildings used in the film as the von Trapp family home, the bus drove by a palatial residence which the guide told us was owned by Mark Mateschitz, the heir to the Red Bull GmbH company, almost as if he was describing a place where royalty lived. Later on, the bus deliberately slowed as the guide pointed out the Red Bull headquarters in Fuschl am See. So how did an energy drinks business end up being mentioned three times on a tour supposedly devoted to *The Sound of Music*? Let's start at the very beginning.

Back in the 1970s, a businessman in Thailand called Chaleo Yoovidhya concocted a drink called Krating Daeng. Made with caffeine, glucose and other ingredients, the drink proved popular with Thai people, but became an international phenomenon following the involvement of an Austrian called Dietrich Mateschitz. Having come across Krating Daeng while travelling in Thailand, Mateschitz went into business with Yoovidhya, establishing a company to make the drink in 1984. The little bottles that Krating Daeng had originally been sold in were replaced by cans, and the drink was renamed Red Bull (a translation of Krating Daeng).

As the Red Bull GmbH company grew, it sought to break into new and lucrative markets by avoiding the usual dependence on advertising through conventional media; instead, the marketing strategy used sport to convey the idea of Red Bull being a new and exciting product, designed to appeal to youthful, energetic and adventurous people, living up to its slogan, 'Red Bull gives you wings.' Red Bull is now as famous for its sporting activities as for the drinks that the sponsorship is designed to promote, being involved in motor sports, ice hockey, sailing, surfing and skateboarding, as well as a number of extreme sports. Telling the story up to 2020, Karan Tejwani's book *Wings of Change* provides arguably the best account in English of how the Red Bull company became involved in football.

Nearly eight billion cans of Red Bull are sold annually in over 170 countries. As well as its headquarters in Fuschl am See, the company possesses two other bases in the Salzburg area. By the time Mateschitz died in 2022 he was a billionaire and Austria's richest man, owning a series of castles and other properties in the Alps. Red Bull employs over 2,000 people in Austria plus many more in other countries, boosting the economy and profile of the Salzburg region. All of this explains why the company was mentioned with such reverence on the *Sound of Music* tour.

Red Bull's involvement with football began in 2005 when it took over SV Austria Salzburg. Formed in 1933 and nicknamed *Die Mozartstädter* ('The People from Mozart City'), SV Austria Salzburg had a proud history, having won three Austrian Bundesliga championships and reached the 1994 UEFA Cup Final. However, by the early 21st century, the club had entered financial difficulty, enabling

Red Bull to acquire ownership of it and immediately order three changes.

Firstly, a new name, Red Bull Salzburg, was imposed. Renaming clubs for commercial purposes is not unusual in Austrian football (SV Austria Salzburg had previously been known for a time as Casino Salzburg, and the previous chapter listed some of the many different names for FC Wacker Innsbruck); consequently, although the change to Red Bull became permanent, it didn't cause that much fuss.

Secondly, Red Bull tried to erase the history of the old club and present it as a totally new one; however, the footballing authorities ordered a stop to this, arguing that it prevented the club being a legal successor to the old one, which would require it starting again in the lower leagues.

The third area of controversy, the *Farbenstreit* ('colour dispute') became one change too far. After Red Bull altered the club's purple and white to red and white, the final straw for some fans came when Red Bull offered to equip the team's goalkeeper with purple socks at away games. Insulted at the paltry concession, a section of the club's supporters broke away and formed their own club, using the old name SV Austria. This phoenix certainly rose from the flames, and after starting at the bottom of the football pyramid it now competes in the third tier.

For the first few years after the takeover, Red Bull hired big-name coaches such as Giovanni Trapattoni and signed experienced players for relatively high transfer fees. In 2012, German coach Ralf Rangnick became sporting director for both Red Bull Salzburg and RB Leipzig (a German club added to the energy drink company's portfolio in 2009). Rangnick supervised a change in strategy, hiring relatively inexperienced coaches and developing an extensive scouting system, particularly abroad, which recruited young players before selling them on at a profit. Rangnick also advocated a high-tempo playing style, forceful in possession with intense pressing out of it.

On Saturday, 16 August 2014, I had my first view of Red Bull Salzburg, away against VfB Admira Wacker in Vienna, part of the fifth round of fixtures in the 2014/15 Austrian Bundesliga season.

The Red Bull Salzburg line-up included 19-year-old Guinean midfielder Naby Keïta, a player who later signed for RB Leipzig before moving for a sizeable fee to Liverpool. The loss of the likes of Keïta to RB Leipzig, and the profits made by the German club, encouraged a feeling of disquiet among some supporters in Salzburg who resented the idea that their club might be a feeder to supply footballers to compete in more lucrative leagues.

While Rangnick still held the post of sporting director at the time of the visit to Admira Wacker, the Red Bull Salzburg coach at the game, Adi Hütter, provided an element of continuity with the old club, having won three Austrian Bundesliga titles for SV Austria as a player in the 1990s.

During the close season preceding the match, Red Bull Salzburg spent more money in that summer's transfer window than the rest of the Austrian Bundesliga combined, giving the club a huge advantage. Seemingly aware of that disparity, both teams appeared to treat the game as a foregone conclusion, meaning that it provided little excitement for me or the 3,949 other spectators.

With Admira's colours being red and white, Red Bull Salzburg opted to wear a horrible change kit of dark-blue shirts and yellow shorts. The visitors immediately imposed themselves on the game, although it wasn't until the 24th minute that they went ahead. Marcel Sabitzer lobbed the ball over the Admira back line, enabling Belgian winger Massimo Bruno to beat the offside trap and volley into the net from just inside the penalty area. Sabitzer and Bruno were on loan from RB Leipzig.

Five minutes into the second half, the Red Bull Salzburg players extended their lead. Admira carelessly lost possession just outside the penalty area and Swiss defender Christian Schwegler hit a low shot from the right which crept in at the near post. With quarter of an hour to go, Peter Ankerson crossed from the left to Sabitzer, who eluded his markers and headed the ball over the keeper and into the far corner to seal an easy 3-0 victory.

Red Bull Salzburg won the 2014/15 Austrian Bundesliga by a margin of six points. Although Rangnick then left the role of sporting director at Red Bull Salzburg to concentrate on performing the role at RB Leipzig, the strategy he helped develop was continued by his successor Christoph Freund.

Following years of trying, Red Bull Salzburg finally reached the Champions League group stage in 2019/20 by qualifying automatically. During that season, a young Erling Haaland starred for *Die Roten Bullen* before joining Borussia Dortmund, but despite losing him Red Bull Salzburg has gone on to regularly appear in the Champions League.

By this time, Red Bull Salzburg's domination of the Austrian Bundesliga had made the division so predictable that the authorities revised the format. From 2018/19, teams have been split into championship and relegation groups at the end of the regular Austrian Bundesliga season. Half of the points accrued in the regular season are then added to points won in the concluding group of matches to determine the overall winner. For the first few seasons since the change, it didn't seem to make any difference, and when Red Bull Salzburg won the Austrian Bundesliga in 2022/23 it meant ten championships in a row and 14 out of 18 since the takeover in 2005.

However, under the old format Red Bull Salzburg would have won the 2023/24 Austrian Bundesliga, but a poor run in the championship group matches allowed Sturm Graz to narrowly snatch the title. Red Bull Salzburg's strategy of selling players on for profit and reinvesting by signing relatively unknown replacements looked to have finally gone too far, with the club allowing no fewer than eight first-team players to leave in pre-season, plus the departures of sporting director Freund and coach Matthias Jaissle.

One notable encounter during the 2023/24 season occurred when Red Bull Salzburg drew SV Austria in the second round of the ÖFB-Cup (Austria's equivalent of the FA Cup), the first time the two teams had met since the takeover 18 years earlier. With SV Austria's usual stadium too small to host the big game, the tie was moved to the Untersberg-Arena in Grödig to the south of Salzburg. The game was played amid an intense atmosphere, with fans of *Die Mozartstädter* displaying banners saying 'In Salzburg spielen wir die 1. Geige!' ('In Salzburg we play first violin!') Despite SV Austria winning the choreography contest, the match ended 4-0 to Red Bull Salzburg.

A few months into the following season, on Saturday, 23 November 2024, I took in an Austrian Bundesliga fixture at the Red Bull Arena. LASK Linz, the club that played Wacker Innsbruck back in 2007, provided the opposition. For Red Bull Salzburg, the background to the game could hardly have been more different to my last sighting of the club ten years earlier, with the team enduring poor form and rumours of unrest.

In the summer of 2024, Red Bull Salzburg appointed the former assistant to Jürgen Klopp at Liverpool, Pepijn Lijnders, as coach. A couple of years earlier, Lijnders had produced a book called *Intensity: Inside Liverpool FC.* Telling the story of the club's 2021/22 season, the book received some criticism for allegedly revealing secrets about team tactics and training.

Lijnders had been recruited by Red Bull so that he could introduce a version of Klopp's *gegenpressing* ('counterpressing') tactics. Lijnders' preferred style involves playing with the ball in the opponent's half, and quickly pressing to win the ball back when possession is lost. Four months into the campaign, Lijnders had succeeded in making the Salzburg team more attacking and increased its share of possession compared to the previous season, but this came at the cost of defensive frailty. The centre-backs were frequently denied adequate protection from the midfielders and gaps appeared for opponents to exploit. The defenders also struggled to deal with pace and showed particular vulnerability to long balls, crosses and set pieces. Such shortcomings were highlighted in a crushing 5-0 defeat away to Sturm Graz at the start of October.

Reports in the Austrian media suggested that some squad members were concerned about Lijnders selecting two of his former Anfield players ahead of already established team members. The two names concerned were Spanish midfielder Stefan Bajčetić on loan from Liverpool, and the permanently signed English midfielder Bobby Clark. Many supporters were also unhappy about fan favourite Alexander Schlager being replaced in goal by Janis Blaswich.

Going into the game against LASK, Red Bull Salzburg had lost three of its opening 11 Austrian Bundesliga games and languished fourth in the table, 11 points behind the leading team albeit with a couple of games in hand. Results were even worse in the Champions League with three defeats from the opening four fixtures.

Following a 2-0 defeat to LASK's neighbours Blau-Weiß Linz in the last round of matches, Lijnders had a two-week gap for international fixtures to try and turn the situation around.

My match ticket cost €43 (£36), which included free travel on public transport in the local region for up to six hours before the game. Using my ticket, I caught a bus from the centre of Salzburg which took me directly to the stadium in plenty of time for the 4pm kick-off.

Located in the western suburb of Wals-Siezenheim, the stadium had originally been built as a venue for UEFA Euro 2008. Completed five years before the start of the tournament, the stadium was immediately occupied by SV Austria Salzburg who had previously played at the now demolished Stadion Lehen, nearer the city centre. After Red Bull took over the club in 2005, Salzburg's stadium was renamed the Red Bull Arena.

Originally, the capacity at the stadium had been 18,250, but in 2006 an additional upper tier was added, increasing the total capacity to more than 30,000. From the 2018/19 season onwards, the upper tier has been largely unused for domestic league and cup matches in an attempt to create a better atmosphere, although it is still used for UEFA fixtures. My ticket got me a seat in the Unterrang Ost, in the lower tier along one of the sides towards a corner.

Being purpose-built for football, the stadium lacks an athletics track surrounding the pitch, bringing the sides closer to the action, although there is still a significant gap between the ends and the goal line. The two tiers run continuously around the playing area with all the seats covered, except for the first few rows in the lower section.

It immediately became apparent that the club is heavily orientated to a youthful market: the stadium walls were 'decorated' with graffiti-style images of Red Bulls and various cartoon characters; the only publication on sale was a comic for children, with no match programme for adults; loads of cardboard clappers were distributed; and groups of youngsters came on to the pitch waving flags before kick-off. On the evidence of this game, the strategy worked, with probably the highest proportion of children at a top-flight fixture I have ever seen. The block to my left contained several rows filled entirely with kids and they made far more noise than the adult home supporters. Interestingly, the young boy sitting immediately in front of me chanted 'Red Bull! Red Bull!' rather than 'Red Bull Salzburg' or 'Salzburg'.

While the view for the home fans was good, the away supporters were crowded into a corner to my left, with their sight lines obstructed by metal fencing and a net, presumably to stop objects being thrown. For the visitors, this particular fixture had recently acquired special significance. In the spring of 2020, LASK had stood top of the table, but then came the COVID-19 pandemic. After the team's training sessions were found to have violated coronavirus regulations, points were deducted and LASK's bid to win only its second Austrian championship subsequently faltered, with Red Bull Salzburg once again retaining the title.

I estimated that LASK brought over 1,500 fans to the game, a sizeable proportion of the total attendance of 9,145. The Linzer ultras, with their loudhailers, choreographed routines and flares, provided most of the noise and atmosphere at the game. Although the home supporters displayed colourful banners and flags advertising a considerable number of ultra groups, the small attendance in the home end suggested that each faction only had a handful of members present. The team's recent poor form undoubtedly contributed to the subdued atmosphere, with the stadium about as soulless as the nearby suburban retail park.

For this game, Lijnders left Blaswich, Bajčetić and Clark out of his starting line-up. LASK's coach, Markus Schopp, had Red Bull connections of his own, having appeared for the empire's Salzburg and New York clubs during his playing days. Both coaches arranged their teams in 4-2-3-1 formations. The Red Bull Salzburg players wore their usual white shirts, red shorts and white socks, while LASK appeared in a black and white kit.

Red Bull Salzburg should have gone ahead after only a minute when a long ball from Kamil Piątkowski reached Karim Konaté on the edge of the penalty area, but the Ivory Coast striker's effort was well saved by Jörg Siebenhandl in the LASK goal. The home side's next chance came after quarter of an hour, but Konaté squandered another opportunity, this time sending a free header over the bar. A couple of minutes later, Austrian international striker Maximilian Entrup had LASK's only decent chance of the first half, but also sent his header over the bar. Red Bull Salzburg's players then failed to take advantage of a few half-chances that came their way.

By the interval, the temperature in the stadium had plummeted to about 2°C but felt colder; despite multiple layers of thermal clothing, I was freezing. Incredibly, many of the locals were downing pints of chilled beer, and although I spotted a man behind me drinking a cup of tea, I couldn't find an outlet selling anything hot.

Seven minutes into the second half, Konaté sent another header wide of the target. That miss was quickly followed by another from Red Bull Salzburg's defender Amar Dedić. The home side finally took the lead after 62 minutes following a corner, with Malian midfielder Moussa Yeo hitting a right-footed shot into the net from close range. With 20 minutes remaining, Konaté had another chance, but blasted his shot over the crossbar. The miss proved costly, because three minutes later LASK equalised. The visitors took a free kick about 30 metres out on the right; the ball was headed back across goal by a LASK attacker, only for Konaté to slice the ball past Schlager to score an own goal. The hapless Konaté was later described as the '*Unglücksraben des heutigen Abends*' ('unlucky raven of this evening') in the club website's report of the match.

Wearing black clothes with white trainers, Lijnders stood in the dugout on the other side of the pitch; images on the big screen in the stadium showed him with arms crossed looking rather concerned. With nine minutes remaining, Bajčetić and Clark came on as substitutes, but although Red Bull Salzburg's players tried to pile on the pressure, they failed to restore their lead. Disaster struck with only two minutes left when the home side lost possession and LASK counter-attacked; a slick passing move ended with Entrup clinically slotting the ball past Schlager with his left foot. The goal was greeted ecstatically in the away enclosure, with smoke from several flares spreading over the pitch.

Several minutes of stoppage time failed to produce an equaliser, so the game ended in Red Bull Salzburg's first home Austrian Bundesliga defeat of the season. Just like the game at Innsbruck in 2007, LASK triumphed 2-1 thanks to a late winner. The result also meant that the Linzers overtook Red Bull Salzburg in the league table, with *Die Roten Bullen* now in sixth place. Once again, Red Bull Salzburg had been undone by poor defending from set pieces and lack of pace at the back.

The second half had been a huge improvement on the opening period; nevertheless, I was glad to board one of the first shuttle buses back to the city centre and warm up.

Two days later, while waiting at Salzburg airport before getting a flight back to Gatwick, I noticed the presence of a film crew interviewing people just inside the terminal building. Seconds later, I recognised the face of someone walking past my seat – it was Pep Lijnders, which seemed weird as I was halfway through reading his book *Intensity*. Looking relaxed, the Red Bull Salzburg coach then joined the rest of his staff and players queuing to catch a plane to Cologne before their Champions League game against German team Bayer Leverkusen the following day. Despite supposedly being in a separate fast-track queue, the Red Bull Salzburg contingent took ages to get through the baggage check; the security evidently tighter than the team's defence. Seeing the coach and his squad at the airport proves that Red Bull definitely gives you wings, although the players may have wished they'd stayed on the ground; Leverkusen won 5-0.

Three weeks after the defeat at home to LASK, the Austrian Bundesliga started its winter break with Red Bull Salzburg occupying fifth place in the domestic league table and having lost five out of six European games. Although the team won its last domestic match 3-0 against Klagenfurt, the Red Bull hierarchy took advantage of the pause to order a change of coach. For Lijnders, it was sadly a case of so long, farewell.

Under new coach Thomas Letsch, Red Bull Salzburg defeated Sturm Graz 3-1 in March 2025, and at the time of writing had narrowed the gap to the leaders in the Austrian Bundesliga table.

In the summer of 2025, Red Bull Salzburg is scheduled to participate in the FIFA Club World Cup, qualifying for the tournament in the USA through the 'ranking pathway', based on the club's recent European performances, helped by the expansion of the competition and limits on the number of entrants from Europe's biggest leagues. Will the team turn out to be as successful in the USA as the von Trapp family? I have little confidence.

ii. Spreading the Wings

During the last couple of decades, Red Bull has acquired several other clubs throughout the world. A year after taking over SV Austria, Red Bull purchased the American club MetroStars, renaming it New York Red Bulls. Then in 2007, the company established a totally new club in South America called Red Bull Brasil. A year later, the empire extended to West Africa with the formation of another new outfit called Red Bull Ghana, which later merged into a football academy.

In 2009, Red Bull purchased the licence of a fifth-tier German club, SSV Markranstädt. This takeover proved to be extremely controversial because of Germany's 50+1 rule, which requires fans to own a majority stake in clubs. Introduced in 1998, the rule made exceptions for Bayer Leverkusen and Wolfsburg because they had already been owned by companies for at least 20 years, but no more allowances were anticipated. To get round the rule, Red Bull bought 49 per cent of the Leipzig club's shares, with the remaining 51 per cent owned by a small number of members, all of whom are linked to the company and pay an initial €100 to register plus €800 per year! The German football association refused to allow the drinks company's name to be included in the club's title; instead, its full name is RasenBallsport Leipzig ('Lawn Ball Sports Leipzig'), invariably abbreviated to RB.

Three years later, Red Bull acquired another club in the Salzburg area. Following a reduction in size of the 2. Liga in 2010, Austrian Bundesliga clubs were no longer allowed to enter reserve teams in the second tier. Determined to field a team in the 2. Liga to test its youth players, Red Bull Salzburg established cooperation with a local club called USK Anif. By 2012, Anif had effectively been transformed into a new club called FC Liefering, named after a suburb in the northern part of Salzburg. Following promotion from the third tier to the 2. Liga, FC Liefering became a farm team for Red Bull Salzburg, helping young players develop by giving them competitive experience out on loan to the second-tier side.

In 2019, the energy drinks company became a sponsor of Brazilian team Clube Atlético Bragantino, and within a year of the sponsorship deal the club had been renamed Red Bull Bragantino. The latest acquisition occurred in August 2024, when Red Bull spread to Asia with its purchase of third-tier Japanese club Omiya Ardija.

The rise of the Red Bull football empire presented UEFA with some challenges. European football's governing body refuses to use the club's sponsored name, referring instead to 'FC Salzburg', and displays a revised version of its badge which omits the name 'Red Bull' although still containing an image of the animal. UEFA rules also stipulate that no person or organisation can have a 'decisive influence' over more than one club in the same tournament. In response, the energy drinks company initiated organisational and personnel changes in 2017 to reduce the overlap between RB Leipzig and the Salzburg club, as well as claiming that Red Bull was now merely a sponsor of the Austrian team rather than the owner. UEFA subsequently accepted these modifications, enabling the two clubs to be drawn in the same Europa League group in 2018/19.

Unlike many of those buying into football, Red Bull avoids splashing the cash on already successful 'elite-level' clubs, because of their cost and greater difficulty in rebranding them; instead, the energy drinks company is more interested in potential.

During the summer of 2024, it was announced that Red Bull would become a sponsor of the team I support, Leeds United. When the drinks company's logo appeared on the front of the team's shirt for the 2024/25 season, it was described as the biggest sponsorship deal in the history of the English second tier. The current LUFC owners, 49ers Enterprises, immediately explained that the energy drinks company's involvement was limited to sponsorship and a minority share without a seat on the board.

The energy drinks giant's conduct during the takeovers in Salzburg and Leipzig prompted considerable criticism from many football fans. Although the way Red Bull got round the 50+1 rule at Leipzig provoked high levels of hostility in Germany, it's less of an issue in England where fan ownership sadly doesn't exist among 'elite-level' clubs. Of more concern to many English football supporters was the rebranding of clubs in the company's portfolio. Red Bull Salzburg, New York Red Bulls, Red Bull Brasil, RB Leipzig, FC Liefering and Red Bull Bragantino are all the products of rebranding, having been given new names, new red and white colours and slight variations of the Red Bull badge. At the time of writing, only Omiya Ardija retains its original name, badge and colours, but it's early days there. Mindful of what happened to those six clubs, LUFC issued a statement following the announcement of Red Bull sponsorship denying that the club's name, colours or badge would change.

During the 2024/25 campaign, Red Bull also extended its reach to include three of Europe's leading football countries, becoming a minority shareholder in French Ligue 2 side Paris FC, as well as the official energy drink partner for Torino FC in Italy's Serie A and a sponsor of Spanish La Liga team Atlético Madrid.

In October 2024, former Liverpool boss Jürgen Klopp announced that he would take on a new role as Red Bull's head of global soccer from the start of 2025. While not involved in the everyday running of teams, his responsibilities include: overseeing the company's international network of football clubs; supporting their sporting directors; working with Red Bull's scouting system; and helping coaches. Sky Sports Germany reported that Klopp's annual salary in his new job at Red Bull would be between €10m and €12m (£8m–£10m).

A few months earlier, in June 2024, I had attended the UEFA Champions League Final at Wembley between Real Madrid and Borussia Dortmund. Before kick-off, the big screens in the stadium showed Klopp in his seat and a huge cheer roared out from the 20,000 travelling German fans acknowledging their former coach. Dortmund supporters have been prominent in the opposition to the undermining of the 50+1 rule at Leipzig, and after Klopp announced his decision to join Red Bull many of the Yellow Wall fans claimed he had tarnished his legacy. Other observers pointed to a comment Klopp made in 2017, where he told BBC Sport, 'I'm a football romantic and I like tradition in football and all that stuff.'

Klopp's recent experience of the English game encouraged speculation about whether Red Bull might be looking to add a Premier League or Championship club to its portfolio. If that does happen, it's likely that Red Bull would bring improvements and success to any English football club, just as the energy drinks company has done in other countries, but probably at the cost of tradition (and all that stuff).

Chapter 4

Austria: Salzburgerland

THE STATE of Salzburg is also known as Salzburgerland, with the area outside the city famous for its natural beauty, including spectacular mountain scenery, valleys, gorges and waterfalls. The contrast with the bustle and sophistication of the city of Salzburg extends to football, with Salzburgerland's smaller clubs the opposite of the corporate image and wealth on show at the Red Bull Arena.

i. Cold-Water Challenge: FC Bad Gastein, 1,081m/3,547ft

About 95km/59 miles south of the city of Salzburg, Bad Gastein is home to just under 4,000 inhabitants, although the number of people in the town is frequently swelled by large numbers of visitors.

Among the attractions in Bad Gastein is the resort's thermal spring water that helps make it the most popular tourist destination in the Gasteinertal (Gastein valley). The therapeutic qualities of the local mineral springs have been known for centuries and provide the resort with its name, *Bad*, being the German word for 'bath'. Today, the Felsentherme complex in the town contains thermal baths, swimming pools and saunas, making good use of the water. The emblem of the town, a jug symbolising water at the thermal baths, also appears on the badge of the local football club.

FC Bad Gastein was established in 1947, shortly after the end of the Second World War. Whereas Vorarlberg and Tyrol were occupied by the French, Salzburgerland found itself in the American zone. At the time of the football club's formation, the town's name still consisted of one word, Badgastein; however, in 1997 it was officially split and became Bad Gastein. The club also changed its name to reflect this, although the team is still abbreviated to FCB rather than FCBG.

During a couple of hiking holidays in the Gasteinertal, I took advantage of opportunities to see the team play at its football ground, the Alpenstadion. Although the older part of Bad Gastein is set in a rocky gorge with spectacular waterfalls at a height of 1,002m/3,287ft, the football ground is situated at the southern end of town, further up the valley. At an altitude of 1,081m/3,547ft, it is one of the highest full-size football stadiums to appear in this book. The Alpenstadion has a small grandstand along part of one side and a clubhouse which serves refreshments; modest but suitable for the size of the local team.

The trainer of FC Bad Gastein at the time of my visits was a man called Alwin Wigele. Born in 1969 and from Bad Gastein, Wigele is a former footballer, once selected to play for the federal state of Salzburg. He later became a youth trainer and technical trainer of the Salzburger Fußballverband (Salzburg Football Association). When I contacted Wigele while researching this book he told me, 'Yes, I've got stories, but the biggest is when we were with the youth team of FCB and were champions of Austria in the Ernst-Happel-Stadion in Vienna in 2005.'

On 26 May 2005, Wigele, then aged 36, was a trainer for the youth team of FC Bad Gastein which won the Baumit Junior Soccer Cup Final for under-nines, the Austrian national championship for that age group. The final took place at the Ernst-Happel-Stadion where Wigele saw the victorious FC Bad Gastein under-nine players being awarded their medals before SK Rapid played FK Austria later that evening in the same stadium. After the awards ceremony, Wigele and the FC Bad Gastein youth players stayed to watch the Vienna derby, played in front of a crowd of over 47,000. Given the small size of Bad Gastein, this was an amazing achievement.

The first game I attended, on Sunday, 25 August 2013, was a fixture in the 1. Klasse Süd, a local league at what is now the seventh tier of Austrian football. UFC Radstadt provided the opposition, coming from a town of that name to the north. Slightly larger than Bad Gastein, the town of Radstadt originated back in the 13th century when a fortress was built by the local river and the settlement became a trading centre, particularly for wine. UFC Radstadt was formed in 1948, a year after FC Bad Gastein.

FCB played in all blue, while Radstadt wore white shirts and black shorts. I nearly witnessed the fastest goal in this collection of Alpine matches, but Radstadt's shot after just ten seconds hit the bar. When a goal did come, nine minutes into the game, it went to the home side, scored by a young Austrian student called Daniel Buhacek. Only just past his 17th birthday at the time of the game, Buhacek's goal was one of 26 he scored that season, making him one of the top scorers in the 1. Klasse Süd.

The lead didn't last long, because Radstadt equalised after 34 minutes through Andreas Trippolt. There had been a mountain storm the night before with heavy rain.

Lighter rain continued for most of the day, producing a soaking playing surface. However, the two teams adapted well to the conditions and managed to produce a decent game with plenty of chances to entertain the 80 people in attendance. The second half, like the first, was closely and keenly contested, but there were no more goals, so it finished 1-1. Good value for the €3 admission charge.

FCB finished the 2013/14 season sixth in the league, half a dozen points ahead of ninth-placed Radstadt, in a division of 14 clubs.

A year later, I returned to Bad Gastein and on the afternoon of Sunday, 24 August 2014, took in another game. Once again, it was a fixture in the 1. Klasse Süd, but this time Sportklub Taxenbach provided the opposition. Despite the cold weather, 150 people attended the game, nearly double the previous year's figure.

SK Taxenbach hails from the small town of Taxenbach about 30km/18 miles to the north. Formed in 1951, SK Taxenbach is a multi-sports club catering for football, tennis, chess and winter sports. After a lengthy period down in the 2. Klasse, SK Taxenbach's football team won promotion to the 1. Klasse Süd in 2009/10. After three years at that level, the club then suffered relegation in 2012/13, before bouncing back immediately with another promotion enabling the team to meet FCB for my match.

SK Taxenbach's Klammstadion stands at an altitude of 744m/2,441ft, meaning that its footballers had to ascend 337m/1,106ft up the valley to reach Bad Gastein. A few hours later, they probably regretted making the effort.

On this occasion, FCB appeared in white shirts, blue shorts and white socks, while Taxenbach wore yellow shirts and shorts with black socks. To begin with, Taxenbach's players held their own and the keeper, Sözen Özgür, pulled off three good saves; however, sadly for him, his team ended up on the end of a thrashing.

Bad Gastein went ahead after 12 minutes with a goal by Rene Rudinger. It remained 1-0 at the break, but in a 14-minute spell in the second half Taxenbach conceded three goals. Midfielder Iskender Kurakaya started it off with a goal after 54 minutes. The pick of the goals came just after the hour and followed a great through ball from Kurakaya to striker Rade Kocic, who finished confidently. It was 4-0 after 68 minutes when Lukas Kendlbacher, who had a chance to score himself, unselfishly passed to the tall striker Elvir Cehajic who shot into the net. The rout was completed in the last minute when Kocic grabbed his second goal to make it five.

A 5-0 scoreline is always memorable; however, even more remarkable was what the victors did by way of celebration.

Earlier in the day, my hike up in the mountains overlooking the Alpenstadion had been curtailed because of snow. Despite wearing layers of thermal clothing, including a special state-of-the-art mountain jacket, I was still cold down in the stadium while watching the football in what was supposed to be summer. The locals are clearly made of stronger stuff, because immediately after the match the FCB players accepted a challenge from UFC Radstadt (coincidentally the team that had provided the opposition a year earlier). Explaining the challenge, the match programme contained an announcement in German which read, 'Im Anschluss, an dieses Spiel findet heute unser Beitrag zur "cold water challenge" statt. Die Mannschaft des FCB wurde von den Kickern des UFC Radstadt däfur nominiert. Natürlich nehmen wir die Nominierung an und stellen uns der Herausforderung, denn dass Fass Bier, welches wir sonst nach Radstadt schicken müssten, trinken wir lieber selber, die Radstädter bekommen nur unser Video zu sehen. Wir freuen uns auf eure lautstarke Unterstützung. Unterstützt wird der FCB bei der "cold water challenge" von der Felsentherme Bad Gastein.'

This translates as, 'Following this game, our contribution to the "cold-water challenge" will take place today. The FCB team was nominated for it by the UFC Radstadt players. Of course, we accept the nomination and rise to the challenge, because we prefer to drink the keg of beer that we otherwise have to give to Radstadt, the people of Radstadt only get to see our video. We look forward to your loud support. FCB is supported in the "cold-water challenge" by Felsentherme Bad Gastein.'

Cold-water challenges have uncertain origins, but became all the rage around the world in the summer of 2014 when various celebrities, such as footballers David Beckham and Cristiano Ronaldo, threw cold water over themselves to raise money for charity. However, what was about to happen in Bad Gastein took cold-water challenges to another level, lasting longer and with colder water.

Immediately after the final whistle, the FCB players left the stadium still wearing their football kit and walked the short distance to the local river, the Gasteiner Ache, to accept Radstadt's challenge.

The Gasteiner Ache is formed by a confluence of two smaller rivers: the Naßfelder Ache, which has its source in the Schlapperebenkees glacier in the nearby mountains, and the Anlaufbach. After the two rivers merge at a small village called Böckstein, the Gasteiner Ache flows down towards Bad Gastein as the biggest river in the area.

After reaching the banks of the Gasteiner Ache, the FCB players entered the glacial meltwater, wearing only their football shirts, shorts, socks and boots. The players stood ankle-deep in the ice-cold river for several seconds, while the captain announced that he and his players were accepting the cold-water challenge. All the players then used their hands to scoop up freezing water and spray it over each other as they went deeper into the river, some becoming almost totally submerged. As the match programme promised, the team's challenge was filmed, so you can view it on YouTube.[6]

Guidelines exist for cold-water challenges, with advice about how to enter the water and the length of time to stay in it. Such activities are potentially hazardous, especially to people with certain health conditions, and anyone considering entering cold water should seek full advice from medical professionals beforehand.

Although cold-water challenges were fashionable in 2014, few participants will have endured one after playing a 90-minute football game in chilly weather at such high altitude, before entering icy glacial meltwater.

Inspired by the FCB players' exploits, I decided to visit the premises of the stunt's sponsor, the Felsentherme, for my own self-imposed test. Whereas the local football team had endured a cold-water challenge, I opted for one with both hot and cold water. My challenge required staying in the sauna's steam room for a full quarter of an hour, the maximum recommended time, followed by total immersion in the icy water of the plunge pool. Unlike in the UK, where you are required to don swimwear in the sauna and nudity is forbidden, the Felsentherme insists that everyone removes all clothing, keeping just flip flops on their feet. The saunas are also unisex, with men and

---

6   Go to tinyurl.com/Yodel05 to see the footage.

women sitting or lying naked, sharing a small cabin with total strangers.

After leaving everything in my locker, I was definitely up for it and keen on an early bath. My tactics involved waiting until all previous occupants had departed before entering the steam cabin. I sat naked alone on the bench, gradually gaining more confidence; but it turned out to be early doors, because with just over seven minutes gone, a woman entered the cabin and sat down further along the bench. Her arrival was a wake-up call, meaning that this was going to be a game of two halves. Mindful of sauna etiquette and football's rules against ungentlemanly conduct, I stared at the floor, making sure my hands were not in an unnatural position. Luckily, there was no fourth official to indicate any added time, so when the clock on the wall showed that the 15 minutes was up, I knew I'd put in a great shift. Staggering out of the steam room drenched in sweat, I headed for the showers as fast as possible, although after the ordeal I'd lost a yard of pace. Not only were the showers communal, they were also unisex and rather crowded. Determined to give 110 per cent, I then submerged myself in the freezing water of the plunge pool. My game plan had worked, and successfully completing the final part of the challenge proved that I could definitely do it on a cold, wet night in Stoke.

Nine years later, the 2022/23 season would prove to be extremely difficult for FC Bad Gastein and SK Taxenbach. A shortage of players forced FCB to drop out of the 1. Klasse Süd; after having its results voided, the team suffered automatic demotion. Taxenbach's footballers had to stop for financial reasons at the end of the campaign, although they later managed to resume competition. Both clubs now play in the eighth-tier 2. Klasse Süd. For football teams in places like Bad Gastein and Taxenbach, simply surviving is the real challenge.

ii. Under the Castle of Eagles: SSK Werfen, 524m/1,719ft

During a long weekend in Salzburg, I headed to Werfen, a small town in the valley of the River Salzach, 40km/25 miles south of the city. Werfen is dominated by the Festung Hohenwerfen (High Werfen Castle) perched on top of a steep cone of rock at the north end of the town. Built by the bishops of Salzburg in the 11th century, the Festung Hohenwerfen was initially a fortress and then a prison. Having never been successfully stormed by attackers, the castle is well-preserved and open to the public during the summer. After appearing in the background in one scene of *The Sound of Music*, the castle then featured more prominently in the 1968 war film *Where Eagles Dare*.

Based on a novel by Alistair MacLean, *Where Eagles Dare* tells the story of a secret service operation to rescue a captured American general imprisoned by the Germans in the Schloß Adler (Castle of Eagles) during the Second World War. Early in the film, the British Major Smith (played by Richard Burton) and the American Lieutenant Schaffer (Clint Eastwood) have their first view of the Schloß Adler from a hillside on the other side of the valley. Looking through binoculars at an area of flat land in between the River Salzach and the bottom of the rock that leads up to the castle, they spot a military barracks used by the Wehrmacht Alpine Corps, with soldiers marching on a snowy parade ground, protected by an electric fence, watchtower and Dobermann guard dogs. In the original novel the Schloß Adler is described as being in Bavaria, west of Garmisch-Partenkirchen; however, for the film, the Festung Hohenwerfen was used as the location for the castle.

Within a year of the actors and film crew leaving the town, local sports enthusiasts set up the Schi- und Sportklub Werfen (Ski and Sports Club Werfen). Although SSK Werfen traces its origins back to a 19th-century gymnastics society, 1969 is regarded as the year when the present organisation was formed. In 1972, four years after *Where Eagles Dare* was made, part of the location for the Wehrmacht Alpine Corps barracks in the film became the site of the town's sports ground, the Sportplatz Werfen.

These days, SSK Werfen offers a variety of sports; as well as skiing, there's mountain running, cycling, gymnastics, tennis and swimming. The importance of the club to the local community is shown by its current membership of 350, more than a tenth of the town's population.

Football was added to the sports club's repertoire in 1974, but stopped after five years before the football team's reformation in 1990. SSK Werfen is not affiliated to the Salzburger Fußballverband, and since the refounding of the team has never participated in league competition, opting instead to have what the club calls on its website *Hobby Fußball Mannschaft* ('hobby football team').

Sometimes known in German-speaking parts of Europe as *Freizeitfußball* ('recreational football') or *Alternativfußball* ('alternative football'), hobby football has become very popular. Originating in the 1970s, hobby football was often influenced by counter-cultural ideas. Being independent, it lacks a strict definition or standardised regulations. Participants usually appear in one-off matches and occasional tournaments, constituting an intermediate type of football; more advanced than casual kickabouts, but without having to play under the control of football associations and deal with their constraints and administration.

Hobby football sometimes involves teams made up of players whose work commitments or age limits their participation, others may simply not want to turn out every week, while some may be limited more by ability than availability. Being independent of the football authorities means that hobby football teams can use this freedom to alter the rules and format of games if they need to, including having smaller teams; using pitches with reduced dimensions; or playing in matches of shorter duration. Whatever the type of hobby football, the emphasis is always on playing for fun and taking the game back to its roots, before commercialisation took over at 'elite level'.

SSK Werfen's footballers play in occasional friendly matches and tournaments during the year, and usually train on Wednesday evenings after work; however, on the day of my visit (Sunday, 24 November 2024) the team hoped to hold a training session on the Sportplatz starting at 10am, weather permitting.

After arriving at Werfen's little railway station early that morning, I followed in the footsteps of Smith and Schaffer, crossing a bridge over the aquamarine-coloured Salzach before continuing up the picturesque main street full of brightly coloured buildings. On the way, I passed the Gasthof Obauer where SSK Werfen had been founded in 1969, before finally arriving at the Sportplatz.

Constructed with the help of the local community and renovated over the years, the Sportplatz consists of a complex which includes a clubhouse, tennis courts, a section of athletics track, plus the floodlit football pitch which has a natural grass surface. Thankfully, the perimeter fence is not electric and there are no Dobermanns! The castle is visible from nearly everywhere in Werfen, but one of the best views of it is from the south goal of the football pitch. The Sportplatz is one of the most spectacular settings for football I have encountered, making it an ideal place to make a short promotional film about this book; a photograph taken from the same spot is included in the central picture section.

Unfortunately, just as the filming of *Where Eagles Dare* had been held up by blizzards and avalanches in the Werfen area during the early months of 1968, it was also very wintry when I arrived in the town. The land that is now the Sportplatz looked rather similar to how it had appeared when used as the location for the army barracks in *Where Eagles Dare*, in other words covered by a blanket of snow. With the temperature only just above freezing and the pitch under several inches of the white stuff, the football training session had to be cancelled. Sometimes it's best not to dare.

Chapter 5

France

FOOTBALL ARRIVED in France via ports, with the first club formed in 1872 in Le Havre on the English Channel, helped by British enthusiasts. The sport then spread inland, reaching the French capital with the formation of a club in Paris in 1879. Organised football then took another 13 years to reach as far as the French Alps, in the south-east of the country.

In 1904, Paris became the birthplace of the Fédération Internationale de Football Association (FIFA). As well as giving the sport's world governing body a French title and a launch venue, France also contributed Jules Rimet, who initiated the FIFA World Cup in 1930 and lent his name to the tournament's trophy.

Domestically, the first national championship for French clubs took place in 1932/33, and over the years it evolved into the present Ligue 1.

A later chapter looks at a football club from the principality of Monaco that regularly competes in Ligue 1, but this chapter focuses on two teams from the Grenoble-Alpes Métropole administrative area more familiar with the lower leagues.

i. Money Doesn't Grow on Trees: Grenoble Foot 38, 217m/712ft

Grenoble is the largest city within the entire Alpine region with a population of about 158,000. Located in a valley, Grenoble is surrounded by mountains and often referred to as the capital of the French Alps. With a reputation for scientific and technological research, the city possesses a youthful buzz as a result of its large student population. In recent times, Grenoble has also become known for environmentalism, as the local football club would discover to its cost.

In 1892, some students from a Grenoble school, the Lycée Champollion, formed a football team which they initially named Association Athlétique du Lycée. Three sports organisations then joined the club in 1911: Cercle Sportif, Stade Grenoblois and Union Athlétique Grenobloise. After that merger, the name Football Club de Grenoble (FC Grenoble) was adopted.

In 1932/33, around the time that professionalism entered French football, FC Grenoble joined a regional league called the Division Honneur Lyonnais. For the first season of FC Grenoble's participation in the Division Honneur Lyonnais it occupied the second tier of the football league pyramid; however, it soon became the third tier, and the club stayed at that level until relegation to the fourth-tier Promoton Honneur in 1937/38.

During the German occupation in the Second World War, Grenoble became part of Vichy France, a regime in the south of the country led by Marshal Pétain in collaboration with the Nazis. Grenoble and the surrounding mountains became a major centre of resistance activity, as remembered by the excellent Resistance and Deportation Museum in the city. In 1943, the Vichy regime reorganised French football and banned professionalism, causing the effective demise of FC Grenoble.

After the war, Grenoble's main football club was relaunched, mainly competing in the fourth tier before reaching the second level and turning professional in 1952. Eight years later, FC Grenoble won promotion to the top division for the first time in its history; unfortunately, that 1960/61 season ended in relegation from the top flight. Although the club immediately bounced back, winning promotion in 1962, Grenoble's second spell in the highest division during 1962/63 also ended in a rapid demotion after just one season. The club then gradually declined, slipping down to the fourth tier in 1972.

After keeping the same name since 1911, the club then changed it six times in a 20-year period between 1977 and 1997, finally settling on Grenoble Foot 38 (often abbreviated to GF 38). Usually, numbers in a football club's name indicate the year of formation, such as Bayer 04 Leverkusen; however, the only significance of 1938 for Grenoble is that the club suffered one of its relegations, hardly a cause for commemoration. According to at least one account, the number 38 refers not to a date but to the start of Grenoble's postcode.[7] Surely, after six name changes, the club's managers should have stamped their authority and delivered a better way to be addressed.

Around the millennium, GF 38 competed in the second tier, but in order to fulfil ambitions of competing in Ligue 1 the club needed a bigger stadium than its old Stade Lesdiguières. The local authorities therefore authorised the

---

7 See tinyurl.com/Yodel06 for the full story.

building of a new stadium in Parc Paul Mistral, which used to be on the outskirts of Grenoble but is now near the city centre. Named after a former mayor of Grenoble, the park had been established in 1925 on land formerly occupied by the military before being used to stage an international exhibition. Parc Paul Mistral also hosted several events during the 1968 Winter Olympics, when the Games were held in and around Grenoble.

The plan to build what would become known as the Stade des Alpes proved to be extremely controversial because Parc Paul Mistral was Grenoble's largest park in a city short of green space. About 500 people formed a campaign called SOS Parc Paul Mistral, collecting over 10,000 signatures calling for a cheaper and smaller stadium to be built elsewhere. The campaigners also initiated legal action against the development.

The most controversial issue concerned the need to fell approximately 200 trees in the park to provide space for the stadium. Most of those to be chopped down were plane trees including some old ones. Campaigners staged what they called a *fête des arbres* ('tree festival') in the park to oppose the development.

On 2 November 2003, three eco warriors climbed one of the plane trees in the park and then set up a table displaying leaflets and petitions at the bottom of its trunk. Huts were constructed high up in three of the trees, a form of protest known as tree sitting. The original three protestors were joined by seven more who started to live in the tree houses. Some local people started bringing food and drink for the protesters and a makeshift kitchen was established in a tent on the ground. Originally intended as a short-lived publicity stunt, the tree sitters ended up staying for several months. Other campaigners started obstructing the arrival of construction workers and blocking deliveries of building materials to the site.

The protests attracted considerable media attention, with the actions backed by environmentalists but opposed by many local football fans keen to have a new stadium. The polarising of opinion was an unfortunate consequence of failing to find a suitable brownfield site. This time, football wasn't parking the bus, but busting the park.

In December, the courts judged that the tree occupations were illegal, but this only prompted 30 additional activists to join in by building and occupying more tree houses. The protest at the bottom of the trees also expanded, including the addition of a small information kiosk distributing environmental booklets. The escalating protests attracted hundreds of visitors to the park and on 24 January 2004 about 4,500 people took to the streets of Grenoble to demonstrate against the construction of the stadium.

However, the authorities refused to back down and on 2 February they began chopping down the first of the trees, starting with ones on the edge of the park. CRS riot police were called in to contain the protests, but this only provoked even more people to join the activities, resulting in violent exchanges and arrests. Campaigners responded by building more tree houses up in the branches and organising events such as concerts in those parts of the park that were still accessible. These events included informal football matches, showing that the protesters weren't against the sport per se, only the location of the stadium.

The climax of the campaign took place over three days between 10 and 12 February, with large numbers of riot police using tear gas to clear the park and evict about 60 arboreal activists occupying 20 of the tree houses.

Eight months after the eviction of the tree sitters, GF 38 became the first French football club to have foreign owners. Formerly owned by the city of Grenoble, the club was bought by Index Corporation, a Japanese mobile software company, in October 2004.

Four years later, the Stade des Alpes was inaugurated, perfectly timed to coincide with GF 38 regaining its place in the top tier. Although the club's president referred in the media to 'the Champions League as a long-term ambition', things turned out rather differently.

In 2009, the new stadium recorded its record attendance when a crowd of 19,662 people turned up to see the south of France's biggest club, Olympique Marseille, visit for a Ligue 1 fixture. The 2008/09 campaign promised much, with the club finishing 13th in Ligue 1 and reaching the semi-finals of the Coupe de France (the French FA Cup). However, a terrible run of 12 successive defeats in 2009/10 contributed to the team finishing bottom of Ligue 1 and being relegated to the second tier.

In July 2011, GF 38 filed for bankruptcy, being unable to repay the €2.9m it owed. The financial problems led to demotion in 2011 to the Championnat de France Amateur 2 (since renamed Championnat National 3) at the fifth level of the French league system. After the conclusion of Index's involvement, the club reverted to French ownership.

GF 38 won promotion at the end of its first year in the fifth tier in 2011/12, but it took five seasons for the club to claw its way out of the fourth tier in 2017. Grenoble finished third at the end of the subsequent campaign, qualifying for a play-off which it duly won to clinch promotion back to the second tier in 2018. Grenoble reached another play-off in 2021, only this time coming up short.

Visiting Grenoble provided my first trip abroad since the COVID-19 pandemic, and the match I attended took place on Saturday, 29 April 2023, with GF 38 facing Niort in Ligue 2 at the Stade des Alpes.

My ticket provided a seat in the Tribune Nord Central and at only €15 provided good value, positioned by the halfway line and high enough to provide a perfect view. A multipurpose venue, the Stade des Alpes hosts rugby as well as football and consists of one all-seater tier going right round the pitch. From my position, I could peep through the transparent roof made with glass panels to see the snow-capped mountains of the Arves Massif on the left.

A crowd of 4,135 attended the game, meaning that the Stade des Alpes was only a fifth full. Many of those present were local ultras occupying the Tribune Ouest (West Stand) behind the goal to my right. Despite GF 38's colour being blue, the club's main ultra group is called Red Kaos because of its left-wing political sympathies. Members of this group waved Che Guevara flags during the game, depicting an iconic image of the South American revolutionary with his black beret and shaggy beard. Another banner hanging behind the same goal showed the presence of another ultra faction, the Diables Bleus ('Blue Devils'), named after French mountain soldiers.

Before kick-off, GF 38 stood in seventh place in Ligue 2, while the opposition struggled at the bottom of the table. The visiting team's full title, Chamois Niortais Football Club, owes its origins to the species of goat-antelopes whose skins were made into leather products by one of the club's founders back in the 19th century.

Niort's form, plus the long distance of 660km/410 miles from near the Bay of Biscay to Grenoble, explained why the visitors only brought seven fans, although the allocation given to them was incredibly generous as they had all of the Tribune Est to choose their places.

Only one of the GF 38 team that started the match actually came from Grenoble, the captain and goalkeeper, Brice Mableu, who was born in Saint-Martin-d'Hères on the outskirts of the city. Mableu played for GF 38 in two spells from 2009 to 2012, then again from 2014 onwards, meaning that he had been at the club during its Ligue 1 days as well as during its time in the lower tiers.

Grenoble's players, appearing in their usual all-blue kit, were arranged in a 4-2-3-1 formation, with two exciting wingers, Matthias Phaëton on the left and Abdoulie Sanyang (known as Bamba) on the right. Niort in white lined up in a more cautious 3-4-1-2, with a bank of four players set up to protect the three-man defence.

Rain produced a slippery surface during the opening phase. Both teams had chances during the early stages, including a header from Niort's Nesta Elphege after 19 minutes which was just off target (a year later Elphege would join GF 38). Thankfully for most of those in attendance, it was the home side that opened the scoring after half an hour when Niort failed to deal with a free kick from the left, enabling Phaëton to fire a shot on goal which was knocked in by Bamba. The defending had been woeful, angering Niort's goalkeeper, Jean Louchet, who was also culpable, remaining static and seemingly taken by surprise. Bamba then nearly scored twice, with Louchet saving one shot, while another effort hit the crossbar.

In the second half, the GF 38 players came close to extending their lead when a cross from the left by Arial Mendy was met by Bamba hitting a shot down on to the ground which bounced up, only to be touched over the bar by Louchet. The Niort keeper then saved a shot from Phaëton, only to be injured by Grenoble's Amine Sbaï when he challenged for the loose ball. Niort gradually got more into the game, nearly scoring from a corner after 64 minutes, and almost nicking an equaliser three minutes from time when one of the many substitutes, striker Yanis Merdji, headed towards goal, only for Mableu to push the ball on to the post. The incident proved crucial, because in the final minute of normal time GF 38 scored a second. Phaëton broke down the left and passed to centre-back Loïc Nestor who crossed for another of the subs, striker Joris Correa, to tap the ball in from close range and secure a 2-0 win. Although both teams enjoyed an equal share of possession, GF 38 deserved the win having created twice as many chances as Niort (17 attempts on goal compared to eight).

GF 38 ended the 2022/23 season in the middle of Ligue 2. The Grenoble club started the 2023/24 campaign impressively, remaining in third place until the beginning of February; however, a poor run of five successive defeats saw any promotion hopes disappear and the team slump to another mid-table finish.

Although GF 38's foreign ownership experiment ended badly, it has since been emulated by other French football clubs. At the time of writing, about half of the teams in Ligue 1 have foreign owners who have increased club budgets and widened the financial gap between their sides and all the others. Sadly, for football in Grenoble and Parc Paul Mistral, money doesn't grow on trees.

ii. Footy and the Chocolate Factory: FC Pays Voironnais, 305m/1,001ft

On Sunday, 30 April 2023, the day after the GF 38 game, I travelled to Voiron, about 25km/16 miles to the north-west of Grenoble. Easily reached by a 15-minute direct train journey from the city, the town of Voiron is the third-largest settlement in the department of Isère with a population of just over 20,000. Standing at the base of the Massif de la Chartreuse, Voiron has a slightly higher altitude than Grenoble.

Voiron has long been an important industrial location, known centuries ago for the production of art canvases, before silk weaving took over as the main activity. In more recent times, Voiron's factories have produced anything from paper to pharmaceuticals to skiing equipment. However, the most significant commercial activity as far as the history of football in Voiron is concerned involves chocolate!

A resident of Voiron, Félix Bonnat, diversified his family's old liqueur and confectionery business and started making chocolate in the town in 1884. After Bonnat's first big success with fondant-filled chocolates, the firm expanded and opened nearly 200 shops across France selling the increasingly sophisticated and elaborate sweets as well as exporting them abroad. The Maison Bonnat factory's next success came in 1936, when it secured the rights to use the famous Chartreuse herbal liqueur in its chocolates. Made since the early 17th century using a secret recipe including ingredients from over 100 plants, the liqueur had been produced by Carthusian monks at the Grande Chartreuse monastery near Voiron. While in Voiron, I called at the Caves de la Chartreuse in the town centre and went down to the cellars where the liqueur aged. Although only one of the huge barrels still contains the liqueur, the cellars in Voiron continue to be the world's longest, stretching over 160 metres.

Today, Bonnat is the oldest family-run chocolate business operating in France, as well as being one of the few to roast its own cacao beans. Today, you can visit Bonnat's premises in the centre of Voiron, only a short distance from the town's local church, Église Saint-Bruno de Voiron. Consecrated in 1883, the year before the company started making chocolate, the church still appears on the beautiful art nouveau wrappers of every bar of Bonnat chocolate.

All very interesting, I hear you say, but what has this got to do with football? The answer is because half a century later, in 1930, employees at Maison Bonnat created the Football Club Voironnais.

Initially a multi-sports club, FC Voironnais became devoted solely to football after dropping rugby and changing its name to Voiron Olympique Club in 1938. VOC's first success came shortly after the end of the Second World War when the club won the Coupe du Dauphiné (the local knockout cup) in 1947. Two years later, VOC won its league and secured promotion. The next silverware arrived in 1963/64 in the form of a league and Coupe du Dauphiné double.

During the 1960s, VOC was coached by Alfred Kaucsar. Born in Târgu-Mureş in Romania, Kaucsar left his country in 1934, following the path of his older brother Joseph, who had become the first Romanian to play football in France a decade earlier. Alfred Kaucsar played for Montpellier, Sochaux, Lyon and Rennes before retiring in 1949. Not only did he coach VOC, but his grandson, Kewin Chamard, is the current president of the club.

In the 1970s, another club appeared in the town called FC Voiron. After co-existing for a few seasons, the two outfits merged in 1982, forming Football Olympique Voironnais. Until then, the club had ground-shared with the local rugby team, but following the merger moved to the adjacent, although much smaller, Stade Plan Menu Est.

In recent times, the club has concentrated on youth and women's football, as well as promoting foot health. A change of management in 2021 saw FOV renamed FC Pays Voironnais (Football Club from the Land of Voiron, often abbreviated to FCPV).

The match I planned to attend had been advertised as a fixture in the District de L'Isère Seniors D1 Pool A, with the opposition provided by ASL St Cassien. I guessed that D1 probably stood for Départemental 1. During my research to confirm the game's exact step on the French football league pyramid, I kept coming across the name Laura, which regularly appeared on various websites and email addresses. Laura was obviously the person to answer all my questions; however, when trying to contact her I discovered that she was actually an acronym, with LAURA standing for Ligue Auvergne-Rhône-Alpes, the local football league.

After looking through the windows of the Bonnat chocolate shop (it's closed on Sundays), then visiting the Église Saint-Bruno de Voiron and the Caves de la Chartreuse, I headed towards the FCPV ground. Having read that the game would start at 2pm, it was rather alarming to arrive at the little stadium 20 minutes before kick-off to find the place totally deserted.

Just when I had abandoned hope of seeing any football and prepared to leave the stadium, a man in a tracksuit appeared. When I asked him if the game was going ahead, he replied positively, but with a 3pm kick-off time. I also took the opportunity to show him my attempt to understand the structure of French football leagues which I had written out earlier on a scrap of paper. The list looked like this (with those from level four downwards divided into groups):

1. Ligue 1
2. Ligue 2
3. Championnat National
4. Championnat National 2
5. Championnat National 3
6. Régional 1
7. Régional 2
8. Régional 3
9. Départemental 1
10. Départemental 2
11. Départemental 3
12. Départemental 4
13. Départemental 5

Thankfully, the tracksuited man confirmed that the match was indeed in Départemental 1, on the ninth tier. Finally, I asked how much it would cost to stay and watch the game, but he just smiled and said that it was free. Only when the same person led his team out just before kick-off did I realise I had been speaking to FCPV's captain, Audric Fontaine.

The Stade Plan Menu Est consists of an artificial pitch surrounded by a new white metal fence, a stall selling refreshments, a marquee and a small block containing the toilets. With rain forecast, it was a bit worrying to discover that there were no covered areas. Although the temperature fell during the game to around 16°C (unusually low for the region at that time of year), fortunately the rain held off.

Association Sports et Loisirs St Cassien (Association of Sports and Leisure St Cassien) only had a short journey to make, coming from a village slightly to the west of Voiron with a population of little more than 1,000 people. Like

Voiron, St Cassien is located within the perimeter of the Alpine Convention.

Before kick-off, FCPV stood tenth out of 12 teams in the league, while ASL St Cassien occupied eighth place.

FCPV kicked off, attacking the goal to my right, wearing a kit of white shirts with grey sleeves, black shorts and white socks, while ASL St Cassien wore all black with yellow trim. By the time the match started, a crowd of 105 people were in attendance, mainly from Voiron but with a noisy group of about half a dozen fans who had made the short journey from St Cassien.

The home side started the stronger and went ahead after 22 minutes when Fontaine gained possession of the ball just outside the penalty area on the left and after evading the attentions of the opposing defenders fired a shot into the far corner of the goal.

St Cassien responded strongly, with Valentin cutting through the Voiron defence down the right and forcing a good save from the keeper. FCPV's task then became a whole lot harder when Vullnet lost possession after effective St Cassien pressing and received a second yellow for a rash challenge on an attacker, reducing the home team to ten men. The visitors then had what looked like a good goal disallowed following a free kick, presumably for some sort of infringement in the crowded penalty area.

Both sides then forced decent saves from the opposing keepers, but the next goal came five minutes before the break when a St Cassien corner on the right was headed in for the equaliser. Congestion in the area made it difficult to be certain who scored, but it looked like the visiting team's number eight, Joaquim.

About five minutes into the second half, FCPV's Matthieu beat several defenders before being brought down in the box for a clear penalty. Naim Fadli calmly hit the ball into the centre of the goal after the keeper had dived to his right. Six minutes later, Matthieu crossed the ball towards Adrien Lucchino who then blasted a left-footed shot from just outside the penalty area against the crossbar. In hindsight, the whole game hinged on that moment, because the ten men of FCPV would probably have hung on with a two-goal cushion; instead, eight minutes later, St Cassien grabbed an equaliser when an attack down the left ended with Maxime finishing from close range.

Six minutes from time, a St Cassien breakaway left Thomas with just the goalkeeper to beat, only for the substitute to hit his shot just wide of the post. Shortly before the end, the same player looked to me to have been sent off for violent conduct, but subsequent reports failed to confirm that; in any case it was too late to make much difference and the game finished in a 2-2 draw, which was probably a fair result.

During the game, a neighbouring spectator heard me talking in English and initiated a conversation, intrigued that anyone from outside France would be watching a game in such a place and at this level. The friendly local proceeded to introduce himself as Adnan Sahin, formerly a youth player at Voiron. Aged 17, Sahin had just signed a contract with Ligue 1 club Clermont Foot as a defender in the youth team. Sahin told me that he was the first footballer from Voiron to join a Ligue 1 club. When asked what he thought of the game we were watching, Sahin replied that in his opinion the two best players were Valentin for St Cassien and Lucchino for FCPV. The woman standing next to me overheard the conversation, and on hearing Lucchino's name being mentioned, she turned and said, 'He's my son.'

A regular in the FCPV first team, 26-year-old Lucchino was completing his third season at the club. Highly versatile and able to play in a variety of positions, Lucchino mainly operated on the right of midfield in this match, beating the opposing defenders several times and getting in decent crosses as well as hitting the bar with a shot. When he's not playing for the first team, Lucchino also helps coach young players at FCPV, as well as being a video analyst for big neighbours GF 38 and the far more distant Haitian women's team. A few months before our match, Lucchino helped the Caribbean country overcome Senegal and Chile to qualify for the FIFA Women's World Cup finals.

Rightly proud of her son's achievements, Lucchino's mother told me that he would be accompanying the Haiti players to Australia for their first appearance at a World Cup finals tournament where the Caribbean team would be competing in the same group as England.

Clearly very busy with different roles and responsibilities, Lucchino told me 'luck helps sometimes, hard work always', summing up his philosophy.

The point earned that afternoon proved to be crucial at the end of the season, when FCPV finished third from bottom of the District de L'Isère Seniors Départemental 1 Pool A, only one point ahead of the lowest-ranked team. ASL St Cassien ended the campaign two places above FCPV.

Two days after the game, my long weekend in France came to an end, but just before boarding the plane at Lyon airport, I spotted some Bonnat chocolate bars on display in a duty-free shop. All of the bars carried a picture of the Église Saint-Bruno and the slogan 'Voiron/Isère depuis 1884' ('Voiron/Isère since 1884') on their wrappers. The different varieties were made with cocoa from various parts of the world, such as Peru, Madagascar and Indonesia; however, I simply had to buy a bar made with beans from Haiti.

At the Women's World Cup finals, Haiti was coached by Nicolas Delépine, a former coach at Grenoble Foot, with five of the squad playing for the French Alpine club. Despite being 500/1 outsiders, Haiti only narrowly lost 1-0 to England, then by the same score to China, followed by a 2-0 loss to Denmark. The side ranked 53rd in the world exceeded expectations, looked dangerous on the counter-attack and only conceded one goal from open play, with the other three coming from penalties.

In 2023/24, FCPV finished in second place, while ASL St Cassien ended seventh. At the end of that same season, Adnan Sahin was transferred to the under-19 team of Tours FC, which as we shall hear in a later chapter, is a former club of Olivier Giroud, the most successful footballer from the French Alps.

Chapter 6

Germany: Bavaria

FOOTBALL ARRIVED in Germany in the second half of the 19th century, but exactly where and when is a matter of dispute, with various places and dates suggested by different historians of the sport. In the early days of German football, competition took place at a local level before the Deutscher Fußball-Bund (German Football Association, or DFB) arrived on the scene in 1900. Three years later, the DFB organised the first national tournament which involved the winners of regional leagues qualifying for a knockout competition to decide the overall German championship.

The southern state of Bavaria is the largest by area and the second largest in terms of population in the Federal Republic of Germany. The oldest football club in the Bavarian capital, TSV 1860 München, had originally been formed for gymnastics in the date of its title, before adding football to its repertoire in 1899, a year before the formation of the city's most well-known club, FC Bayern München.

Munich is only about 20km/12.5 miles outside the perimeter of the Alpine Convention; nevertheless, such a location means that its famous football club doesn't feature in this book. Of Bavaria's seven administrative regions, only the most southerly portions of Oberbayern (Upper Bavaria) and the Allgäu are within the Alps; the next two chapters look at clubs from both those areas.

i. Knees like Pudding: 1. FC Garmisch-Partenkirchen, 704m/2,310ft

Approximately 90km/56 miles south-west of Munich, the town of Garmisch-Partenkirchen in Oberbayern can easily be reached by a direct train from the Bavarian capital. Full of brightly coloured Alpine chalets, Garmisch-Partenkirchen has been described as 'Bavaria's largest village', although with a population of just over 27,000 the settlement has long been a fully fledged town.

At 21 letters long, the name Garmisch-Partenkirchen is rather protracted, but outsiders should be wary of shortening it because this is a rather sensitive issue. Some residents of Partenkirchen get irritated when people refer to the whole town as 'Garmisch'. If you need to shorten it, 'Ga-Pa' is acceptable, but whatever you do, make sure you don't stroll around drunk in the Partenkirchen half chanting 'small town in Garmisch, you're just a small town in Garmisch'.

Although these days Garmisch-Partenkirchen is one place, until 1936 it consisted of two separate settlements: Garmisch to the west and Partenkirchen in the east. The arrival of the railway line in 1889 allowed visitors to come and view the Alps, or hike, climb and ski on them. At that time, Partenkirchen was the more developed of the two places and hosted a local market, while Garmisch was still a farming village separated from its neighbour by a strip of land.

On four occasions between 1893 and 1897, the famous English composer Edward (later Sir Edward) Elgar and his wife Alice holidayed in Garmisch. During their breaks in the village, the Elgars stayed in a guest house called the Villa Bader run by an English couple, Mr and Mrs Slingsby-Bethell. Peter Greaves's book *In the Bavarian Highlands: Edward Elgar's German Holidays in the 1890s*, details Elgar's itinerary, telling us 'On a "rest day", Saturday, 1 September 1894, he played football with the Slingsby-Bethell boys.' At that time, there were no local teams in Garmisch, making the then 37-year-old composer's kickabout one of the earliest recorded examples of football being played in the area.

Those surprised to hear about Elgar playing football might be interested to know that a couple of years later the famous composer attended his first match at Molineux, home of Wolverhampton Wanderers. In 1898, Elgar composed the words and music for what is reputedly the first song or chant specifically written for football. Usually referred to as 'He Banged the Leather for Goal' (although the handwritten score reproduced in Mrs Richard Powell's book *Edward Elgar: Memories of a Variation* looks to me like 'We' not 'He'), the song had been inspired by Wolves striker Billy Malpass. Unfortunately, the song didn't catch on with fans at Molineux, which explains why most people have never heard of it.

Back in Garmisch, Elgar saw performances of folk dancing in the Drei Mohren hotel during his 1893 holiday. Coincidentally, 35 years later, the Drei Mohren became the location for the founding of 1. FC Garmisch-Partenkirchen, after two local football enthusiasts organised a meeting at the hotel in March 1928. Sadly, the Drei Mohren suffered demolition in 1980, but at least the football club is still with us.

Consisting of 59 characters, the football club's full unabbreviated title, 1. Fußball-Club Garmisch-Partenkirchen 1928 eingetragener Verein, is a bit of a mouthful and also requires some explanation. The '1. Fußball-Club' bit is invariably abbreviated to '1. FC' and is quite common in Germany, meaning 'first' or 'leading football club'. The main part wisely includes both components of the town's name, while 1928 denotes its year of formation. Finally, 'eingetragener Verein' (usually abbreviated to eV) means 'registered association'. In this book, the club will sometimes be referred to as FCGP.

In 1931, FCGP decided to construct a permanent home, encouraged by promotion up through the local leagues. The original name for the football ground was Stadion am Gröben.

Two years later, the Nazis came to power in Germany, and in 1935 local councillors were pressured to vote in favour of merging the two settlements of Garmisch and Partenkirchen in preparation for hosting the Winter Olympics. Held in February 1936 and personally attended by Adolf Hitler, the Winter Olympics became a propaganda success for the Nazis, giving the world a false impression of the Third Reich after antisemitic posters were temporarily taken down in the town.

The Stadion am Gröben's unsuitability for sports such as skiing, skating, bobsleigh and ice hockey meant that it could not be used as a venue for the Winter Olympics. The president of the organising committee for the Games was a man called Karl Ritter von Halt. As well as being a Nazi party member, Ritter von Halt rose to become Reich Sports Leader during the Second World War. He performed a similar role as a sports administrator in post-war West Germany, and during the 1950s it was decided to change the name of Garmisch-Partenkirchen's football ground to Ritter-von-Halt-Stadion in his honour. Only as late as 2006 did the local authorities decide to rename the club's football ground following objections to Ritter von Halt's Nazi past, restoring its original name, Stadion am Gröben, instead.

To be fair to FCGP, the club's football ground wasn't the only one to have been named after a former Nazi; even the home of the famously left-wing and anti-fascist FC St Pauli kept the title Wilhelm-Koch-Stadion until as recently as 1998, before being renamed Millerntor-Stadion following complaints about Herr Koch's Nazi party membership.

In 1937, the year after the Winter Olympics, FCGP experienced a shortage of players, so a mixture of reserves and youth were joined by soldiers to make up a team. Garmisch-Partenkirchen's Alpine location had made it a suitable base for some of the Wehrmacht's elite mountain troops who were garrisoned in the town.

Fortunately, Garmisch-Partenkirchen escaped the heavy bombing which devastated so much of Germany during the war. After the defeat of the Third Reich, the town became part of the American occupation zone. The Americans were slightly more liberal than the British, and far more tolerant than the French and Soviets who administered the other zones. Consequently, the Americans allowed sporting events to take place much earlier than elsewhere. Competitive football restarted with the launch of a Bavarian Oberliga in November 1945, while the Bayerischer Fußball-Verband (Bavarian Football Association or BFV) was formed the following year.

The town soon became the main winter sports recreation centre for US military personnel. In April 1946, with their town still teeming with GIs, a couple of locals, Josef Hinfner and Paul Fischer, took the initiative to reconstitute 1. FC Garmisch-Partenkirchen. However, American liberalism had its limits, because the US authorities continued to commandeer the Stadion am Gröben, making it difficult to play matches.

Within a few years, some of the old pre-war footballers returned to play for FCGP. In 1949, the new country of West Germany came into being, and a crowd of 1,500 turned out to watch Bavarian giants 1. FC Nürnberg in a friendly at Ga-Pa. As in other parts of Europe, football provided a welcome escape from hardship and misery.

The club spent the post-war years competing in the lower leagues of the A-Klasse and B-Klasse, until in 1959 it reached the Landesliga (sometimes translated as either National League or Country League). Despite its grandiose name, the Landesliga was a regional league in southern Germany, and the club would spend much of its subsequent history as another 'elevator club', yo-yoing between that division and the lower level of the Bezirksliga (District League).

Launched in the 1963/64 season, the Bundesliga became the first league covering the whole of West Germany, replacing the old knockout competition between regional champions. Five years later in 1969, a crowd of 6,000 spectators filled the Ritter-von-Halt-Stadion to watch FC Bayern München (who had just clinched the Bundesliga title) defeat FCGP by the hefty score of 11-3.

The 1995/96 season turned out to be one of FCGP's most notable campaigns, with the team securing promotion to the Landesliga and reaching the Bayerische Pokalfinale (Bavarian Cup Final) for the first and only time, losing 3-1 to Schweinfurt.

FCGP struggled to stay in the Landesliga, and briefly appointed Norbert Eder as coach in 1998. Eder had played for West Germany as a full international, including an appearance in the 1986 World Cup Final when the national team lost to Diego Maradona's Argentina. However, Eder couldn't halt the slide, and FCGP suffered two successive relegations.

As in some other countries featuring in this book, the German football league pyramid is complicated, with regional variations and reorganisations. A new fifth tier called the Bezirksoberliga was added in 1988; Regionalligas then replaced the previous level three in 1994; followed by the 3. Liga becoming the new third tier in 2008. With each change, all divisions below these additions were bumped down a rung on the German league ladder.

At the time of my visit to Ga-Pa in 2012, the football pyramid in the local area looked like this (confusingly, both Bezirksliga and Kreisliga translate as 'District League'):

1. Bundesliga 1
2. Bundesliga 2
3. 3. Liga
4. Regionalliga
5. Bayernliga
6. Landesliga
7. Bezirksoberliga Oberbayern
8. Bezirksliga Süd
9. Kreisliga Zugspitze
10. Kreisklasse

When I saw 1. FC Garmisch-Partenkirchen in 2012, appearing in the team that afternoon was a footballer called Christoph Saller. Born in 1973 in Ga-Pa, Saller mainly played for FCGP, but also had a three-year spell at nearby FC Oberau. Six years before I saw him, Saller played in one of the most crucial matches in the history of FCGP. In the 2005/06 season, the team competed in the Bezirksliga Süd and needed to win its final match of the season against SC Maissach to avoid relegation down to the Kreisliga Zugspitze. Three minutes into stoppage time it was 2-2, when the referee dramatically awarded Saller's side a penalty.

The club's website says of the crucial 2006 penalty, 'Christoph Saller confidently converted the penalty kick to the cheers of the entire team.' However, when I asked Saller about the vital penalty, he replied in English, but told me a different story, saying that he was far from confident: 'The situation was very difficult. One of the players of SC Maissach had a long discussion with the referee about the penalty decision while I waited to take the kick. This situation is horrible. You know, if you don't score, the team goes down to the lower league. I began to think about where to shoot the penalty: in my preferred corner, flat right or should I change it? After three minutes the referee confirmed his decision to award the penalty, but after all this time waiting my knees were like pudding. Finally, I decided to shoot hard into my favourite corner, flat right, directly beside the goalpost. The keeper dived towards this corner, but had no chance of keeping out my shot. So, we finally avoided relegation and it was the beginning of a long and happy boozy evening with the team which went on into the night.'

Two years later in 2008, Saller was at it again, scoring the winning goal as FCGP defeated SV Ohlstad in another crucial match to help his team avoid relegation. However, the following season the club experienced financial problems and multiple injuries, causing a drop to the Kreisliga Zugspitze.

On the afternoon of Sunday, 20 May 2012, I headed towards the Stadion am Gröben to see FCGP in action. At that time, the team played in the ninth-tier Kreisliga Zugspitze.

I took a seat in the grandstand along the north side of the little stadium. Covered since 1975 when a roof had been constructed and floodlights installed, the grandstand provided superb views of the Wetterstein Mountains.

On the right of the Wetterstein range stands the Zugspitze, the tallest peak in Germany at 2,962m/9,718ft high. This mountain has three connections to football.

Firstly, a view of the Zugspitze appears on the badge of FCGP. Secondly, the mountain lends its name to the local football division, Kreisliga Zugspitze (which literally means 'District League Zugspitze').

The third, and most bizarre, connection occurred 11 years after my match and involved the former German international, Andre Schürrle, who I first saw playing for Bayer Leverkusen in the Champions League in 2011 against Chelsea, a club he later joined. A devotee of extreme physical activities, Schürrle went shirtless, completing an eight-hour ascent of the Zugspitze bare-chested, wearing just a helmet, shorts, socks and boots, together with a rucksack. Schürrle also climbed during the night, when the temperature on the snow-covered mountain would be at its coldest.[8] Thirty-two years old at the time of his climb in July 2023, Schürrle had given up football at the age of just 29 having tired of the game only six years after providing the assist for the winning goal in the 2014 World Cup Final in Brazil. Some people claim that exposure to extreme cold can be beneficial for your health, but others argue that

---

8 See tinyurl.com/Yodel07 for the full story.

such exploits potentially put the rescue services at risk. For what it's worth, my advice is that people should always wear proper mountain clothing when hiking or climbing at altitude and never attempt ascents at night.

Although the view of the mountains from the grandstand at the Stadion am Gröben was impressive, the view of the pitch wasn't quite so good because of the athletics track running around it. Practically all the spectators watched from the grandstand, with just the odd individual preferring the grass banking on the other side.

Formed in 1947, the opposition, Sport Verein Eberfing, came from a small village of that name with fewer than 1,500 inhabitants, about 42km/26 miles to the north. Although Eberfing is within the Alpine region, it is further from the mountains and at a slightly lower altitude.

FCGP wore its usual blue kit, while SV Eberfing appeared in all white. The home side included Christoph Saller in its starting line-up. By then aged 39, Saller's high level of fitness was shown by the fact that he later became the Sportlicher Leiter, the football club's athletic supervisor.

With just over a minute played, Eberfing's Martin Plonner dribbled unopposed in a straight line from the centre circle towards the FCGP goal. No defenders closed Plonner down, allowing him plenty of time to kick a weak shot which slowly bobbled along before the goalkeeper, Hannes Maurer, dived over the ball, Gary Sprake 1970 FA Cup Final-style, letting it trickle into the goal. Despite this unpromising start, the match improved and turned out to be quite watchable.

FCGP equalised after ten minutes when Florian Sporer delivered an accurate cross for Günter Kellner to knock into an empty net. Sporer then turned from assister to scorer, putting the home side ahead after 27 minutes.

FCGP led 2-1 at half-time, and I took advantage of the interval to buy an excellent beer from the clubhouse. Built in 1981, aided by sponsorship from the famous Paulaner brewery in Munich, the clubhouse served as the social hub for the crowd of about 100 people, all enjoying a live football game amid a genuine family and community atmosphere.

Midway through the second half, Hannes Mohr extended FCGP's lead. Plonner then got his second goal for Eberfing a couple of minutes before the end of normal time with a shot from distance, making it 3-2 and setting up an exciting finish. However, the visitors proved unable to score again, so it ended in victory for the home side.

At the conclusion of the 2011/12 campaign, FCGP finished 12th out of 14 teams in the division, while Eberfing ended up one place higher. The conclusion of the season saw yet another change to the structure of Bavarian football, with the former seventh-tier Bezirksoberliga Oberbayern and eighth-tier Bezirksliga Süd merged to create a single Bezirksliga Oberbayern-Süd division. FCGP won promotion to the new division in 2012/13.

During 2013/14, FCGP found itself struggling at the bottom of the table. Saller took over as coach in the winter break, initiating a dramatic improvement with the team winning eight games in a row. However, a 3-1 defeat in the decisive game at SC Gaißach led to relegation to the Kreisliga.

FCGP stayed at that level for three seasons before winning promotion back to the Bezirksliga Oberbayern-Süd at the end of the 2016/17 campaign. Saller then secured a second successive promotion, returning the club to the Landesliga. In March 2022, after eight years as FCGP's coach, Saller quit, reportedly following a dispute with the club's sporting director. Saller then became coach of

SC Eibsee Grainau, a team based just outside Ga-Pa that competes in the A-Klasse.

FCGP finished the 2021/22 season in the relegation play-offs and ended up being demoted from the Landesliga back to the Bezirksliga Oberbayern-Süd. The club then secured an instant return to the sixth-tier Landesliga Südost-Bayern where it still played at the time of writing. SV Eberfing competes down in the A-Klasse, in one of those merged *Spielgemeinschaft* ('game community') joint teams under the name SG SV Eberfing/SV Söchering.

ii. From Villa Bader to Bad Villain

Earlier we heard about Elgar watching folk dancing being performed at Garmisch's Drei Mohren hotel in 1893. The particular type of dancing that the English composer saw is called the *Schuhplattler*, a dance which gets its name from part of the routine where performers slap the soles of their shoes (*Schuhe*) with their hands held flat (*platt*). The performance of the *Schuhplattler* that Elgar witnessed in Garmisch inspired the first part of *From the Bavarian Highlands*, which he composed on his return to England. Elgar later dedicated that piece of music to Mr and Mrs Slingsby-Bethell, the people he had stayed with at the Villa Bader and parents of the boys he played football with in the village.

Over 130 years later, an international footballer performed the *Schuhplattler* in Garmish-Partenkirchen. The story goes as follows.

Like most Alpine resorts, Garmisch-Partenkirchen is fairly quiet during the summer, resting up for the skiing season. Foreign football teams often take advantage of the relatively empty hotels and sunny weather for their pre-season preparation. A notable example occurred when Garmisch-Partenkirchen provided the base camp for Scotland during UEFA Euro 2024. Ga-Pa was chosen partly because it provided easy access to Munich where the Scots faced host country Germany in the opening match of the tournament.

According to *The Scotsman* in June 2024, 'Scotland came here for clear air, tranquillity and first-rate facilities,' adding: 'With apologies to Fort William FC, Stadion am Gröben, as the ground is now known, must be the most breathtaking spot to play football in Europe.' Unfortunately, when Scotland's squad held an open training session on the pitch of the Stadion am Gröben, grey cloudy skies meant that the Zugspitze struggled to be seen and the players needed umbrellas to shelter from the rain. However, the weather failed to dampen the enthusiasm of dozens of local children who excitedly watched Steve Clarke put his players through their paces.

The Obermühle Hotel, just the other side of the River Loisach from the Stadion am Gröben, provided the squad's accommodation and offered the players use of its private spa, sauna, swimming pool and rooftop terrace with glorious mountain views. The hotel proudly announced on its website that it would be hosting the Scottish team, possibly until the closing stages of the tournament, 'until 13 July at the latest'.

The *Schuhplattler* made its appearance when the Scottish squad arrived in the resort and attended a reception in the Bayernhalle, an indoor venue on the edge of town. After an oompah band welcomed the players, three locals wearing traditional lederhosen costumes started to perform the *Schuhplattler*. At the beginning of the display, the Scottish players were standing behind the dancers. Scotland and

Aston Villa midfielder John McGinn tried to mimic one of the performers, but that backfired when the dancer grabbed the Glaswegian and added him to the troupe, plonking a feathered hat on his head.

Despite the title of this section of the book, the tracksuited McGinn went on to deliver a mean *Schuhplattler*, learning the routine very quickly, with some impressive side-to-side movements, accompanying his knee, thigh and foot-slapping. Although I was sadly not in Ga-Pa at the time to see his moves, they are available to watch on several online sites.

Unfortunately, Scotland's footballing performances were not as good as McGinn's dancing. After finishing bottom of the group, the Scots checked out of the Obermühle Hotel halfway through their booking.

Chapter 7

Germany and Austria: Junior Football

THE PROMOTION and development of football among young people is obviously crucial for the future of the game in the Alps, just like it is everywhere else. This chapter considers recent changes at junior level in Germany, followed by eyewitness accounts of under-nines and under-11s games played under the new guidelines.

i. Primary Objective

Since 1972, *Junioren* ('junior') football in Germany has been structured as follows:

> G-Junioren for under-sevens (also called Bambini)
> F-Junioren for under-nines
> E-Junioren for under-11s
> D-Junioren for under-13s
> C-Junioren for under-15s
> B-Junioren for under-17s
> A-Junioren for under-19s

Following several disappointing performances from the German national side around the millennium, the Deutscher

Fußball-Bund initiated its Talentförderprogramm (Talent Development Programme). In addition to the work already done by schools, scouts and football clubs, the programme launched during the 2002/03 season involved setting up nearly 400 bases across Germany with over 1,000 coaches catering for players over the age of 11. One particular purpose of the bases was to try and reach youngsters showing potential who had not been signed up by one of the top clubs. The bases aimed to give these youngsters training tailored to their individual needs, in tactics and technique, with the ultimate aim of creating more 'elite-level' footballers. The DFB hoped that the bases would help promote unified training and playing methods throughout Germany.

The DFB also ordered all 18 clubs in the Bundesliga to establish football academies which would be centrally regulated. Since then, thousands of young players have been trained in these academies, with some of them going on to join professional football clubs. These initiatives contributed to a revival in German football, culminating in the country winning the 2014 World Cup. According to Raphael Honigstein in his book *Das Reboot*, all but two of the players in Germany's squad in Brazil were products of the academies.

At the time of writing, for German under-13s the top tier is at state level; for under-15s it is at regional level; while for under-17s and under-19s the highest tier is national (albeit initially divided into regional groupings ahead of a national final). For all these age groups, the highest leagues have several more localised divisions below them.

Despite German success in 2014, football goes in cycles, and when disappointing performances by the national side returned at the 2018 World Cup and the European

Championship in 2021, the DFB ordered changes to how the game is played by children under the age of 11. Football for older age groups remained largely unaltered, the earlier reforms deemed sufficient, although there were some modifications to tournaments. The new strategy was designed to ensure more children continued playing through the G-, F- and E-Junioren levels (under-sevens through to under-11s); something that would produce a larger pool of potential talent for the academies and clubs to draw on.

In response to concerns about the high drop-out rate among younger children, many countries have introduced reforms designed to make football more enjoyable and encourage kids to continue in the game as they grow up. Countries such as England, the Netherlands, Austria and Switzerland had already implemented changes by the time Germany followed suit at the start of the 2024/25 season.

It could be argued that the reforms were a reaction to the over-coaching of youngsters, with formations, positions and set ways of playing drilled into them at too early an age by adults; instead, the changes aimed to boost individual creativity. In some ways, the reforms were a throwback to children's informal kickabouts in the street, activities that used to be common but rarely happen these days.

The reforms were inspired by *Funino*, which despite being a combination of the English word 'fun' and the Spanish word *niño* – meaning 'child' – had actually been developed by a German sports coach, Horst Wein. The guidelines include the following changes.

Previously, football in Germany for younger children had tended to involve seven-a-side games. Under the new arrangements, kids take part in short games on smaller pitches, with constant rotation of players ensuring that all children get their share of possession to help develop their individual skills, particularly ball control in tight spaces and dribbling. At the youngest Bambini level, only three youngsters actually play for a team at any one time; each team defends two mini goals rather than just one; and there are no goalkeepers (partly to stop conditioning kids for specific roles too early in their development). Throw-ins and goal kicks are replaced by 'dribble-ins'; heading of the ball is discouraged for health and safety reasons; while smaller and lighter footballs are used. Coaching and refereeing are reduced to a minimum during the games, with children encouraged to oversee the rules themselves.

As the juniors get older, their games gradually begin to bear more resemblance to regular football, with slightly longer match duration; more players on the pitch; bigger playing surfaces; two goals instead of four; heavier balls; the introduction of throw-ins and goal kicks; the appearance of goalkeepers; and eventually toleration of heading.

German football up to and including under-nine level had previously been part of league competition, but under the changes there are no competitive divisions or tables for these age groups. Instead, games are billed as one-off events or 'festivals' to emphasise the joy of playing (particularly the thrill of scoring goals) rather than the pressure of grinding out results. It was also felt that the recording of scores might discourage children whose teams were frequently on the end of thrashings. The absence of matches in a competitive league has the added advantage of making the presence of parents less common, with dads shouting out ill-informed or negative comments during youth games having been specifically recognised as detrimental.

The ending of competitive leagues and the publication of results proved to be the most controversial change.

Supporters of the new policies argue that children are naturally competitive enough already and want to win every game; the only thing that has changed is removing the external pressure from adults, particularly coaches and parents, created by the recording of scores and league tables. For an eight-year-old goalkeeper who has just conceded his age in goals, telling everyone about it could be quite dispiriting. Furthermore, removing competitive leagues and their focus on results means there is no longer a need to always select the strongest team, or encourage other children to quickly give the ball to the best player. The new approach ensures more kids get adequate game time and share of ball possession.

On the other hand, prominent figures such as Hans-Joachim Watzke (vice-president of the DFB) and Ralf Rangnick (by now coach of the Austrian national side) have criticised the demise of competitive leagues for the youngest children. Opponents argue that life is competitive with plenty of disappointment and stress, casting doubt on whether such a policy can help prepare children for dealing with both grown-up football and adult life. Less importantly, not publicising results of games, or the names of goalscorers also makes things challenging for authors of football books, as I soon discovered.

Unfortunately, the changes were accompanied by quite a lot of confusion. Reports on some websites said that competitive football would be stopped up to and including under-nine level, but others stated that it would end for under-11s too. I have also read accounts providing conflicting information about whether games should be refereed. The reforms were also ambiguous about heading, saying there was no need for younger players to head the ball, but stopping short of an actual ban. The DFB also allowed local federations to implement their own slightly different versions of the guidelines, with the Bayerischer Fußball-Verband (Bavarian Football Association or BFV) deciding to rebrand junior football in that state as *Minifußball* ('Mini Football'). Although in some ways laudable, this devolution may have added to the mixed messages.

In September 2024, during a holiday in the Bavarian resort of Oberstdorf, I had the chance to see for myself how the reforms were going, by attending games for under-nines and under-11s played according to the new regulations.

ii. Mini Football in the Little Valley: SV Kleinwalsertal, 1,108m/3,635ft

Kleinwalsertal is a small triangular part of the Austrian state of Vorarlberg protruding towards Germany. Most of the 5,000 inhabitants of Kleinwalsertal live in four settlements: the small town of Mittelberg, the villages of Riezlern and Hirschegg, and the tiny hamlet of Baad, all along the valley of the River Breitach.

The name Kleinwalsertal literally means 'little Walser valley', derived from the migration of the Walser people who left the Swiss canton of Valais (Wallis in German) and settled in the valley from the year 1302. Aspects of Valais culture are still celebrated in this remote part of Austria, including an alphorn festival dedicated to the iconic Swiss musical instrument. Fortunately, the festival coincided with my visit, so I was able to hear 53 of these horns being played together during a memorable and highly atmospheric finale.

The surrounding mountains create a natural barrier between Kleinwalsertal and the rest of Austria; consequently, people leaving the valley have to use the only main road which leads to Oberstdorf in Germany.

Travellers can then continue by road or join the German rail network to complete their onward journeys, either back into Austria or to other destinations.

In the 1890s, Kleinwalsertal's isolation from the rest of Austria encouraged it to develop a closer relationship with Germany by using the mark as currency, joining a customs union and having an open border with its bigger neighbour. This special relationship continued until Austria joined the European Union in 1995, followed by the mark being replaced by the euro a few years later; developments that rendered the old arrangements superfluous. However, addresses in Kleinwalsertal still have German as well as Austrian postcodes.

It isn't just transport, business, finance and mail deliveries where Kleinwalsertal established closer ties with Germany, because sportsmen and women living in the valley have also found it easier to compete against teams from Bavaria than travel to play opponents elsewhere in Austria. Kleinwalsertal's footballers are no different, and play matches under the auspices of the BFV, while the local club is a member of both the Österreichischer Fußball-Bund (Austrian Football Association or ÖFB) and the DFB.

Football in the valley can be traced back to 1958, when members of a local ski club started to play the beautiful game before breaking away a couple of years later to form an independent team.

A pitch at Bödmen, a hamlet near Mittelberg, provided the first home for Kleinwalsertal's footballers. Undoubtedly the biggest match at Bödmen occurred in 1968, in the form of a friendly against 1. FC Nürnberg. Practically the entire population of the valley turned out, with a crowd of 4,000 spectators seeing the team that had just won the German

Bundesliga beat Kleinwalsertal 13-1. Nothing remains of the old venue, and the site is now occupied by a large Aparthotel on the road up the valley to Baad.

Like many Austrian football clubs, the Walser footballers have gone through a series of name changes. Since 1975, the valley's footballers have joined other athletes as part of Sportverein Kleinwalsertal (Sports Club Kleinwalsertal), a multi-sports organisation, not only offering football, but activities such as skiing, tennis, volleyball and yoga. However, the book *Vorarlberger Fußballgeschichte* lists the team as having been a member of the Vorarlberg Football Association for three seasons between 1980 and 1983 under the name FC Kleinwalsertal. These days, the club is officially known as SV Casino Kleinwalsertal, because of sponsorship from the gambling house in Riezlern.

A remote location and a small population have sometimes made it difficult to find enough players, causing the club to periodically drop out of competition. The men's first team last played in the 11th tier of German football (the B-Klasse Allgäu 8), but stopped competing at the end of 2017/18, and at the time of writing has yet to restart. In recent seasons, SV Kleinwalsertal's football department has decided to concentrate on developing junior talent.

Until 2019/20, the E-Junioren was SV Kleinwalsertal's only team involved in competitive matches, playing in the U11 (E1-Jun.) Liga organised by the BFV. During the COVID-19 pandemic, not only was football suspended but it became difficult to cross the border between Germany and Austria, putting the whole of Kleinwalsertal in a very tricky situation.

For a brief period following the pandemic, SV Kleinwalsertal contributed footballers under the age of

11 to a joint *Spielgemeinschaft* ('game community') with FC Oberstdorf. Called SG Oberstdorf/Kleinwalsertal, the merged team played home games at the Bavarian club's Oybele-Stadion. SV Kleinwalsertal then resumed its independence, operating junior squads for the three youngest categories: G-Junioren, F-Junioren and E-Junioren.

To reach Kleinwalsertal from my holiday apartment in Oberstdorf meant taking one of the regular buses operating on the 20-minute journey. Interestingly, it was a bendy bus, like the ones used in London between 2001 and 2011 except it was blue rather than red. The bendy bus wound its way up a road which sometimes lacked crash barriers despite significant drops down the hillside, then drove past the Breitachklamm, the deepest rocky gorge in central Europe; as it did so, it occurred to me that Friday the 13th was perhaps not the best day for such a journey.

Fortunately, the road soon levelled out, and a sign saying 'Republik Österreich' meant that the bus had crossed into Austria, but there were no border checks so passports stayed in pockets. It quickly became apparent that Kleinwalsertal is something of a mini paradise, with opportunities to hike amid beautiful Alpine scenery, plus picture-postcard villages and obvious wealth combining to produce a luxury mountain resort.

I got off the bus at Breitachbrucke, a bridge over the river in the middle of the valley, and it then took just a few minutes to reach Kleinwalsertal's football ground. A slight breathlessness when walking up the sloping pavement could have been caused by altitude, having been down at sea level at my home in England only two days earlier.

At 1,108m/3,635ft, the Walser-Arena, to give the little stadium its official name, possesses the highest full-size permanent football pitch to feature in this book. Although a later chapter describes my visit to the even higher Ottmar Hitzfeld Gspon Arena in Switzerland, that pitch is smaller, designed for eight-a-side games. To put the Walser-Arena's altitude into perspective, it is higher than the summit of any mountain in England or Wales.

After years of hard work as well as financial assistance from the local community, SV Kleinwalsertal managed to leave Bödmen and move to its current site. According to the valley's newspaper *Der Walser*, a local pastor formally inaugurated the new football ground in August 1983.

The Walser-Arena's location, in a hamlet called Au near the village of Hirschegg, explains why it's sometimes referred to as the Sportplatz Au or Sportplatz Hirschegg. One end of the pitch backs on to a car park, while the other merges with a smaller field near the Walmendinger hotel. Floodlights and trees run along the touchlines, while a fast-flowing stream called the Schwarzwasserbach runs behind the clubhouse on the south side. When matches take place, a net is installed to try and stop balls landing in the stream; those that do splash in the water tend to get rapidly washed downstream and eventually into the Breitach, with many of them lost.

Summer is definitely the busiest time for the Walser-Arena, when the likes of German football school Anstoß-Die Fußballschule and Bundesliga club FC Augsburg hold pre-season training camps for youngsters there. Just before winter, any perimeter fencing or advertising boards as well as the goalposts have to be removed to avoid damage from snow and ice. When SV Kleinwalsertal's men's team functioned, the players had to travel over the border to use artificial pitches in Bavaria for any 'home' fixtures during the winter.

The week before my visit, it had been 32°C just over the border in Oberstdorf, but by the time I arrived in Kleinwalsertal the temperature had plummeted to 4°C, with snow on the grass bank next to the pitch. The earlier than expected snowfall caused Kleinwalsertal's herders to bring their cows down from the mountain pastures a few days earlier than planned.

Despite the weather, the game I attended on 13 September 2024 proved to be timely, because it was the first official fixture played by SV Kleinwalsertal's F-Junior team under the new guidelines introduced by the DFB and the BFV for the start of the 2024/25 season.

At the time, the Walser club had two teams for children under-nine: SV Kleinwalsertal 1 and SV Kleinwalsertal 2, which were in U9 F1 OA/KE Gruppe 5 and Gruppe 5a respectively. These two groups were organised by the BFV, and under the new system the match results were not recorded, nor did they count towards a league competition; instead, the only function of the groups was to arrange opponents for stand-aione matches. Both of the club's under-nines teams train for an hour and a half after school on Monday and Wednesday, then play their matches on Fridays. That afternoon, it was the turn of the SV Kleinwalsertal 1 under-nines, with the opposition provided by FC Oberstdorf.

Formed in 1921, FC Obertsdorf men's team currently competes in a local league on the seventh tier of German football. The club also has a second team for men, plus teams for under-nines and under-11s. Kleinwalsertal and Oberstdorf are friendly rivals, because the two settlements are only 13km/8 miles apart and many of the valley's children go to school over the border in Oberstdorf so know their opponents well. The two clubs also recently shared the previously mentioned *Spielgemeinschaft*, and still joke that matches between them are 'internationals'.

The BFV directed that F-Juniors should play four-a-side with each team defending two mini goals, or five-a-side with each team defending one slightly larger goal and using a goalkeeper. By way of comparison, English under-nines play in seven-a-side teams, each defending a single goal.

I arrived 20 minutes before the 5pm kick-off; in time to see both teams warming up and doing little drills and some shooting practice. Although the Walser-Arena has a full-size pitch, the children played on just a part of it and used small goals, in accordance with the regulations. The playing area was marked off by plastic cones along the touchlines and red tape for the goal lines.

SV Kleinwalsertal's team lined up in an all-red kit, while FC Oberstdorf appeared in black-and-white-striped shirts, black shorts and white socks. Each team defended just one goal and it was five-a-side with four outfield players and a goalkeeper per team. The match consisted of two halves, each lasting 20 minutes. Although some versions of the new DFB guidelines discourage the involvement of match officials for F-Junior and G-Junior age groups, this particular game was refereed.

During the game, goal kicks and throw-ins were replaced by passing in or dribbling in from where the ball left the pitch, all in accordance with the new regulations. However, I was interested to see that twice during the second half, Kleinwalsertal defenders firmly headed the ball clear following Oberstdorf balls into the box, despite deliberate headers being discouraged by the recent guidelines.

The DFB had hoped that the ban on competitive games would discourage unsolicited 'coaching' from the sidelines. There had been no parental involvement in the first half, but that changed during the second period, when a few more family members turned up, presumably having come straight from work. However, their contributions from the benches outside the clubhouse were shouts of encouragement rather than anything negative, and even after the late arrivals the number of spectators remained in single figures.

Towards the end of the game the visibility worsened, with the top of the mountain above the pitch called Gottesacker ('God's Field') disappearing into the heavens (or more accurately behind the clouds). Sleet began to fall, adding to the moisture on a pitch already sodden from the recent rain. As the weather deteriorated, the ball slowed or even got stuck in the surface water. Following modern trends, the kids continued to try and play out from the back, whereas in my day we would have hoofed the ball clear in such conditions. The sleet turned to snow during the last few minutes, but fortunately the game was completed in full, and without any balls being lost in the stream.

Despite the cold, sleet and snow at well over 3,000ft, not all of the young footballers had leggings, only half of them opted to wear warm hats, while gloves were just for the goalkeepers. Remember this when you next see a millionaire Premier League star dressed in thermals during mild weather down near sea level in England.

As with other under-nine games, the BFV declined to publish the result, possibly to stop anyone aggregating the final scores and formulating their own league tables. Instead, next to the fixture, the federation's website merely said 'O.E.', standing for 'Ohne Ergebnisbekanntgabe' ('without announcement of results').

Following such guidelines, I have decided not to provide the result or list the goalscorers in this account. What I can say is that the kids clearly enjoyed the game and the absence of a competitive league structure didn't seem to dampen their commitment. Although there were a couple of tearful moments following collisions and tumbles, those involved soon recovered and carried on playing. Multiple substitutions throughout the game ensured that all children had an opportunity to participate.

SV Kleinwalsertal's under-nine teams have two coaches, and I spoke to one of them, Florian Nyer (known as Flo), after the final whistle. When I commented that the children had done very well considering the rain, sleet and snow, Flo replied that they have to play in this kind of weather or miss lots of matches. He added that they hope to carry on playing at the Walser-Arena until October then use the Turnhalle, an indoor sports centre in Hirschegg. After I returned to England, Flo told me that despite snowy weather, SV Kleinwalsertal's juniors actually continued playing in the open at the Walser-Arena until the start of November.

Originally from Kleinwalsertal, Flo went to primary school locally and then crossed over the border to attend secondary school in Oberstdorf, before completing his studies in Vienna. Flo has been involved in football for much of his life, telling me, 'As a child, I played football almost every day as long as the garden was free of snow. We had a flat area of about 10x10m, which is not a given for a house on a hillside. Either I played there or on the football field in the Au. In my childhood and youth, I played for SV Kleinwalsertal. Since I was doing competitive cross-country skiing, I stopped playing club football at some point. In Vienna I only played football occasionally and not in a club.'

After working as a children's trainer in Vienna, Flo returned to Kleinwalsertal with his young family in 2021. The following year he became a coach at SV Kleinwalsertal, and since 2023 has also taken on the role of *Jugendleiter* ('youth leader'), a responsibility which he described to me as follows, 'I have a wide range of tasks as youth leader. My main goal is to get as many children as possible interested in football and at the same time to specifically promote talented players. Of course, this includes a variety of organisational tasks: from registering children for player passes, to ensuring that the game runs smoothly, to communicating with parents and coaches on all relevant topics.'

When I asked Flo what he considered to be the biggest achievement since he became *Jugendleiter*, he said, 'Since this summer there has been a girls' soccer team in Kleinwalsertal for the first time with 24 games for ages five to ten. Unfortunately, this is not a given, especially in a small club like ours, and we are therefore particularly pleased.'

The Walser-Arena's high altitude means the pitch is usually only playable from May to October, as Flo explained, 'Unfortunately, due to the cold in autumn and the snow conditions, we can only play on grass for six months of the year, with training taking place in the gym for the other six months. Unfortunately, the soccer field is in the shade for a long time, where the sun does not melt the snow so quickly.'

Following the controversy about recent changes to Bambini, F-Junioren and E-Junioren football introduced by the DFB and BFV, I was keen to know Flo's opinion, and his response made it clear that he was fully behind the measures, 'I am a big supporter of mini football or *Funino*. For me, this is the right approach to teaching children how to play football in the best possible way. It makes perfect sense to focus on giving as many children as possible lots of ball contact and scoring experiences in order to promote fun in the game. The less talented children also benefit from this, which will hopefully help to reduce the drop-out rate in youth football in the long term.'

iii. Off the Hook: TSV Fischen, 760m/2,493ft

On Friday, 20 September 2024, a week after the Kleinwalsertal under-nines game, I travelled 7km/4 miles north from Oberstdorf to Fischen im Allgäu to see an under-11s match. Luckily, the weather improved considerably, and instead of the previous week's sleet and snow it was a sunny 20°C with a long queue at the ice-cream kiosk.

Known for short as Fischen, this settlement in the Oberallgäu district of Bavaria is home to about 3,000 people, and although a town according to my definition, seemed more like a sleepy village. In 1888, the railways arrived at Fischen and easier access enabled it to develop as a resort. These days, Fischen is a spa and health destination, and among the treatments available is a form of hydrotherapy involving walking through water. Other people relying on their feet are the players of the local football team.

Turn-und Sportverein Fischen (Gymnastics and Sport Club Fischen) was founded in 1908. Another of the region's multi-sports clubs, these days TSV Fischen has just over 800 members and specialises in three sports: football, tennis and gymnastics. The German word *Fischen* means 'fishing' and a couple of fish appear on the badge of TSV Fischen proudly displayed at the club's stadium.

Located on the edge of town, Fischen's football ground, the Weidachsportanlage, consists of a natural grass pitch, with perimeter fencing, floodlights and a short straight section of athletics track in front of a rather grand clubhouse. The benches in front of the clubhouse offer an unobstructed panorama of the Sonnenkopf and other peaks of the Allgäu Alps; however, the stadium's position on flat land squeezed between the River Iller and its tributary the Grundbach means that the mountains are more distant and the view less dramatic than in Oberstdorf or Kleinwalsertal.

TSV Fischen's men's team stopped functioning independently at the end of the 2023/24 season, merging into another *Spielgemeinschaft*, in this case with 1. FC Sonthofen's second team. However, TSV Fischen continues to operate independently at junior level with two under-11 teams and three at under-nine. The under-11s train once per week in the summer, then twice a week during the football season.

TV Hindelang provided the afternoon's opposition, coming from the town of Bad Hindelang, a short distance to the north-east but still within the Oberallgäu district and the Alpine region. Bad Hindelang has a slightly larger population and also a marginally higher altitude. As its name suggests, Bad Hindelang is another spa and health resort; this time people head to the town because of its low level of pollen and spores, together with dozens of allergy-friendly hotels, restaurants and shops; facilities that are certainly not to be sneezed at.

Formed in 1893, Turnverein Hindelang (Gymnastics Club Hindelang) is also a multi-sports club. These days football is the largest section with no fewer than 12 teams: three men's teams and nine junior teams. TV Hindelang's under-11s train twice a week, for an hour and a half after school on Mondays and Thursdays.

For under-11s, the new BFV regulations stipulate that games can be either five-a-side or seven-a-side, and for the match at Fischen it was the larger number of players. The guidelines also say that each team defends just one youth-size goal; goalkeepers are allowed; deliberate heading of the ball is still discouraged; however, when the ball crosses the touchline, throw-ins can now be used to restart play. With regard to the playing area, the new regulations require pitches to be 55m long and 35m wide. By comparison, English kids of that age have nine players per side and play on larger surfaces.

The game I had come to see was in the second round of matches in the U11 (E-Jun.) OA/KE Gruppe 2, and featured the first teams of the clubs at under-11 level. TSV Fischen 1 played in white shirts, red shorts and white socks, while TV Hindelang 1 appeared in a rather snazzy turquoise kit with a blue and yellow trim.

As the Weidachsportanlage has a full-size playing surface, the game was played across the pitch with slightly smaller youth goals temporarily placed by each of the touchlines. This meant that the clubhouse where the 40 spectators were gathered was behind one of the goals, rather than along the side as it is for adult matches.

Kicking off at 6pm, the game consisted of two halves each lasting 25 minutes, making it slightly longer than the previous week's under-nine encounter. Like that earlier game, this one was also refereed.

Hindelang went ahead after four minutes, with Fischen equalising nine minutes later through a deflected shot. Only two minutes elapsed before the home side made it 2-1 with a firm shot into the goal. Within seconds, Hindelang levelled the scores through a header. As with the under-nines in Kleinwalsertal, I was surprised to see deliberate heading of the ball continuing at this level. At half-time it remained 2-2, partly thanks to the Fischen goalkeeper who pulled off several decent saves.

At the Kleinwalsertal versus Oberstdorf under-nine game the previous week, all the players had been boys, but when the teams returned after a five-minute interval, I noticed that TV Hindelang had brought on a girl as a substitute. Hindelang's female player stayed on the pitch for just under 20 minutes before herself being substituted; the new guidelines encourage regular rotation of players during a match, so this was not unusual. Although the young girl made minimal impact on the game, she made no obvious errors and certainly didn't look out of place among the boys.

In Germany, girls are allowed to play in the same team as boys up to and including under-17 level. The consent of the parent or guardian is required before a girl can participate in an under-15 team or older with boys, but not required for under-13s or below. At the time of writing, female participation in under-19 teams with boys is being tried in German football as part of a pilot project, but only allowed under certain conditions.

Midway through the second half, Fischen went ahead, but the home side's lead only lasted five minutes before the visitors equalised following a quick attack down the right flank which was finished with a powerful and accurate shot from a wide angle by Hindelang's number seven. Three minutes from time, the same youngster probably thought he had clinched victory, after rounding the keeper and slotting the ball into the net; however, Fischen grabbed a rather fortunate equaliser through another deflected shot only seconds from the end.

All the confusion about whether competitive football would continue beyond under-nine level left me curious about whether to report the score of the game in this book, but I later saw that the BFV website not only displayed the 4-4 result, but also compiled a league table for the U11 (E-Jun.) OA/KE Gruppe 2, updated after this round of matches. However, neither the BFV website nor those of TSV Fischen and TV Hindelang listed the identities of the young participants or the goalscorers, so I have followed that lead.

What I can also report is that the Fischen players were rather fortunate to get a draw; just when it looked like they had been filleted, it took a second deflected goal to get them off the hook. As to whether the reforms at junior level will increase the number of entrants into the academies, the Germans, like all good anglers, will need to be patient before knowing the size of their catch.

Chapter 8

Italy

MODERN FOOTBALL arrived in Italy via the Mediterranean port of Genoa, with the Genoa Cricket and Athletic Club forming a team in the 1890s. The first Italian football championship began on a regional basis in 1898, staying like that until 1929 when a national league, Serie A, was established.

Although near Italy's northern boundaries and not far from the mountains, the cities of Turin, Milan, Como, Bergamo, Brescia, Verona and Udine are all just outside the Alpine region; consequently, their football teams don't feature in this book. Instead, this chapter will focus on clubs from the Dolomites and Lepontine Alps, areas where football took some time to arrive.

i. Where Am I? FC Südtirol, 261m/856ft

About 160km/100 miles south of the Austrian border, the city of Bolzano in north-east Italy is part of Trentino-Alto Adige/Südtirol, one of the country's 20 administrative regions. Since 1972, the region has had more autonomy than most parts of Italy, reflecting its unusual history and culture. Today, Bolzano has a population of over 100,000 and is regarded as a gateway to the Dolomites. Composed of various types of rock that erode at different rates, many of the Dolomites have developed into jagged peaks and near vertical pillars. Suddenly rising from a relatively low level, these mountains were too steep or dangerous for me to hike up during my holiday. Whereas, in most other parts of the Alps you are hiking on the mountains, with the Dolomites you are merely looking at them from a distance. Consequently, although I loved Bolzano as a city, the walking proved to be disappointing.

Until 1919, this region was part of the Habsburg Empire, but after the First World War, Austria-Hungary, as one of the defeated Central Powers, lost the territory which went to Italy under the terms of the Treaty of Versailles. Known by the German name Bozen during Habsburg times, most of the population of Bolzano spoke German. In the 1920s and 1930s, the fascist dictator Mussolini introduced measures to make the area more Italian, and a similar policy impacted on the game of football throughout the country.

During the late 19th and early 20th centuries, Italian clubs playing association football usually referred to the sport by its English name, acknowledging English invention of the modern game and the frequent involvement of UK nationals in the formation of clubs in Italy. However, in the 1920s during Mussolini's nationalistic rule a more Italian word started to be preferred, namely *calcio*. The word originated from *Calcio Fiorentino* ('Florentine Football') and *Calcio Storico* ('Historic Football'), which were games dating back to the 16th century and more like a violent form of rugby, according to Chris Lee's 2021 book, *Origin Stories*. Although some changes to the names of Italian football clubs, such as AC Milan becoming Milano, were later reversed, *calcio* continued to be the popular term long after Mussolini's corpse had been hung upside down in that city's centre.

These days, although over 60 per cent of the people living in South Tyrol still speak German as their first language, this proportion falls to about a quarter in Bolzano itself. The smaller towns and villages outside Bolzano have proved more resistant to change, but better communications aided Italianisation of the city. The area also includes a small minority of people who speak Ladin, a tongue similar to the Swiss Romansh language.

The *Lonely Planet* guidebook to Italy sums up this particular part of the country very well when it says, 'Biergartens, pizzerias, hearty *guten morgens* and flirtatious *ciao bellas*; where the heck are you? It doesn't take long to decipher that cultural generalisations don't apply in Bolzano.' The combination of Italian and German extends beyond cafe society to include traffic signs and information at local attractions, as well as the city's football club.

Football reached the area in 1931 with the formation of AC Bolzano, the city's first team. After AC Bolzano dropped out of professional football into the amateur level, another club in the area, SV Milland Fussball, was taken over in 1995 and transformed into FC Südtirol. Initially based outside of Bolzano, the club had the name Fußball Club Südtirol-Alto Adige (*Südtirol* being the German for South Tyrol, while *Alto Adige* is its Italian name). A bilingual name had been chosen in a conscious effort to unite and appeal to both linguistic communities.

Over the decades, the Italian league structure has changed, but at the time of the matches I attended, the country's football pyramid looked like this (from the third tier downwards the levels consist of several regional and local divisions):

1. Serie A
2. Serie B
3. Serie C
4. Serie D
5. Eccellenza
6. Promozione
7. Prima Categoria
8. Seconda Categoria
9. Terza Categoria

The region's new club started out in the Promozione, but by 2000 when the club moved to Bolzano it had reached the fourth tier. That same year, the club removed the Italian part of its name, becoming just FC Südtirol, although both Bolzano and Bozen still appear on its badge, with the Italian name of the city appearing before the German translation. At the end of the 2009/10 season, FC Südtirol secured promotion to Serie C for the first time in the club's history.

In 2019, my wife Josie and I noticed that FC Südtirol would be playing at home during our summer hiking holiday in Bolzano. Before flying out to Italy, we checked the club's website and saw that the game was part of the second round of fixtures in the northern group of Serie C for the 2019/20 season, with the information available in Italian, German and English.

On the day of the match, Sunday, 1 September 2019, we walked to the stadium and went to the ticket office a couple of hours before kick-off. Given the club's name and the popularity of the German language in the city, we were surprised to find that when Josie asked for 'Zwei karten bitte' ('Two tickets please') the woman at the counter replied, in rather flustered Italian, 'Non capisco il Tedesco' ('I don't understand German'). Fortunately, Josie speaks Italian and could complete the transaction, paying €17 per ticket. When I glanced at the ticket, all the details printed on it, such as kick-off time, row and seat number, were just in Italian, not German.

The second task was buying a match programme. As in England, football programmes are very much part of the German and Austrian football culture, but get one in Italy or Spain? Forget it. However, I did find a programme, although it too turned out to be linguistically confusing. Despite its title being in English ('News'), all the text on the inside pages was in both German and Italian, except for the part devoted to our match, because the details of the fixture, including date and kick-off time were only in Italian.

Next, it was time to buy some food before the match started. In the same year as our trip, the Italian chef and broadcaster Gino D'Acampo had written in one of his cookery books that in Bolzano, 'As well as the culture, the local cuisine is very Germanic. The bread is dark and seeded and *wurstel* sausages (basically Frankfurters) are widely available.' Consequently, I had looked forward to some of these sausages, only to discover there was no German food of any kind in the stadium. The only grub available was as Italian as it gets; yes, you've guessed it, pizza!

The Stadio Druso not only has an Italian title, but one that is arguably anti-German, being named after Nero Claudius Drusus, a commander in ancient Rome who launched military campaigns against people in what is now Germany. Built in 1930, the stadium had a grand terracotta entrance to its main western grandstand, where we sat. The sector opposite was also seated and covered. Visiting supporters were housed in the end to the right, consisting of uncovered terracing. The end to the left looked like a building site, evidence of extensive redevelopment to bring the stadium up to Serie B requirements and triple its capacity from just over 3,000 to 10,000, in case the club achieved promotion; however, for our game, I estimated that only about 1,000 people were present.

Beautifully located, the stadium offered views of the highest mountain in the vicinity, Monte Pozza at a height of 1,616m/5,302ft; however, even this peak had a different name among German speakers, who call it Titschen.

When the public address system announced FC Südtirol's line-up, I noticed that most of the players had Italian-sounding names. The home fans also generally sung in Italian, although some reports say that the crowd is usually equally split between the two main linguistic groups. The club's nickname also appears in both languages: *Biancorossi* in Italian and *Weiß-Rote* in German (both meaning 'white and reds').

In terms of ownership, the club is controlled by several businesses, rather than any one individual or organisation, with German the first language of most of the club's directors.

FC Südtirol's players appeared in their usual kit of all white with red trim, arranged in a 4-3-1-2; while the opposition, Carpi FC from the province of Emilia-Romagna, wore an all-red kit and adopted a similar formation.

Carpi's Saber Hraiech opened the scoring after 11 minutes, receiving the ball midway in the home side's half before hitting a perfectly flighted lob from the edge of the penalty area past a defender and over the keeper. Hraiech then had the opportunity to repeat the feat from a similar position, but this time sliced his effort wide. Both sides had further chances, but it remained 1-0 to the visitors at the break.

Needing at least one goal, FC Südtirol decided on a change at half-time, bringing on 20-year-old Matteo Rover. The club magazine contained a feature on all its players in both Italian and German, although there were more details in the Italian version. From the information provided, I gathered that Rover had been born in Motta di Livenza near Venice in 1999, then started to play at youth level for his local side Liventina. After being spotted by Inter, Rover moved to the Italian giants in 2015 where he scored 14 goals in 19 games and won two trophies at under-17 level. After loan spells at Serie C clubs Vicenza and Pordenone, Rover then joined FC Südtirol six weeks before the Carpi game. A right-footed attacker, Rover's loan to FC Südtirol later became a permanent move at the end of the 2019/20 season. His arrival in Bolzano enabled him to be reunited with FC Südtirol's coach, Stefano Vecchi, who had previously coached him at Inter.

Within seconds of the restart, we witnessed a real case of 'Matteo of the Rovers' as the young player scored his first goal at full professional level; Gianluca Turchetta crossed from the right into a crowded area and Rover headed the ball in at the far post.

After 57 minutes, Michele Vano restored Carpi's lead, finishing an attack by slotting the ball past the keeper. Six minutes later, FC Südtirol's Tammaso Morosini evaded the challenge of an opposing defender and cut inside to hit a terrific shot from the left on the edge of the penalty area into the far corner of the goal, making it 2-2.

With 87 minutes gone, the home side's Alessandro Fabbri received his marching orders after accumulating two yellow cards, the second of which was for pulling the shirt of an opponent near the halfway line. It was a silly foul, far away from a dangerous position. However, at least it wouldn't be difficult for Fabbri to get an early bath, with his team's shirt displaying the name of Duka, a shower cabin company based in the South Tyrolean town of Bressanone.

A minute into stoppage time, Carpi's Vano scored his second goal, this time a header from a corner on the far side, out-jumping the surrounding defenders. There was still time for FC Südtirol's Niccolò Romero to hit a shot across goal which struck the inside of the far post before bouncing out. It could have rebounded towards a totally unmarked Matteo Rover, with the keeper helpless on the ground and the goal wide open, but sadly there was no *Roy of the Rovers* finish on this occasion as the ball ricocheted harmlessly back into the arms of the grateful goalie.

Carpi's 100 or so travelling fans rapturously greeted their side's 3-2 victory at the final whistle. During the match many of them had chanted abusively towards FC Südtirol, inferring that it was a German rather than an Italian club. The following day's local newspaper, *Dolomiten*, headlined its report, entirely in German, 'Diese Niederlage tut gewaltig weh'. ('This defeat hurts a lot'.)

So, that's football in Bolzano: German was used for FC Südtirol's name; the match report in the local newspaper; as well as being the first language of most of the club's directors. However, the person at the ticket office only spoke Italian; the name of the stadium and the information on our tickets were Italian; most of the players had Italian-sounding names; the home fans chanted in Italian; and the only food available was Italian. On the other hand, the club's badge displayed the Italian as well as the German name of its home city; most of the match programme and the website were bilingual; and the club has nicknames in both languages. As the guidebook says, where the heck are you?

After 27 games, the team stood fourth in its Serie C group; however, in March 2020 the season was suspended because of the COVID-19 pandemic and the remaining matches were never played. FC Südtirol finished the following 2020/21 campaign one place higher in third, only four points off the top, narrowly missing out on a chance of promotion. Renovation of the Stadio Druso was also completed by the end of that season, with both grandstands extended along the full length of the pitch and the running track removed. Thankfully, the impressive 1930 entrance was preserved and incorporated into the new design.

The completion of the building work couldn't have been better timed, because the summer of 2021 saw the arrival of a new coach, the Croat Ivan Javorčić. Ten games into 2021/22, FC Südtirol took over top spot in the Serie C Girone A (northern group) table and remained there until the end of the campaign, winning a total of 90 points from 38 games and only losing twice. FC Südtirol's promotion made it the first club from the Italian Alps to reach Serie B since the start of Italy's national football leagues (remember, Como is marginally outside the region).

Controversy followed promotion with an intervention from the club's ultras, the Gradinata Nord Bolzano (Italian for 'North Terrace Bolzano', named after the part of the stadium where its members usually congregate). The ultras chose the occasion to raise objections to the all-German title of the club, wanting the restoration of the bilingual name FC Südtirol-Alto Adige that had been used earlier in its history.

After the departure of Javorčić, Pierpaolo Bisoli took over as coach in the summer of 2022. Despite losing the first three Serie B matches, FC Südtirol qualified for the promotion play-offs at the end of the season. In the preliminary round, FC Südtirol faced AS Reggina in a single-legged tie and won courtesy of a dramatic last-minute goal from Daniele Casiraghi. A midfielder, Casiraghi had joined FC Südtirol a few weeks before my game in 2019 and had been one of the players subbed at half-time against Carpi. In the play-off semi-final, FC Südtirol met SSC Bari, this time over two legs. In the first leg, it was none other than Matteo Rover who headed the ball home in the second minute of stoppage time to give his team a slender lead to take to southern Italy. Unfortunately for FC Südtirol, Bari scored towards the end of the second leg, and the peculiar rules of the play-offs meant that although the tie was now level on aggregate there would be no extra time or penalties; instead, the tie was awarded to Bari courtesy of a higher-placed finish in the league season.

In 2023/24, FC Südtirol had a less successful campaign, ending in mid-table, but at the time of writing the club continues to fly the flag for the Italian Alps in Serie B.

ii. Patience is a Virtue: ASD Virtus Villadossola, 281m/922ft

Located in the north-west of Italy, the region of Piedmont means 'foot of the mountains', so named because no less than six Alpine ranges encroach on its territory. In the far north of Piedmont is an area called Ossola where the biggest settlement is the town of Domodossola, home to 18,000 people.

Domodossola is a stop on the railway line between Switzerland and Milan, with the two countries connected by the Simplon Tunnel. For centuries the Simplon Pass had been a high route over the Alps, before a tunnel through the mountains opened in 1906. At 19km/12 miles, the tunnel is one of the longest in the world, with trains taking more than ten minutes to travel all the way through it. My visit to Domodossola took place during a holiday in the Swiss resort of Stalden in 2023. With just one change of train at Brig, the journey was a quick and easy way of taking in a match in the Italian Alps.

One potential limitation of a book like this is that it can easily turn into a eulogy about the Alps, with resort after resort fulsomely praised for beauty, comfort and efficiency. I am grateful to Domodossola for breaking the pattern and restoring some variety and credibility.

Near the top end of Italy, Domodossola conveyed the feeling of a remote frontier town, peripheral, almost forgotten. Arriving at the railway station, passengers disembarking from the train immediately encountered Italian border police; uniformed and uneasy they scrutinised the newcomers, creating a sense of transience and tension. On another platform, a locomotive stood rusting and covered in graffiti, weeds entangling its wheels. In the centre of the Old Town, road works had dug a huge dusty trench running along the length of one of the main streets, leaving it gashed, slashed, disfigured. A smartly dressed hotel doorman looked despairingly at the excavator responsible, abandoned with one caterpillar track leaning into the ditch; the crooked angle symbolising neglect. Even the much-hyped market in the Piazza Mercato turned out to sell little more than tat, with its stalls obscuring the buildings surrounding the square; only when the traders and bargain hunters had vanished at the end of the afternoon did it become possible to see the 15th-century porticos and archways and appreciate their faded elegance. Memorials of better times. My attempts to check in at a run-down hotel on the edge of town were frustrated by the front door being locked. Ringing the bell produced no response, and a peep through smudged and smeared windows revealed that the place was empty, silent. After returning later and finally gaining entry to the hotel, what was the reward for such patience and persistence? Getting locked in the toilet. Panic ensued.

In the English phonetic alphabet, D is for delta, but following a popular television game show Italians say 'D come Domodossola' ('D for Domodossola'). It looked like only the football match could prevent my overnight trip becoming a case of D for disappointing.

The town's biggest team Juventus Domodossola (widely known as Juve Domo) should not be confused with the famous Turin club. Over the years, a number of Italian clubs have used the Latin word *Juventus* (meaning 'youth') or its shortened form *Juve* in their names, such as Juventus Siderno from the foot of Italy and Juve Stabia near Naples. With Juve Domo playing away that weekend, I decided to take in a game featuring ASD Virtus Villadossola.

The ASD part of the team's full name stands for Associazione Sportiva Dilettantistica (Amateur Sports Association); *Virtus* is Latin for 'virtue;' while Villadossola is a settlement with 7,000 inhabitants a few kilometres to the south of Domodossola. Virtus Villa, as the club is often known for short, had formerly played at the Stadio Felino Poscio in Villadossola, but in 2018 the running of that stadium was taken over by another company, forcing the club to play its home games in Domodossola at Juve Domo's Stadio Silvestro Curotti.

The name of the Domodossola stadium originates from Ossola's turbulent history during the Second World War. After Italy surrendered in 1943, Mussolini led a rump puppet regime in the north of the country, backed by the Nazis. A member of a local partisan group, Silvestro Curotti, died fighting German troops during a gun battle in 1944. According to documents stored in the Archivio storico del Comune di Domodossola (Historical Archive of the Municipality of Domodossola), the stadium was officially renamed the Stadio Silvestro Curotti on 30 August 1945, just four months after the end of the war, and still retains the name today. A monument to the partisan hero greets visitors immediately to the right of the stadium's main entrance.

Ossola and its mountains became one of Italy's main centres of partisan resistance. Amid what was effectively a civil war in Italy between 1943 and 1945, it is hardly surprising that football was abandoned during those years, resuming a few months after the end of the conflict. ASD Virtus Villadossola came into being on 6 November 1945, playing its first match against local rivals, Juve Domo, a fixture known to locals as the Villa-Domo derby.

Virtus Villa claims to be the oldest club in continuous existence in the Ossola region, having avoided the financial collapses and renamings that Juve Domo has endured. Between 2015 and 2017, Virtus Villa suffered relegations from the Prima Categoria to the Seconda Categoria then down to the Terza Categoria, in other words from the seventh tier of the Italian league structure down to the ninth tier. However, the club has since recovered, with successive promotions in 2018 and 2019 restoring its former place. In 2022/23, Virtus Villa ended in second place in the Prima Categoria, but missed out on promotion to the Promozione following defeat in the play-offs.

The match I attended on Saturday, 9 September 2023, was the opening fixture of the Prima Categoria Girone A (First Category Group A), in the seventh tier and one level below Juve Domo. ASD Agrano Sportiva from Omegna provided the evening's opposition. Located about 30km/19 miles to the south, Omegna like Domodossola and Villadossola is comfortably within the Alpine region. Formed in 1964, ASD Agrano Sportiva has, like Virtus Villa, spent recent times competing in the seventh, eighth and ninth tiers.

Located in the north of Domodossola, the Stadio Silvestro Curotti underwent refurbishment in 2017/18, and is part of a complex with a swimming pool, tennis courts, a seven-a-side pitch, plus other sports facilities. The main football part of the complex consists of a full-sized pitch with an artificial surface, surrounded by a blue six-lane running track, four floodlights, an open area of seating on one side and a covered main grandstand on the other.

At the entrance to the stadium, a lady sitting down at a table sold match tickets for €7 per person. Spectators were able to go anywhere, so I chose a seat by the halfway line towards the back of the main grandstand, offering a perfect view of the pitch. Even more impressive was the panorama of the Lepontine Alps to the east, with the peaks of Monte Navone, Pizzo Locciabella and Monte Alom silhouetted against the sky as the sun set.

The previous chapter looking at youth football in Germany and Austria mentioned problems with parents 'coaching' their children from the sidelines during matches.

This has evidently been an issue in Domodossola, because on the side of the main grandstand at the Stadio Silvestro Curotti there was a sign which read, 'Advice for parents on the sidelines. The trainer trains, the referee referees, you have fun! Your job is to support the team and your child, so don't think about technical advice. Don't insult your opponents, they are kids like your son, clap as loudly as you can and enjoy the game!'

By 8.30pm when the match kicked off, it was dark, and the temperature which had been a sweltering 30°C at the time of my arrival in the afternoon, dropped to a more comfortable 21°C.

Virtus Villa appeared in an all-white kit, while Agrano wore a maroon one with white sleeves. By the time the match started, the attendance had grown to about 100, and the small size of the crowd meant that the players' voices could easily be heard, including a few blood-curdling screams when players went down from challenges hitting the hard synthetic playing surface. Also clearly audible were trains on the track running immediately behind the grandstand, either travelling towards or coming from the Simplon Tunnel.

In the first half, Virtus Villa attacked the south end of the stadium, the goal to my right. The hosts came closest to scoring after 12 minutes with a move that culminated in a long-range shot which hit the crossbar. Agrano's forward Simone Tacchini provided his side's best attacking outlet; however, despite both teams' efforts, the opening period ended goalless.

Two minutes after the restart, Virtus Villa's Fabio Martinella bent a free kick from about 25 metres around the keeper to make it 1-0 to the hosts. After 52 minutes, Agrano nearly equalised, hitting the bar from another free kick, but wouldn't have to wait too long to get on level terms because three minutes later Riccardo Ardizzoia headed a corner into the net. Only then did I realise that there were quite a few visiting fans sitting in the grandstand, but despite the lack of segregation there was no hostility between the two sets of supporters who were even allowed to drink beer from glass bottles while watching the match.

Goalscoring opportunities were few and far between during the next phase of the game, with a Virtus Villa attack down the left which ended with a shot going wide providing one of the few chances. About ten minutes from the end of normal time, Agrano attacked, and after Virtus Villa failed to clear the ball, Ardizzoia scored his second goal. There seemed to be a hint of offside, possibly explaining why one of the locals behind me got up and stormed out of the stadium shouting 'Ladro!' ('Thief!'). He should have been more patient and stayed, because three minutes into stoppage time, a ball from the left found Martinella unmarked, and the Virtus Villa player scored his second goal of the game.

Even then the action wasn't over, because both teams came close to nicking a winner. A Virtus Villa shot was pushed around the post by the keeper, followed by an Agrano player being upended in the penalty area. The visiting coaching and training staff rushed from the dugout in front of me, frantically appealing for a spot kick, but referee Anthony Pio Fornaro waved play on. The game ended moments later in a 2-2 draw.

The following morning, I decided not to bother with the hotel's meagre breakfast and headed to a cafe instead. Just when I was trying to look cool like James Richardson from Channel 4's *Football Italia* in the 1990s by drinking a cup of coffee and skim-reading a local sports newspaper, an Italian man in a white string vest sat down next to me. Unfortunately, the Rab C. Nesbitt lookalike was accompanied by a savage dog which reluctantly settled under the table. A few minutes later, the animal took exception to another of its kind walking by, resulting in a brief but fierce dog fight. Abandoning my coffee and the newspaper, I headed for the railway station to get the next train. James Richardson never had to put up with anything like this.

At the end of the 2023/24 season, Virtus Villa finished ninth in the league, with Agrano one place below. By then, Virtus Villa had secured an agreement allowing the club to move back to the Stadio Felino Poscio in Villadossola. After a six-year exile in Domodossola, the club's patient wait was over.

Chapter 9
Liechtenstein: Women's Football

SANDWICHED BETWEEN Switzerland and Austria, Liechtenstein is located entirely within the Alps. About two-thirds of the country consists of mountainous terrain, while the remainder runs along the valley of the River Rhine.

Liechtenstein gets its name from a family of landowners who acquired the territory 20 years before it became a principality in 1719. Initially within the Holy Roman Empire, Liechtenstein then became part of the Confederation of the Rhine and the German Confederation, before gaining full independence in 1866. The country's small size encouraged it to forge links with Austria-Hungary, but after the collapse of the Habsburg Empire following the First World War, Liechtenstein developed closer ties to Switzerland, adopting the Swiss Franc as its currency and joining a customs union with its neighbour to the west. Like Switzerland, Liechtenstein remained neutral during the Second World War.

One of the smallest countries in Europe, Liechtenstein has an area of about 160 square km/62 square miles. Formerly undeveloped and agricultural, Liechtenstein has changed enormously over the last three-quarters of a century, with the population of 39,300 now enjoying the world's second-highest GDP per capita (after Monaco) in what has become a tax haven for the wealthy. Many people are employed in the financial sector of the economy, including a large number of foreigners who commute to the country for work.

Although Liechtenstein has been transformed economically, political change has been slower, with the prince retaining considerable powers, including the ability to veto legislation he dislikes. All attempts to make the country a more modern constitutional monarchy have so far failed to gain enough popular support.

i. Women on the Ball

Although the Liechtensteiner Fussballverband (Liechtenstein Football Association or LFV) was formed in 1934, the country's national men's side didn't play its first official international fixture until 1982, narrowly losing 1-0 to Switzerland. A member of both FIFA and UEFA, Liechtenstein has competed in qualifying matches for the men's Euros and World Cups since 1994, but without managing to reach any final stages.

Being too small to maintain its own football league, the principality's seven men's club teams play in Swiss leagues. The top club is currently FC Vaduz, from Liechtenstein's capital, whose team currently competes in the Challenge League, the second tier of Swiss men's football. In 2022/23, FC Vaduz became the first Liechtensteiner club to reach the group stages of a UEFA tournament; entering the Conference League after winning the principality's domestic cup and then successfully negotiating a couple of qualifiers. Liechtenstein's other six teams are USV Eschen/Mauren, FC Ruggell, FC Schaan, FC Triesen, FC Triesenberg and FC Balzers. The last of these attracted considerable publicity in January 2025, when Valen Scarsini, a 'football influencer' from Argentina, identified the club as having one of the smallest fanbases in the world and resolved to help it. In no time, FC Balzers, currently competing in the Swiss fifth tier, attracted hundreds of thousands of social media followers, more than any other club in the Swiss leagues, reported *World Soccer* in February 2025.

Readers wanting to know more about men's football in Liechtenstein, particularly the national side, might want to take a look at Charlie Connolly's book, *Stamping Grounds: Exploring Liechtenstein and its World Cup Dream*, which covers the years around the millennium. However, the focus of this chapter is on the women's game.

In many European countries, women's football briefly blossomed in the early 20th century before being banned in the 1920s and 1930s, either by conservative national football associations or repressive political regimes. The women's game then revived in the late 1960s and early 1970s; for example, either side of Liechtenstein, Switzerland launched a national women's football league in 1970, followed two years later by one in Austria.

If the swinging 60s led to notable steps towards women's liberation elsewhere in Europe, the phenomenon made little impression on Liechtenstein. A socially and politically conservative country, Liechtenstein's women didn't even have the vote in 1970 let alone anything like sporting equality. The franchise was only extended to women as late as 1984, when a referendum involving an entirely male electorate voted narrowly in favour, making the principality the last country in Europe to do so. In the 21st century, Liechtenstein has made considerable progress with the political representation of women, appointing its first female deputy prime minister in 2001, followed by another in 2021.

Although a few individual women had played football in Liechtenstein as part of men's teams, the country's first major all-female team was FC Ruggell, from a settlement of that name in the extreme north of the principality. Like the men, women's teams from Liechtenstein compete in Swiss leagues. After starting to play against Swiss opposition in 1987/88, FC Ruggell rose to the highest tier of Swiss women's football before financial problems caused the demise of the team in 2008.

One year later in 2009, the number of licensed female players in Liechtenstein stood at about 110. Since then, the LFV and the country's seven clubs have worked hard to get more women involved in the sport, particularly at youth levels. Initiatives include local versions of the UEFA Playmakers campaign focusing on encouraging girls aged between five and eight years old; Girls on the Ball Camps; and the Liechtensteiner Frauen-und Mädchenfussballtag (Liechtenstein Women's and Girls' Football Day). The results have been impressive: by 2023 the number of licensed female players in Liechtenstein had more than tripled to 360, according to the LFV.

In 2021, the LFV set out a five-year plan called Gemeinsam.2026 (Together.2026). Part of the plan included Frauen am Ball 2026 (Women on the Ball 2026) with four key aims for women's football in the principality: developing the game at club level; increasing the number of players; promoting more competition; and improving the image of the sport.[9]

---

9   https://www.uefa.com/news-media/news/026e-1395de6b964a-7602df68ccad-1000--new-women-s-football-strategy-in-liechtenstein/

Known as the Frauen Nationalteam (Women's National Team), Liechtenstein's international women's side played its first unofficial friendly in 2019. These unofficial games provided opportunities for useful practice, with the opposition coming from other small nations, club sides or youth teams.

The Frauen Nationalteam competed in its first official friendly as recently as April 2021. Despite taking the lead, the team eventually lost 2-1 to Luxembourg. Sadly, no fans were allowed in the stadium to see Liechtenstein's first women's international game because of the COVID-19 pandemic; however, the match was heralded by campaign group The Borgen Project as 'a historic moment for women's rights in Liechtenstein'.

By the end of 2024, Liechtenstein's women had played ten further official international friendlies, meeting Gibraltar six times (four victories, one draw and one defeat); two defeats against Andorra; together with a draw and a defeat versus Namibia. The Frauen Nationalteam also entered the FIFA world rankings, and at the end of 2024 stood in 189th place out of 195 countries.

ii. Football is Female: FC Triesen, 466m/1,529ft

Following the demise of FC Ruggell's team, the most senior women's club side in Liechtenstein has been FC Triesen Frauen whose website boasts, 'The fact that football is female is part of everyday life at FC Triesen.' On Sunday, 14 April 2024, I visited the club to check that out.

Despite having fewer than 6,000 inhabitants, Triesen is the third-largest settlement in Liechtenstein. Like the principality's two biggest towns, Schaan and Vaduz,

Triesen is positioned in the valley of the Rhine, straddling the main road that runs north to south, with the river to the west and a range of mountains to the east. As with these other two towns, many of Triesen's buildings are modern and functional, rather than the chalets usually associated with the Alps (to see the latter you need to take a bus to Triesenberg up the mountainside above Triesen).

With the game kicking off at 1pm, there was plenty of time to walk along the riverside path from the youth hostel in Schaan where I was staying to the stadium in Triesen.

At about 1,230km/764 miles, the Rhine is the second-longest river in western and central Europe. Partly supplied with glacial meltwater, the Rhine's two main tributaries, Vorderrhein and Hinterrhein, merge in the Swiss Alps to create the Rhine. The river marks Liechtenstein's western boundary with Switzerland, and after leaving the principality it flows through Austria, Germany, France and the Netherlands, before emptying into the North Sea. The river serves a considerable amount of agricultural and industrial activity, and further downstream, when it is deeper and wider, transforms into a major shipping route.

In the past, the Rhine was more than a kilometre wide as it flowed by Triesen, many times its current width. However, the river was straightened about a century ago with stronger and higher embankments constructed to reduce the danger of flooding. This canalisation has saved Triesen's football stadium and other places along the riverbank from occasionally disappearing underwater, but leaves the Rhine looking rather tamed and controlled, a bit like a dog in a muzzle.

FC Triesen's stadium, Sportanlage Blumenau (Blumenau Sports Facility), is less than the width of the pitch from the Rhine which runs parallel to it. I expected a few balls to be lost in the river after wayward kicks during the match, but the high embankment that starts to rise immediately behind the dugouts on one side of the pitch usually prevents that from happening.

Alpine rivers are often aquamarine in colour, but as I walked alongside the Rhine it looked more like an icy grey, despite the bright blue sky above. Straight ahead, the outlines of the Mittagspitze and Mittlerspitz, a couple of peaks in the Rätikon Alps, were silhouetted by the sunlight.

Later on, the Rhine flows through the Germany of Richard Wagner's operatic *Ring Cycle*, where the composer imagined Rhinemaidens guarding gold; however, today was all about different kinds of Rhinemaidens – those guarding goals.

FC Triesen was one of four founder members of the LFV. All 18 of the people who established the club back in 1932 had been male. These days, the club's men compete in the 3. Liga, the Swiss seventh tier, but the focus of my visit was women's football.

FC Triesen started football training for girls in 1997, then set up its women's team a year later. After steady progress during the first 20 years, things have developed very quickly in recent seasons.

In 2018, the LFV decided to create two *Stützpunkten* ('bases') in Liechtenstein to encourage the growth of women's football; one in the north of the principality, the other in the south. FC Triesen's geographical position meant that it became part of the southern base, together with FC Balzers and FC Triesenberg.

That same year, FC Triesen hosted the first of the LFV's previously mentioned Liechtenstein Women's and Girls' Football Days. Held on 23 June 2018 at the

Sportanlage Blumenau, this event attracted over 100 female participants of various ages and involved training sessions and the chance for young girls to meet and discuss with players in the women's national team. The success of the event meant that Triesen also hosted another one the following year.

FC Triesen offers the opportunity of playing football to girls and women of all ages. To start with, the youngest girls play in teams with boys, before moving up to all-female sides.

In 2021, the LFV submitted an application to the Ostschweizer Fussballverband (Eastern Switzerland Football Association or OFV) for FC Triesen's women's team to be admitted to the Frauen 2. Liga, the fourth tier of women's football in the neighbouring country. The LFV chose FC Triesen because it possessed Liechtenstein's best women's team, and the federation hoped that the move would encourage the development of women's football throughout the principality.

After the OFV agreed to the request and admitted the team to the Frauen 2. Liga, FC Triesen became the first women's team from Liechtenstein to participate at such a level in the Swiss leagues since FC Ruggell.

The Frauen 2. Liga is the highest regional league for women's football in Switzerland and is divided into local groups; above that level the leagues are national. The whole structure for women's football in Switzerland currently looks like this:

1. Women's Super League
2. Nationalliga B
3. Frauen 1. Liga
4. Frauen 2. Liga

5. Frauen 3. Liga

6. Frauen 4. Liga

FC Triesen's first season in the Frauen 2. Liga (2021/22) ended with the team fifth out of 11 places, a comfortable 29 points off relegation. In 2022/23, Triesen improved by finishing the campaign in fourth position.

Before the start of the 2023/24 season, Adrienne Krysl became the new coach of FC Triesen Frauen. Then aged 35, Krysl had played for several Swiss clubs and the national side. After retiring from playing, Krysl helped found a women's football team in her hometown Winterthur and led it up to the Nationalliga B. At the same time that Krysl joined Triesen, she also became coach of the Liechtenstein national women's team and head of the LFV's women's football department. The appointment demonstrated the partnership between the LFV and FC Triesen, which aims to use the club to boost women's football throughout the principality.

The opposition for the match I attended, FC Ems, had travelled from the town of Domat-Ems further up the Rhine in eastern Switzerland. With a population of 8,000, Domat-Ems is the fourth-largest settlement in the canton of Graubünden. The town's double-barrelled title reflects the fact that it is the northernmost town where a significant number of people speak Romansch, a local language derived from Latin (Domat being the minority language's name for the town, while Ems is the German). However, the club's website appears in German, with no option to read it in Romansch.

Formed in 1919, FC Ems only fielded men's teams until 1996 when a women's team was formed. The FC Ems women's team had finished towards the bottom of the Frauen 2. Liga at the end of the previous, 2022/23, season. On its website, the club cited shortages of players for training sessions and matches as reasons for the team's struggles, but hoped that its focus on younger women and girls would provide long-term benefit.

Going into the game, FC Triesen occupied sixth place in the Meisterschaft Frauen 2. Liga Gruppe 1 table, with FC Ems a couple of places below.

FC Triesen's home since 1943, the Sportanlage Blumenau consists of a complex with several pitches, volleyball courts, a skateboard park and a climbing wall. Platz 1, the main football pitch, is a natural grass surface surrounded by an athletics track, perimeter fencing and floodlights. Along the eastern side is a clubhouse, with a refreshment area at ground level and a viewing platform on the flat roof.

Before the 1pm kick-off, I had arranged to meet Fredy Wolfinger, president of FC Triesen. Aged 63 at the time of our meeting, Fredy, like many of his compatriots, works in finance, having been a business economist and banker both in the principality and abroad, including a spell in London. These days, Fredy is the president of the Association of Independent Asset Managers in Liechtenstein.

Fluent in German, French and English, Fredy told me that he is originally from the town of Balzers in the south of the principality. During his youth, Fredy played football in Vaduz, but gave up the game to concentrate on studying at college. Fredy began his involvement with FC Triesen in 1987, training the juniors, and has been president of the club since 2014.

Fredy told me that the FC Triesen Frauen squad included no fewer than six Liechtenstein internationals, and that three of them would start in the afternoon's match:

right-back Sina Kollman; defensive midfielder Elena Lohner; with Camilla Kind in a more forward role. Two others would start on the bench: defender Lara Uebersax and striker Mia Rinderer. Fredy added that the last of the six, midfielder Eva Fasel, was unavailable that day.

When I asked Fredy about how far FC Triesen Frauen could realistically progress, he was surprisingly frank, saying, 'Up another level, but not with this team.' Fredy explained that the present objective was consolidation in the Frauen 2. Liga, but when more of the younger players progress through the junior ranks into the first team the club would then aim for the Frauen 1. Liga. Hopefully, the junior women players would benefit from having received more training than the current team. As that third tier is a national league, competing with teams from all over Switzerland rather than just the east of the country, it would be a major step up for Triesen, requiring extra time and money for travelling.

The weather had been hot all weekend, with the temperature reaching 28°C that afternoon. When I asked Fredy about this, he said that it was usually between 12 and 14°C in mid-April, but was predicted to plummet to slightly below its normal temperature in three days' time, so I had been extremely lucky.

As I munched a *wurst* (sausage) which Fredy kindly brought to the table in the clubhouse, it became clear while listening to him talk enthusiastically about football why he had received the award of LFV 2023 Volunteer of the Year in recognition of his commitment. Pleased that someone from the UK was writing about the important story that is women's football in Liechtenstein, Fredy gave me copies of the annual reports of FC Triesen and the LFV, both of which contained useful coverage of the women's game.

Our conversation ended abruptly when the two teams came out on to the pitch, with Triesen in all blue and Ems in white shirts with black shorts and socks. The small crowd of about 40 people reflected the novelty of women's football in Liechtenstein, as well as the small size of the town and the principality as a whole.

Like lower-league stadiums in England, it's possible to walk all the way around the pitch at the Blumenau. I decided to do this during the first half, to get the benefit of different views and angles, and then try out the view from on top of the clubhouse after the break.

Triesen nearly went ahead after three minutes when Melina Meyer burst through, only to hit her shot wide with just the keeper to beat. That miss looked costly when Ems scored ten minutes later, with a shot by Romina Cavegn.

The hot weather meant that after another ten minutes it was time for a drinks and cooling break. When the game resumed, Triesen's two wingers, Jasmin Ackermann on the right and Jana Tipura on the left, both had shots in quick succession, with the first saved by the keeper and the second hit wide of the goal. These two wingers then swapped sides for the last part of the half.

During the interval, I climbed the steps up to the viewing platform above the clubhouse from where there was a fine view of the Churfürsten range: seven jagged peaks constituting the most southerly part of the Appenzell Alps on the Swiss side of the Rhine.

The second half began with Ackermann and Tipura reverting to their original positions, with the latter getting in a couple of crosses from the left wing, although both were wasted. Soon after that, it became Ackermann's turn to attack down the right, only to blast her shot off target.

Triesen's pressure eventually led to a goal after 55 minutes, finished from close range by another Liechtenstein international, Rinderer, who had come on as a substitute a few minutes earlier.

Just after the hour, another of those national team members, Lohner, went on a long run with the ball up the left, only to shoot tamely straight at the keeper. The closest Triesen came to scoring a second goal was a shot from the edge of the penalty area after 71 minutes; unfortunately, Viola Sinnesberger, who had come on as a substitute earlier in the half, hit her effort against the crossbar. After that, Triesen had five more attempts on goal, but failed to get that all-important winner.

Nine minutes from time, the last of the Liechtenstein internationals, Lara Uebersax, put in an appearance from the bench. Although Triesen fielded five internationals and looked to have the better players, Ems performed more effectively as a team, operating well as a unit, particularly by repeatedly catching the home team offside.

During the match, several large tractors drove by on the road topping the river embankment that ran along the far side of the stadium, many of them pulling trailers full of straw or grass cuttings. Amid all that agricultural activity and the sweltering heat, Triesen's women footballers were unable to take advantage of having most of the possession and chances on goal, clearly failing to make hay while the sun shone.

At the end of the 2023/24 season, FC Triesen Frauen finished fourth in the 2. Liga, repeating the achievement of the previous season.

The following morning, I left Liechtenstein, catching a train to Zürich airport. Although my impressions were undoubtedly influenced by the unseasonably good weather,

I have nothing but fond memories of Liechtenstein, that small strip of land between the mountains and the Rhine. The principality has something of an oddball reputation, partly because of its political system and reliance on finance, but also complaints about its lack of facilities or attractions. Some of these criticisms are unfair, because Liechtenstein's small size means that its amenities shouldn't be compared to larger countries; instead, a more realistic comparison is with other towns and resorts in the Alps.

The following year, the LFV's hopes of entering major women's tournaments were realised sooner than expected when the Frauen Nationalteam gained admittance to the 2025 UEFA Women's Nations League, playing its first competitive games in League C Group 3 against Armenia, Luxembourg and Kazakhstan. It proved to be a baptism of fire, with heavy defeats in the first couple of matches: losing 6-1 away to Armenia and 7-0 in Luxembourg. Despite those results, considering that women in Liechtenstein only received the vote a little over 40 years ago, and the Frauen Nationalteam played its first official match as recently as 2021, the development of the women's game in the principality in the last few seasons constitutes one of the sport's more interesting and largely untold stories.

Chapter 10

Monaco

WITH A population of approximately 38,500 inhabitants crammed into a total area of just 2 square kilometres/0.8 square miles, Monaco is the second-smallest country in the world.

Despite much of its territory standing only slightly above sea level on the Mediterranean coast, and also being separated from the main part of the Alpine Convention by a narrow strip of French land, Monaco signed up to the treaty in 1994. Being close to the Maritime Alps, as well as awareness of environmental factors in the region impacting on the principality, were factors in the decision to join.

The area spent much of its early history under rulers from Italy, Spain and France, but eventually gained its independence. Despite being the size of a town, Monaco is regarded as a city-state.

Since 1911, Monaco has been ruled by a constitutional monarchy. In recent times, Monaco's setting on the French Riviera, its famous casino, luxury hotels and favourable taxation arrangements, have attracted many of the world's super rich, as evidenced by all the yachts in the harbour and expensive cars driving around.

During my brief visit, the presence of Monaco's rulers loomed large, whether in the form of Rainier III's car collection, the Prince's Palace, or the crown on the badge of the local football team reflecting the third of the club that they still own. Such a high local profile meant that the House of Grimaldi appeared less stuffy or remote than our royal family.

i. Just Short of Football's Summit: AS Monaco, 21m/69ft

The principality's football team, Association Sportive de Monaco (known as AS Monaco, ASM, or just plain Monaco), was formed between 1919 and 1924, although the later date is regarded as the official founding year.

Monaco is far too small to support enough teams for its own football league, so the new club became affiliated to the Fédération Française de Football (French Football Federation or FFF) and entered its competitions. The principality is not a member of UEFA or FIFA and cannot enter a national team in the European Championship or World Cup. At club level, AS Monaco qualifies for UEFA competitions through its performances in the French league.

Despite all the wealth in the principality, the local football team lacked a proper ground until 1939 with the arrival of the first Stade Louis II, named after the prince of Monaco at that time.

The club turned professional in 1948 when it joined the French second division, then five years later gained promotion to Division 1 (the name for the top tier of French football until its rebranding as Ligue 1 in 2002).

AS Monaco has always worn the red and white colours of the principality, but until 1960 this took the form of shirts with vertical stripes. After the club won its first Coupe de France, a new shirt was adopted to celebrate the victory. Based on the Monaco flag, which consists of a red horizontal band above a white one, the new shirt incorporated a diagonal division running from the right shoulder down to the left hip, with red above white. Known as *La Diagonale*, the new shirt had a rather surprising designer.

One of the most popular Hollywood actresses of the 1950s, Grace Kelly became a style icon, famous for her spectacular wardrobe. Four years after marrying Monaco's Prince Rainier III and becoming Princess Consort of Monaco, she used her fashion sense to design *La Diagonale* for her local football club. First worn in 1960/61, Princess Grace's *La Diagonale* proved to be immediately inspirational, with AS Monaco winning its first Division 1 championship that season. The team has worn the same basic design for its home shirts ever since. Sadly, Princess Grace died from injuries sustained in a car crash in 1982.

AS Monaco added a second Division 1 title in 1962/63, by which time the team included Armand Forchério, who went on to become arguably the most famous Monégasque (person from Monaco) footballer of all time. Forchério played for the team until 1972 and coached it from 1976 to 1977. After his departure, AS Monaco won a third French league championship in 1977/78 and a fourth in 1981/82.

In 1987, Arsène Wenger became Monaco's coach and established the side as one of the top teams in the French league, attracting stars like Glenn Hoddle. The reward proved to be instantaneous, with another Division 1 title secured at the end of the 1987/88 season. After Hoddle returned to England, Monaco reached the final of the 1992 European Cup Winners' Cup and the semi-final of the Champions League in 1994, followed soon after by Wenger's departure.

AS Monaco won another Division 1 title in 1996/97 (helped by a young Thierry Henry) and made a further appearance in a Champions League semi-final in 1998, followed by a seventh French league title in 1999/2000.

Despite those achievements, the French football authorities ordered AS Monaco to be relegated to Ligue 2 in the summer of 2003, after accruing debts of over €50m (£33m). However, the decision was reversed on appeal, allowing the club to not only resume playing in Ligue 1 but embark on an epic European run.

Coached by French World Cup winner Didier Deschamps, Monaco topped a Champions League group containing PSV Eindhoven, AEK Athens and Deportivo La Coruña, then beat Lokomotiv Moscow, Real Madrid and Chelsea in the knockout rounds, qualifying for the final. The achievement was all the more remarkable because of continuing financial worries with the club searching for new investors.

On Wednesday, 26 May 2004, I attended the biggest game in AS Monaco's history, with José Mourinho's Portuguese side FC Porto providing the opposition in the Champions League Final. The venue chosen couldn't have contrasted more with the Côte d'Azur, because the final that year took place at the AufSchalke Arena in the drab and grey city of Gelsenkirchen, part of Germany's former industrial Ruhr region. One of the least attractive cities to have hosted European club football's showpiece event, the final went there to commemorate the centenary of local club Schalke 04.

The AufSchalke Arena was one of the first stadiums to have a retractable roof; however, warm weather meant that the roof remained open for the final. Instead, its beams and struts were used to support bungee jumpers and trapeze artists who were suspended over performers in strange costumes playing huge drums during a mystifying opening ceremony.

My seat was in a corner, next to the Portuguese fans, meaning that the Monaco supporters faced towards me. Each finalist had been allocated 14,000 tickets, not nearly enough for Porto, but plenty for Monaco, giving nearly half of the principality's population at the time a chance of going to the final. I could see quite a few empty seats in the Monaco end, with remaining tickets reportedly on sale on the morning of the game, almost certainly the last time that has happened at a Champions League Final. However, the official attendance was reported to be 53,053, only fractionally below the stadium's all-seated capacity.

After emerging from the tunnel to my right, the two teams lined up with the Monaco players in their usual red and white *La Diagonale* shirts, white shorts and socks, while Porto wore blue and white. Monaco's fans, occupying the two tiers at the other end, waved thousands of flags to create red and white vertical stripes in a rather uninspired mosaic. Although ASM's support wasn't particularly impressive, it did include some famous fans.

One of the club's celebrity backers in the stadium that night was Michael Schumacher, the Formula One motor racing driver. Apart from winning Monaco's famous Grand Prix five times, Schumacher also lived in the principality for a time as well as being a keen football fan.

Being such a big event in so small a location, the Monaco Grand Prix inevitably takes over the entire principality for several days when it's held once a year. The 2004 race took place just three days before the Champions League Final, prompting the ASM squad to travel to Germany on the Saturday to avoid the inevitable distractions.

With overtaking notoriously difficult on the principality's narrow street circuit, getting off to a good start in the Monaco Grand Prix is crucial. Similarly, AS Monaco looked to begin the Champions League Final strongly, and after just two minutes, Ludovic Giuly had a chance to score, running on to a long pass from Lucas Bernardi in midfield. Unfortunately, Giuly hesitated and lost the opportunity to chip the ball over the onrushing Porto keeper, Vítor Baía, who was able to clear the ball despite being way out of his goal.

Another famous Monaco fan at the final in Gelsenkirchen was Prince Albert. Then aged 46, and son of Prince Rainier III and Princess Grace, he would become ruler of the principality as Albert II following the death of his father a year later. A keen sportsman, Albert competed in bobsleigh events at five Winter Olympics between 1988 and 2002.

Rather like Albert's bobsleigh, AS Monaco's fortunes went downhill following Giuly's early missed chance and his departure through injury midway through the first half. Normally a winger, Giuly had been deployed as a fast-running central striker in the final; however, his injury wrecked Deschamps's plans as the coach later admitted.

There were few real goalscoring chances until six minutes before half-time, when Porto went ahead slightly against the run of play. The goal came after the ball had been hit from the right into the penalty area, and two Monaco defenders failed to clear it, enabling Carlos Alberto to shoot home.

Forced to search for an equaliser, Monaco allowed Porto to play on the counter-attack and get a couple more goals in quick succession midway through the second half. Dmitri Alenichev broke down the left and passed the ball to his team-mate, the Brazilian-born Portuguese player Deco, who shot from near the penalty spot past Monaco's Italian goalkeeper, Flavio Roma. Roma dived too early to his left, allowing the Porto midfielder to calmly slot the ball into the other side of the goal.

Roma was also at fault for the third goal, four minutes later. Another counter-attack involved Brazilian forward Derlei breaking down the left to provide an assist for Alenichev; this time, the Russian smashed the ball into the net from about ten metres, with the keeper actually jumping out of the way; had he stayed stationary he might have saved it.

Despite three goals, the match was disappointing, with the football more functional than exciting, providing little entertainment for the estimated 250 million people who watched on television. The Monaco players didn't manage a single shot on target in the whole game, although it should be pointed out that at least four incorrect offside decisions went against them, disrupting their attacks. ASM's successes against the likes of Real Madrid and Chelsea in the knockout rounds hadn't prepared the Ligue 1 club for counter-attacking opposition like Mourinho's Porto.

Although that season's UEFA Champions League campaign ended with Monaco falling just short of the summit of European club football, it still provided the principality with a major sporting claim to fame: despite being the second-smallest country in the world, Monaco is the only place within the Alpine region to possess a team that has reached the final of European football's premier club competition.

The former Stella Matutina school in the Austrian town of Feldkirch, arguably the birthplace of football in the Alps.

The Festung Hohenwerfen castle above SSK Werfen's football stadium.

Entrance to the Stade des Alpes in the French city of Grenoble, controversially constructed after the felling of 200 trees in a public park.

SV Kleinwalsertal and FC Oberstdorf under-9s line up in the Walser-Arena, higher than the summit of any mountain in England or Wales.

Flo Nyer gives last-minute instructions to players before the under-9s match in Kleinwalsertal.

Dolomites towering over the Stadio Druso in Bolzano, Italy.

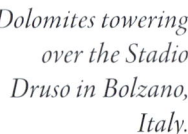

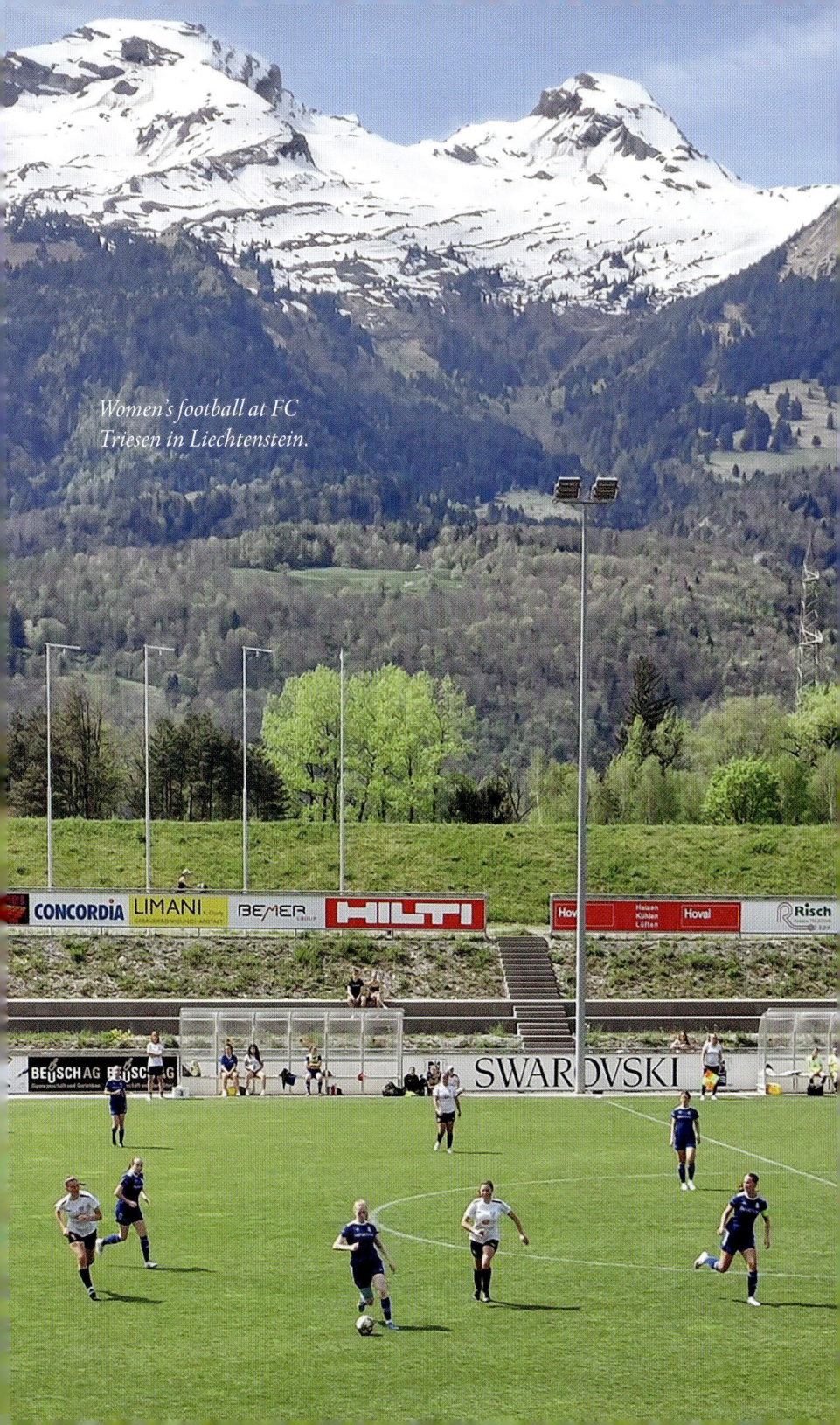

Women's football at FC Triesen in Liechtenstein.

A goal at the Schaan-Vaduz YMCA in Liechtenstein with the Appenzell Alps in the distance.

The peak I called K9 above the Stade Louis II at AS Monaco.

Škofja Loka's football stadium beneath the town's medieval castle, with Kamnik Alps in the background.

Swiss team FC Isérables playing FC Vionnaz 2. The slope of the land on the right shows the gradient that the 'Impossible Stadium' had to be built on.

Looking towards the 'Balfrin End' of Europe's highest permanent football stadium in Gspon at 1,923m/6,309ft. The home side is in the process of losing 10-1 to FC Inter Wiler!

Facing the other end of the Ottmar Hitzfeld Gspon Arena, FC Siders meets FC Visp in a veterans' tournament. In the background, the Bietschhorn does its best Toblerone impression.

The Fee Glacier in the Swiss Alps, venue for one of Europe's highest football matches at an altitude of 3,451m/11,322ft. The snow ploughs behind the author show the location of the temporary pitch.

Seven years after Gelsenkirchen, AS Monaco suffered relegation to France's second tier. A majority share of the club was then bought by a Russian billionaire, Dmitry Rybolovlev. Claudio Ranieri led Monaco to promotion in his first season as the club's coach in 2012/13 before clinching second place in Ligue 1 in 2013/14. Three years after Ranieri's departure, Monaco, coached by Leonardo Jardim, won Ligue 1 in 2016/17, the eighth and most recent league championship in the club's history.

That season, Monaco achieved arguably the best European results of any Alpine team in the last decade, when Pep Guardiola's Manchester City provided the opposition in the first knockout round of the Champions League. After losing 5-3 in Manchester, a Monaco team containing Kylian Mbappé and Bernardo Silva triumphed 3-1 in the second leg at Stade Louis II. With the tie level 6-6 on aggregate, Monaco went through on away goals; the first time that Guardiola had been eliminated at such an early stage of the Champions League. Monaco then overcame Borussia Dortmund in the quarter-final 6-3 on aggregate, only to lose 4-1 to Juventus in the semi.

Towards the start of the 2023/24 season, I visited Monaco and took in a game at Stade Louis II. The price of accommodation in Monaco led me to choose Nice as my base during the trip as it is just a 20-minute train journey away. The match was in the ninth round of fixtures in the new 18-team Ligue 1. Before the weekend, Monaco stood top of the table, while the opposition, FC Metz from Lorraine in eastern France, struggled in fourth from bottom.

A 5pm kick-off on Sunday, 22 October 2023 provided plenty of time for sightseeing, most of which involved the principality's famous Grand Prix. I walked along most of the route of the motor racing circuit (apart from the tunnel section which was out of bounds), followed by viewing the collection of vehicles belonging to the Prince of Monaco which is open to the public as a museum and contains several Formula One cars. After bringing down the chequered flag on my self-guided tour, there was time for a quick walk up to the Rock of Monaco to look at the Prince's Palace, before heading towards the football stadium in the south-eastern district of Fontvieille.

Built on land reclaimed from the sea, Stade Louis II is squeezed next to the French border which runs on the other side of Avenue du Port, immediately outside one end of the stadium. The road also marks the perimeter of the Alpine Convention, making Stade Louis II closer to the edge of the region than any other football ground featuring in this book.

Completed in 1985, the new stadium retained the name of the club's previous football ground, but is otherwise different in every respect. Fundamental to the design was maximising use of the limited space available. The pitch is at an altitude of 21m/69ft, considerably higher than the surrounding streets because underneath it there are four storeys: three above ground, one subterranean. These levels contain parking spaces for 1,750 cars; an Olympic-sized swimming pool; a sports hall capable of holding up to 3,500 people; a restaurant, shops and offices. In the words of Simon Inglis in his book *The Football Grounds of Europe*, 'Quite simply there exists no other sports-orientated structure in the world which packs so much into such a small space, so lavishly and with such ingenuity.'

Since Inglis wrote his book in 1990, even more has been packed into the area immediately surrounding Stade Louis II. Along Avenue des Castelans, next to one side of the stadium, there are now several apartment blocks; while across Avenue du Port behind one of the ends stands another football ground.

Formerly called Stade Marquet, this little venue consists of an artificial pitch surrounded by fencing and a small spectator area on one side. The stadium was renamed Stade Didier Deschamps in 2018 in honour of the man who had just coached the French national side to its second World Cup triumph. Deschamps had also captained France to its first World Cup win in 1998 in addition to taking AS Monaco to that 2004 Champions League Final. Although Stade Didier Deschamps is only a road's width from Stade Louis II, it is nevertheless a few metres outside the perimeter of the Alpine Convention; consequently, the youth game under way at the time of my visit can't feature in this book.

All-seated, Stade Louis II consists of a three-tiered main grandstand along one of the sides; a single-tiered Première Laterale ('First Lateral') on the opposite side; as well as a single-tiered Populaires ('Popular') end behind one of the goals. These three sections are all covered, but the remaining end where the away fans sit is uncovered, partly to encourage ventilation of the pitch. This end is called Pesages, which translates as 'Weighings', but after searching unsuccessfully for an explanation I can only guess that this could have something to do with toll gates that may once have existed at the French border. Nine elegant arches at the back of this end provide the stadium's most distinctive architectural feature.

Although I travelled from Nice to Monaco by train, I had noticed that the club's website advertises a different way of completing the same journey, saying, 'Want to reach Monaco from Nice in less than seven minutes? There's only one way: via helicopter. The Monaco heliport is next to the Stade Louis II.' It's a statement that reveals quite a lot about the club's fans.

Famous for being a playground of the rich, about a third of Monaco's population are millionaires, including a significant number of multi-millionaires. With the club promoting access to the stadium via helicopter, I feared that football there would be extremely corporate and commercialised.

Such fears seemed to be confirmed the moment I entered the stadium and took my seat in the Première Laterale, six rows from the front. On the running track surrounding the pitch was a cordoned-off area. A couple of men wearing smart white shirts stood next to a pedestal table, on top of which rested an ice bucket containing bottles of wine and champagne. Nearby, a woman in a red dress greeted people and ticked off their names from a guest list before admitting them to the enclosure. I assumed it was a hospitality event for 'VIPs' who were probably more interested in being seen than watching the football, and more worryingly, threatened to disturb my line of vision. However, the casual attire of the guests who began to arrive (more jeans than suits) suggested that it was much less formal. More importantly, fears that the gathering would obstruct my view of the game proved unfounded when the woman in red, the waiters and their guests dispersed quarter of an hour before kick-off and the enclosure was hastily dismantled.

These days, Stade Louis II can hold about 18,500 spectators, or nearly half the principality's population, but that afternoon it was only a third full with just 6,200 attending. The only vocal supporters were a few dozen gathered behind a single Ultras Monaco banner at the

Populaires end; but their support was limited to drumming and chanting, with no flags or choreography.

The two teams emerged from the underground dressing rooms with the Monaco players wearing their red and white *La Diagonale* shirts, white shorts and red socks, while Metz appeared in a change kit of all black. Monaco's coach was Adi Hütter, who had previously coached Red Bull Salzburg at the match against Admira Wacker mentioned in chapter three. Hütter had joined the club in the summer, and arranged his team in a nominally 4-4-2 formation, but with two wingers it looked more like 4-2-4. The Metz players were arranged in a solid 4-5-1, and it became clear that they liked to hit lots of long balls to run on to.

After four minutes, a different kind of long ball made an impact when Takumi Minamino attempted a short pass to one of his Monaco colleagues, Youssouf Fofana. Metz's Senegalese international Lamine Camara intercepted the ball in his own half and spotted that Monaco's goalkeeper Philipp Köhn had strayed outside his penalty area. The quick-thinking Camara immediately hit a lob which soared over Köhn and into the net. Sports paper *L'Équipe* subsequently reported that the goal was scored from an astonishing distance of 58.37m, or over 63 yards. Nineteen-year-old Camara's first goal in French football since moving from Senegal in February of that year also made the news in the UK, with *The Sun* headlining 'Senegalese wonderkid Lamine Camara scores "insane" goal from inside his OWN HALF leaving fans stunned'.

Camara's strike is the only time that I have seen a footballer score from his own half on a full-sized pitch. The approximately 100 travelling Metz supporters gathered at the end to my left cheered loudly, as did quite a few people sitting near me in the Première Laterale; fortunately, the home fans didn't object to their presence and there wasn't any trouble.

With AS Monaco's place at the top of the league table under threat, the team created a couple of chances, only for Metz keeper Alexandre Oukidja to save them both. The crowd remained patient until the 38th minute, but when Russian international winger Aleksandr Golovin took a corner by kicking the ball back to the centre circle he was booed. The reaction from the home fans seemed to galvanise Golovin, because a few minutes later, he received a pass from Chrislain Matsima just outside the penalty area, then beat a defender before hitting a powerful right-footed shot which curled past Oukidja into the far corner of the goal.

At half-time, ASM needed to push on and get a winner, so Hütter brought on Maghnes Akliouche. An attacking midfielder, the 21-year-old was a product of the club's highly rated youth academy. With a very small pool of local talent, the club looks to recruit youngsters from all over France. In the past, this has included Paris-born Kylian Mbappé who spent a couple of years as a youth player at Monaco before making his senior debut in the principality. The crowd reacted positively to the change, correctly anticipating that Akliouche's arrival would add speed and creativity to the team.

In the opening minutes of the second half, both sides had a chance to score; however, when a goal came it was for the home team. Ten minutes after the break, ASM won a free kick about 25m from goal, enabling Golovin to hit a right-footed shot which bent inside the post. *L'Équipe* described Golovin's goals as 'Deux coups de genie' ('Two strokes of genius').

ASM proceeded to dominate the game, creating chances for Minamino, Akliouche and strikers Folarin

Balogun and Wissam Ben Yedder, only for Oukidja to save them all. The failure to extend Monaco's lead nearly proved costly when Metz substitute Kevin Van Den Kerkhof had a chance to score in the last minute of normal time, only for Köhn to make a vital save. After three minutes of stoppage time, the contest ended with a 2-1 victory for Monaco, restoring the team's position at the top of Ligue 1.

Overall, my matchday experience at Monaco turned out to be far more positive than expected. Stade Louis II is a lovely little stadium, and the spectators included significant numbers of family groups, attracted by the price of match tickets: mine cost just €35, considerably cheaper and easier to obtain than at most Premier League grounds. Although I stuck to non-alcoholic drinks, it was nice to see people being able to take beers to their seats.

AS Monaco finished the 2023/24 Ligue 1 campaign in second place, nine points behind Paris Saint-Germain. Metz ended in a mess, dropping down to Ligue 2 after losing a play-off. That relegation contributed to Lamine Camara, who made such an impression with his long-range goal, being transferred to Monaco in a €13.5m deal at the end of the season. In August 2024, Camara scored the first of ASM's goals in an impressive 3-0 away win against FC Barcelona in the Joan Gamper Trophy. Since the start of that annual pre-season game in 1966, only 12 clubs have defeated Barcelona, with Monaco becoming the first from the Alps. Camara and Monaco followed that up by beating Barcelona again, this time in a much more important Champions League game, a few weeks later.

Returning to Stade Louis II, my seat provided a fine view of Tête de Chien, a prominent rock formation with a name that translates as 'Dog's Head' because of its shape.

I suppose if the Himalayas have a K2 why shouldn't the Alps have a K9?

A more serious question is whether Monaco can really be considered Alpine. Although dominating the view from inside the stadium, Tête de Chien is only 550m/1,804ft high and actually in France. The hill looked impressive merely because Monaco is so low. The principality may be within the perimeter of the Alpine Convention, but for me it's more maritime than mountainous.

If Monaco's Alpine status is debatable, Metz is definitely too far from the mountain range; however, in 1979 FC Metz had coincidentally also been ASM's surprise opposition in a little-known competition highly relevant to this book: the Coppa delle Alpi.

ii. Coppa delle Alpi

Launched by the Italian and Swiss football associations, the Coppa delle Alpi (Italian for 'Cup of the Alps') was contested by club sides between 1960 and 1987. Initially, the tournament only involved Italian and Swiss teams, but they were later joined by ones from France, West Germany and Belgium, with the latter stretching the definition of Alpine beyond reasonable limits. Over the years, the format of the tournament changed and competing countries came and went. The complete statistical record of this little-known competition is contained in Alfredo Corinti's booklet *La Coppa delle Alpi*.

AS Monaco's first Coppa delle Alpi victory occurred in 1979. After topping a group containing Servette FC and Neuchâtel Xamax FCS from Switzerland together with Olympique Lyonnais from France, Monaco met FC Metz in the final. Played at Metz in front of 4,400 people, the home side led at half-time only for Monaco to score three goals in the second half and secure a 3-1 win. ASM's third goal came from Cameroonian striker Roger Milla, two minutes from time. Another goal from Milla, 15 years later in 1994, would establish his fame as the oldest player to score in a World Cup finals tournament at the age of 42.

In 1983, ASM secured a second Coppa delle Alpi. Monaco finished first in a group containing previous opponents Servette, Neuchâtel Xamax and Metz, before beating French side AJ Auxerre 2-1 in the final. Monaco's third and last Coppa delle Alpi came the following year. After finishing first in a group including Auxerre and Swiss teams FC Sion and FC La Chaux-de-Fonds, ASM overcame Grasshopper Club 2-0 in the final, both goals coming in the last three minutes.

The Coppa delle Alpi came to an end in 1987, partly as a consequence of clubs preferring to concentrate on the more lucrative UEFA competitions. Servette's four triumphs made it the most successful club in the 27 years of the tournament, followed by FC Basel and Monaco in joint second with three wins each. However, both Geneva and Basel are outside the perimeter of the Alpine Convention, meaning that the most successful club within the region is AS Monaco. Today the Coppa delle Alpi is largely forgotten; AS Monaco doesn't even mention its three successes in the tournament on the list of honours on the club's website.

Chapter 11

Slovenia

THE MOST easterly of the Alpine nations, Slovenia is also the youngest of the eight countries, gaining independence only 34 years ago. Two-thirds of Slovenia, including the capital Ljubljana, stands outside the Alpine region; however, the focus of this chapter is on Škofja Loka, a town in the northern and more mountainous third of the country by the foot of the Julian Alps.

Football arrived in Slovenia when the area was part of the Habsburg Empire. In 1900, Austrians from Graz visited Laibach (the German name for Ljubljana) to play football against a scratch team put together at a gymnasium used by the German-speaking community. After the match, the gym established Slovenia's first dedicated football club, Laibacher Sportverein. Interest in football among the German-speaking population soon waned and by 1907 the club ceased to exist; however, the Austrians had unwittingly planted the seeds of the sport, and within a few years locals began to form clubs of their own. Students set up a team called Hermes in 1909, then two years later SK Ilirija became the first club for the general public; both based in Laibach.

After Austria-Hungary's defeat in the First World War in 1918 led to the collapse of its empire, Slovenia joined a union with Croats and Serbs which developed into the Kingdom of Yugoslavia.

i. The Gloves are Off: NK Škofja Loka, 340m/1,115ft

About 22km/14 miles north-west of Ljubljana, Škofja Loka is home to around 12,000 people. Often overlooked by the hordes of tourists heading from the capital to the lakeside resort of Bled, Škofja Loka possesses one of the best-preserved medieval Old Towns in Slovenia, dominated by an imposing castle. Although Škofja Loka possesses an attractive centre, there are a number of reminders of its communist past, including ten hideous Yugoslav-era high-rise housing blocks on the edge of town. Although carefully omitted from postcards and other tourist publicity, these eyesores are clearly visible from the lower slopes of hills surrounding the town.

Škofja Loka dates from the tenth century, when the Holy Roman Emperor gave the territory to the bishop of Freising in Bavaria. In the early 13th century, Loka Castle was constructed for a later bishop's governor on a promontory overlooking the town, then rebuilt following an earthquake about 300 years later. After the dissolution of the Holy Roman Empire in the early 19th century, Škofja Loka, like the rest of Slovenia, came under Austrian rule.

Since 1959, Loka Castle has housed the local museum which contains beautifully displayed artefacts recording the history of the area. Particularly memorable is the museum's collection of locally made clothing, with various garments made from lace, linen, cotton and felt, including traditional Slovenian costumes, hats and shawls. Also on display are two black and white gloves, but these date from the 21st century and are made from modern synthetic material. The gloves belonged to Škofja Loka's most famous person, who autographed them before they were placed in a protective glass cabinet; to discover why they take pride of place in the museum we must turn to the history of football in the town.

The story of football in Škofja Loka began in 1929 when a local gymnasium decided to add a football team to its collection of sports so that it could compete against other local sides. This team developed into Nogometno Društvo Sora Škofja Loka (Football Club Sora Škofja Loka, or NDS Škofja Loka for short). The Sora part of the team's name refers to the local river, which would have a huge impact on football in the town nearly a century later, as we shall hear.

During the inter-war period, the Slovenian football league acted as a feeder into the Yugoslav championship (called the First Federal Football League). Teams from the Croatian city of Zagreb and Belgrade in Serbia dominated the Yugoslav First Federal Football League during this time. NDS Škofja Loka initially played friendlies then participated in the Gorenjska liga, named after the local region.

Sadly, Yugoslav football largely came to a halt following the German invasion in April 1941. After 11 days, Yugoslavia surrendered and Slovenian lands were occupied either by the Nazis or their allies, Italy, Hungary and Croatia. The area around Škofja Loka became incorporated into Großdeutschland ('Greater Germany'), with thousands of Slovenians deported to make way for German settlers or to work as forced labourers.

Several resistance groups developed during the occupation, including one that adopted the symbol of a stylised silhouette of Slovenia's highest mountain, Triglav, with its distinctive three peaks plus the letters OF, standing for Osvobodilna Fronta ('Liberation Front'). Yugoslavia suffered more than most countries during the war, and nine footballers from Škofja Loka died: one in the Yugoslav army during the initial German invasion; two in concentration camps; and six while fighting for the partisans against the occupiers.

Josip Broz, better known as Tito, led the communist partisans who became the strongest resistance movement during the war. Following the defeat of the Third Reich in 1945, Tito's forces took control of Yugoslavia. Like many Slovenian towns, Škofja Loka has several mass graves nearby, containing the bodies of people killed by the partisans soon after the end of the war. Those executed were either Germans, collaborators or locals accused of being anti-communist. Hushed up by the communists, the existence of these mass graves has been acknowledged since independence, enabling Slovenia to try and face up to its dark past.

On 30 September 1945, less than five months after the end of the conflict, a new multi-sports club was founded in the town, offering gymnastics, athletics, skating, skiing and shooting to its members. Called TVD Partizan Škofja Loka, named after the resistance fighters, the club also formed a football team.

Compared to the pre-war regime, the new communist authorities were more positive about sport and acted quickly to revive the First Federal Football League in time for the 1946/47 season. A new Yugoslav-wide second division was also introduced, meaning that the old Slovenian football league remained the highest level in Slovenia, but now became the third tier in Yugoslavia rather than the second.

Under communist rule, the football pyramid in this part of Yugoslavia was arranged as follows (in Slovenian, lower-case letters are used for some words in the names of the leagues):

1. Prva zvezna nogometna liga (First Federal Football League)
2. Druga zvezna liga (Second Federal League)
3. Slovenska republiška nogometna liga (Slovene Republic Football League)
4. 2. Slovenski ligi (2. Slovenian League)
5. Local leagues including Gorenjska liga

TVD Partizan Škofja Loka competed in the fifth tier of Yugoslav football, winning its first Gorenjska liga championship in 1947, earning promotion to the fourth-tier 2. Slovenski ligi. Whereas the Gorenjska liga only involved matches against local teams, the 2. Slovenski ligi involved travelling to play clubs all over Slovenia; however, the team only managed to stay in the fourth tier for two seasons before relegation in 1949.

Around this time, the team's goalkeeper, Urho Kalan, developed an unusual way of saving penalties. Kalan had started to play football for Škofja Loka's youth team in the 1930s. Following an important penalty save at a TVD Partizan Škofja Loka away match in Ljubljana in the late 1940s, Kalan became an expert in saving spot kicks, using what he called a *psihološkega trika* ('psychological trick'), which he described, as reported in a later article on NK Škofja Loka's website, as follows, 'Before the player took the penalty, I always moved half a metre from the middle of the goal to the left. When the player kicked the ball, of course, where there was more space, i.e. to the right, I threw myself in that direction and most of the time I succeeded, and they applauded me. I saved the penalty.'

As often happened in communist countries, the Škofja Loka football team underwent several reorganisations and name changes, including spells as ŠD Ločan and NK Ločan. In 1969, the team secured another promotion to the fourth tier, only to slip back down to the Gorenjska liga.

Tito liked football, but despite having a Slovenian mother and a Croatian father, he decided to support FK Partizan from Serbia. Highly charismatic, Tito broke with Stalin in 1948 and advocated an alternative form of socialism based on workers' self-management. He repositioned Yugoslavia as one of the non-aligned countries, independent of the two superpowers. Heading a one-party dictatorship, Tito ruthlessly suppressed political opposition and kept tight control on Yugoslavia as a multi-national federation. After his death in 1980, political and economic problems eventually led to the country's violent disintegration.

Amid the collapse of communism throughout eastern Europe, Slovenia broke away from Yugoslavia following the Ten-Day War between 27 June and 7 July 1991, becoming a separate state. It was no accident that Slovenia, as the most prosperous part of Yugoslavia and the region geographically closest to western Europe, should be the first to break away from the federation.

Since independence, football is now organised as the Slovenska nogometna liga (Slovenian Football League), with the old Slovenian top division being renamed and raised from the third to the first tier. Today, the structure looks like this:

1. Slovenska nogometna liga (Slovenian Football League)/1. SNL

2. Druga slovenska nogometna liga (Second Slovenian Football League)/2. SNL
3. Tretja slovenska nogometna liga (Third Slovenian Football League)/3. SNL (divided into west and east divisions)
4. Slovenske regionalne lige (Slovenian Regional Leagues)

NK Olimpija from Ljubljana and NK Maribor from the country's second-largest city have dominated Slovenian football since independence; however, both clubs are located outside the Alpine region.

Despite having a population of just over two million (smaller than Greater Manchester) Slovenia has punched above its weight at sport, winning dozens of Olympic medals; however, these were achieved in winter sports or the likes of athletics, judo, rowing and cycling, not football. The 2000 edition of *The Rough Guide to European Football* introduced its section on Slovenia by saying, 'With a great tradition in skiing and other Alpine sports, not to mention a passion for basketball, this tiny former Yugoslav state had for years shown a palpable indifference to football, while all around it were entranced by the beautiful game.'

However, such apathy began to change when Slovenia qualified for Euro 2000, followed by the World Cup finals in 2002.

Slovenia went on to also qualify for the World Cup finals in South Africa in 2010. One year after that tournament, Ljubljana lawyer Aleksander Čeferin became president of the Nogometna Zveza Slovenije (Football Association of Slovenia or NZS), then five years later he became the elected president of UEFA, massively increasing the international profile of Slovenian football.

The successor club to ND Sora Škofja Loka, TVD Partizan Škofja Loka, ŠD Ločan and NK Ločan now goes by the name of Nogometni Klub Škofja Loka (Football Club Škofja Loka or NK Škofja Loka). These days, the team competes in the western division of Slovenia's third tier, the Tretja slovenska nogometna liga/3. SNL (West).

So, now we can finally deal with the question as to why those gloves are prominently displayed in Loka Castle. The answer is because of Jan Oblak, the town's biggest contribution to Slovenian football. Born in Škofja Loka in 1993, Oblak started playing as a five-year-old for his hometown club NK Ločan (forerunner of NK Škofja Loka) in 1998. After progressing from the little club's youth team, Oblak moved to the capital to become the goalkeeper for Olimpija. In 2010, Oblak joined Portuguese giants Benfica and following several loan spells he signed for Atlético Madrid. The only time I saw Oblak was in 2016 after travelling to Milan for the Champions League Final, where his Atlético team faced city rivals Real Madrid in the San Siro. Although Oblak ended up on the losing side after failing to save any penalties in the decisive shoot-out, he is regarded as one of the world's top goalkeepers as well as one of the best footballers in Slovenian history.

In 2022, Oblak received the title of Honorary Citizen of the Municipality of Škofja Loka and appeared in a promotional video for Škofja Loka Tourism, filmed on the pitch of his first football club's tiny Nogometno Igrišče Puštal (Puštal Football Field). Loka Castle appears prominently behind Oblak in the film, with the museum inside the old building proudly displaying his goalkeeping gloves as well as a pair of his football boots.

At the end of each season, the NK Škofja Loka children's football school organises a huge tournament for under-12s, supported by Oblak, with over 120 clubs and 1,400 children participating.

Just before the 3. SNL match I attended on Saturday, 18 May 2024, NK Škofja Loka stood eighth in the table out of 14 clubs, with the opposition, NK Šobec Lesce, down in 12th. The game was the penultimate fixture of a 26-game season.

Slightly to the north of Škofja Loka, the small town of Lesce is also within the Alps and the region of Upper Carniola. Originally a small village, Lesce grew in size because of its strategic location on a shelf above the river valley of the Sava Dolinka. Like many Alpine locations, Lesce's later development owed a great deal to the coming of the railway, constructed lower down in the valley during the second half of the 19th century. Lesce's football club traces its origins to 1946; a few months after the communists came to power in Yugoslavia. During its early years, the club oscillated between the local district league and more senior regional competitions.

NK Škofja Loka moved to its current location in Puštal in the southern part of the town in 1941, during the year of the German invasion. These days, the Nogometno Igrišče Puštal stadium consists of a perimeter wall with a gateway, dugouts on one side of the pitch, and two tiny grandstands on the other side. Both grandstands were wooden with three rows of benches to sit on. The one I chose turned out to be a rickety structure with large cracks and holes in the wood. In the far corner stood a clubhouse which contained the players' dressing rooms. The pitch was a natural grass surface, and the absence of any floodlights made night games impossible. Also impossible was viewing the game from the far side by the dugouts or behind either of the goals; those areas were fenced off, possibly to protect the grass, whereas the one accessible side was concreted.

In the distance, the Kamnik Alps, where I had attempted to hike the previous day but been driven back by terrible weather, appeared over the tops of trees and buildings on the eastern side of the stadium. Luckily it was dry and sunny on matchday with a pleasant temperature of 24°C, which was just as well because there were no covered areas at the stadium.

About three-quarters of an hour before the 5.30pm kick-off, a car with a trailer appeared and drove behind one of the goals before taking up a position over by the clubhouse. A tap on the side of the trailer provided the main clue: this was the mobile beer stall, and tables and chairs that soon appeared outside it confirmed this.

The match kicked off five minutes late, with the home side wearing yellow and black shirts and the visitors in red and black ones. Although both teams wore black shorts and socks, everyone seemed happy despite the colour clash. The official attendance was later given as 80, although it looked more like 60 to me. As with many games at this level of football, most of the spectators appeared to be friends or family of the players.

Soon after the start, Uroš Palibrk, Škofja Loka's number 10, became the first player to catch my eye. A recent recruit to the team, Palibrk had once been a Slovenian youth international. Born in Slovenia's third-largest city, Kranj, in 1992, Palibrk started his career at his local team, NK Triglav Kranj, named after the country's highest mountain. Palibrk's goalscoring prowess for the Kranj youth team led to him being hailed as one of the top footballing talents in the Gorenjska region and earned him a move to Italy in 2007 to join mighty AC Milan at the age of 15. Although Palibrk managed to score a goal every other game for the *Rossoneri* youth team, he failed to break into the senior side. Palibrk subsequently played for clubs in Croatia, Belgium and Austria, leaving SAK Klagenfurt to join NK Škofja Loka a few months before my game. Aged 32 at the time of the match against Šobec Lesce, Palibrk demonstrated some skilful flicks and twists in attack, although his impact later faded.

Sixteen minutes in, Lesce nearly went ahead with a free kick taken by pacy midfielder Zufer Shaini; Škofja Loka's goalkeeper, Patrik Mesarić, saved the shot but failed to hold it and was fortunate that the loose ball didn't reach an opponent. Arguably Škofja Loka's best chance of the opening period came with just over half an hour played; Bojan Bauloski shot from a tight angle on the left, but Timon Popelar in the Lesce goal saved well. Škofja Loka looked vulnerable at the back, with three players in defence and wide gaps between them. However, through blocks and interceptions, the visitors were kept at bay.

Škofja Loka livened up in the early stages of the second half. Eight minutes after the restart, Maks Lotrič Škoda received the ball with his back to goal on the edge of the D and did well to turn and get a right-footed shot on target which Popelar saved. Midway through the second period, Lotrič Škoda was substituted, which surprised me because the 20-year-old striker had seemed to be his team's most likely scorer. However, although skilful, Lotrič Škoda was sometimes crowded out by the Lesce defence, and his coach, Andrej Janežič, may have opted for a more physical presence up front. If so, the change didn't seem to make much difference. In the closing moments of the game,

Škofja Loka had three corners in quick succession but failed to make any of them count.

The game ended 0-0, and despite being the only goalless draw to feature in this book, it had been keenly contested and good value for the €2.50 admission fee. I imagine that Urho Kalan and Jan Oblak would approve of Mesarić keeping a clean sheet for their old club.

Šobec Lesce made up for not scoring by getting six goals in the final game of the season a week later against bottom club Brda Dobrovo. Despite that win, Šobec Lesce ended the campaign still in 12th place, while Škofja Loka's defeat away at Adria saw the team drop to tenth.

Overall, I found Slovenia an intriguing country; far more developed than Belgrade where I had travelled eight years earlier, it was certainly more Alpine than Balkan, with much of it resembling Austria.

That summer at Euro 2024 in Germany, Škofja Loka's most famous former resident, Jan Oblak, played his part as Slovenia secured three draws against Denmark, Serbia and England in the group stage. The tournament's new structure meant that third place was enough to qualify for the next round. A hard-working team with a well-organised defence, Slovenia drew 0-0 with Portugal in the last 16, Oblak pulling off a spectacular save from a Cristiano Ronaldo penalty in extra time. However, despite being fast on the counter-attack, Slovenia's strikers wasted the few chances that came their way, and the team missed every penalty in the shoot-out, with Oblak failing to repeat his earlier heroics. Nevertheless, it was the first time Slovenia had reached the knockout stages of a major international competition, and the little country had remained unbeaten in open play.

ii. *Poplava*: Football and the Alpine Environment

For NK Škofja Loka, 2023/24 will not be remembered for anything that happened during a match; instead, the season was dominated by the *poplava* ('flood').

The first half of 2023 had seen higher than normal rainfall in much of Slovenia. During the night of Friday, 4 August 2023, a month's rain fell in a single day. The downpour continued for the next three days, and with much of the land already saturated, many parts of northern and central Slovenia suffered flash floods and landslides.

In flatter terrain, floodwater often seeps up and spills over riverbanks into the surrounding area; whereas in areas like the Alps, steeper gradients cause the water to travel much more quickly as it races down the mountainside. The speed and force of the water as it pours down brings with it rocks and stones, and this debris is often at least as destructive as the water.

The result was the worst natural disaster in Slovenia since independence. At least seven people were killed, a number which would have been higher without the severe weather warnings that were issued in advance. The floods caused widespread destruction of buildings, roads, bridges, vehicles and farmland. Many people suffered losses of power supply and drinking water in their homes, while others had to be evacuated and army helicopters were hastily brought in to rescue those trapped by the water. Across the whole of Slovenia, the flood damage is estimated to have cost more than ten per cent of Slovenia's annual gross domestic product.

Škofja Loka suffered particularly badly, being located below hills and at the confluence of two rivers, Poljane

Sora and Selca Sora, which merge to form the Sora. Over 400 buildings were flooded in Škofja Loka, of which ten were totally destroyed. Extensive damage was done to local roads and sewers, as well as agriculture with loss of crops and livestock. Altogether, there was over €65m worth of damage in the municipality of Škofja Loka alone, according to local media reports.

During my visit nine months later, I crossed over Capuchin Bridge, one of Slovenia's biggest tourist attractions. Built out of stone in a perfect semi-circle in the 14th century, the bridge is the only one of its kind still standing in central Europe. On Capuchin Bridge stands a statue of Saint John of Nepomuk, who became a Catholic martyr after being thrown off Charles Bridge in Prague for refusing to betray the secrets of the confessional. His death by drowning in a river has made him a patron saint of bridges and protecting people from floods. Although Capuchin Bridge survived the 2023 flooding, Saint John of Nepomuk couldn't save another of Škofja Loka's bridges, because the modern one in the suburb of Suha was destroyed. When I went to the spot, all that could be seen was the road ending suddenly on both sides of the River Sora.

For NK Škofja Loka the impact of the flood was devastating. Positioned near to the confluence of the two rivers, the town's Igrišče Puštal football stadium was deluged by over a metre of water, with only the tops of the perimeter walls and entrance gate protruding above what looked like a muddy sea. The stadium stayed submerged for several days, and even when the water finally drained away the pitch remained totally unplayable.

The 3. SNL season had been scheduled to start the following weekend on 12 and 13 August, but with matches at the Igrišče Puštal clearly impossible, the club played its 'home' fixtures in Gorajte, a few kilometres to the north. Regular fixtures were only resumed in Škofja Loka from 23 March 2024, less than two months before my visit.

Local authorities across the country had their hands full dealing with the devastation, arranging infrastructural repairs and compensation. One relatively minor consequence of this was the withdrawal of a football team of Slovenian mayors from the seventh Alpencup (Alpine Cup). First held in 2011, the Alpencup is a competition for municipal leaders, involving teams from Italy, Austria, Germany and Slovenia. The Slovenian mayors were forced to withdraw from the tournament (held in the Austrian town of Melk an der Donau on 10 September 2023) in order to concentrate on the crisis in their country caused by the flooding.

The local authorities did an excellent job clearing up and repairing the damage. During my visit to Škofja Loka, I observed rebuilt and stronger embankments along the sides of the Sora, and apart from the road ending abruptly by the destroyed bridge at Suha, the only remaining signs of the devastation were a couple of wrecked cars and rock debris by the river.

The extent to which disasters such as the one in Slovenia in 2023 are a consequence of global warming and human impact on the environment is a hugely important and contentious issue, with full consideration of the arguments beyond the scope of this book.

Some of the worst floods in Alpine history occurred in Switzerland in 1868, long before modern global warming. Those 19th-century floods were the result of a perfect storm, with warm air from the Mediterranean moving north and colliding with cooler air in the Swiss Alps, producing torrential rain which fell on saturated ground and on rivers and lakes already full after wet weather. The 2023 floods in Slovenia had similar causes, only in this case the warm and moist air came from the Adriatic Sea, cooling suddenly as it reached the Slovenian Alps, resulting in the deluge. Storms earlier in the year had also caused damage to parts of the terrain, uprooting some of the trees and impeding the ability of the land to retain water.

While the 1868 flood and the one in 2023 might appear to have similar causes, global warming has made such extreme weather more common. Many of the highest global temperatures since records began have occurred in the last couple of decades. This book looks at the history of football in parts of the Alps since the 1870s, yet the two stadiums to feature that have been seriously flooded were both inundated in recent times: Thun in 2005 (mentioned in the next chapter) and Škofja Loka in 2023.

Global warming may partly be explained by natural fluctuations in the world's temperature; however, many people point to human impact on the climate, releasing greenhouse gases such as carbon dioxide which heat up the planet by trapping the sun's heat. Another major factor is population growth, with the number of people living in the Alpine region doubling since the middle of the 19th century and now standing at approximately 13 million.

Since reliable temperature recording started in 1860, temperatures in parts of the Alps have increased by nearly 2°C, twice as rapidly as the global average. The Alps heated up more quickly than lower areas because whereas in the past snow and ice reflected sunlight, newly uncovered rock absorbs the sun's heat at an increased rate, causing the temperature on the mountain and consequently its surrounding area to rise more than areas at lower altitude that weren't covered in snow or ice. In Switzerland, for example, the country's glaciers are estimated to have lost about two-thirds of their volume since 1860.

A later chapter will refer to the Feegletscher in Valais and its significance in football history; I was shocked at the scale of the shrinkage of that glacier between my first visit to it in 2001 and my return in 2023. If present trends continue, Alpine glaciers may disappear altogether by 2100, exposing even more rock to the sun's rays and prompting further increases in temperature.

Alpine glaciers act as massive frozen reservoirs supplying meltwater that eventually flows into the Danube, Po, Rhine and Rhône, providing millions of people with water. However, without meltwater running down from the glaciers, the levels of these rivers could plummet during summer droughts, with a potentially devastating impact on areas far from the mountains.

Apart from shrinkage of glaciers, another consequence of warmer weather in the Alps is more of the precipitation in the winter falling as rain and pouring down the mountainsides, instead of settling as snow. This threatens to damage tourism, of vital importance to local economies, with snow needed for skiing. This is particularly important when it is remembered that more than ten per cent of employment in the region depends on tourism.

Although the exact figure is unknown, some sources estimate that football is responsible for between 0.3 and 0.4 per cent of global emissions contributing to global warming. In other words, approximately the same as a small country like Denmark.

Football impacts on the environment by its use of natural resources and production of greenhouse gases through things such as the transportation of players and spectators to matches; construction of stadiums;

floodlighting; waste disposal; manufacture of football kits and merchandising; and the production of those half-time meat pies. However, I have chosen to focus on football pitches, as this is a particularly important issue.

Artificial playing surfaces are attractive to many Alpine clubs because of weather conditions in the mountains. Seven of the 25 football events featured in this book were played on such surfaces: Voiron; Domodossola; Bern; Thun's new stadium; as well as two matches and a half-day tournament at Gspon. The popularity of artificial pitches in the Alps makes their environmental impact compared to natural surfaces significant; however, this is a rather complicated subject.

Artificial pitches do have some environmental advantages. They need less watering and don't require pesticides or fertilisers which may produce greenhouse gases. Artificial surfaces don't have to be cut by mowers powered by petrol or electric motors, nor do they consume vast amounts of electricity through the use of rigs with lamps to encourage grass to grow by providing light when it's dark and heat when it's cold.

On the other hand, there are also disadvantages with artificial pitches. Firstly, they absorb more of the sun's radiation than grass, causing temperatures in the vicinity to be up to 4°C hotter than pitches with a natural surface. Artificial pitches can also contribute to global warming by replacing grass which has the ability to absorb CO_2. The habitat of earthworms and other creatures living in soil is also restricted by artificial rather than grass surfaces. Most harmful are the small rubber granules used in some types of pitch to provide infill as support for the artificial grass blades and to provide cushioning. These microplastics contain harmful chemicals which may escape from the pitch and pollute nearby land and the water supply, as reported in *Sustainable Football: Environmental Management in Practice.* So-called 'elite-level' football leaves a bigger carbon footprint, because of its larger stadiums, greater use of air travel transporting squads to away matches, and more fans driving cars to games. However, in the Alps, only AS Monaco and Red Bull Salzburg qualify as 'elite', with most clubs from the mountain region contributing much lower carbon footprints than those from Europe's top leagues because of their smaller stadiums and crowds, as well as reduced air travel to games.

In recent years, several clubs and organisations have launched initiatives in response to climate change.

Bidding processes for the hosting of UEFA tournaments and finals now consider the environment. UEFA's Sustainable Infrastructure Guidelines focus on the environmental impact of venues and facilities. All 55 affiliated football associations have been encouraged to reduce the sport's impact on the environment and appoint their own sustainability managers. UEFA has also signed up to the United Nations Race to Zero campaign, aiming to achieve net zero carbon emissions by 2050, or sooner. More recently, holders of tickets for the UEFA Women's Euro 2025 football tournament benefitted from free public transport on matchdays, providing a second-class return trip between anywhere in Switzerland and the stadium in an attempt to reduce car journeys.

Returning to Slovenia, in 2019, climate activists from that country suggested using football's high profile to raise awareness of the threat of air pollution. The Slovenian activists claimed that poor air was responsible for one death in eight, as well as slowing the pace of football matches by up to 15 per cent as a consequence of impairing players' breathing. UEFA agreed to adopt what became known as the Cleaner Air Better Game campaign and chose the 2021 Under-21 Championship, jointly hosted by Slovenia and Hungary, as the opportunity to launch it. The initiative aimed to promote the idea of sustainability to teams and supporters, and included a tree-planting programme as well as funding for children's bicycles. The campaign culminated in the staging of a conference on 7 June 2021 to discuss climate change and the environment, with Slovenia's Aleksander Čeferin, in his capacity as UEFA president, one of the key speakers.

Unfortunately, football has also been accused of 'greenwashing', by making false claims of environmentally friendly practices. In 2023, the Swiss Fairness Commission ruled that FIFA had misled the public by claiming that Qatar the previous year had been the first carbon-neutral World Cup. The regulator found that the Zürich-based federation's estimates of how much CO_2 the finals had produced could not be verified, as reported by BBC Sport.

UEFA also came in for criticism in 2024 when the Nyon-based organisation announced its carbon footprint calculator to help clubs measure their environmental impact, while simultaneously increasing the number of matches in European club competitions, many of them requiring air travel. In UEFA's defence, the increase in matches was partly forced upon the federation by the threat of a breakaway so-called European Super League from greedy clubs, keen to boost their revenues. Sadly, under the present system, environmental considerations will struggle to compete with the commercialisation of the game.

Chapter 12

Switzerland: Bernese Oberland

FINALLY, WE reach Switzerland, arguably the nation most associated with the Alps. The perimeter of the Alpine Convention runs diagonally through Switzerland; the north-west of the country, containing its five biggest cities (Zürich, Geneva, Basel, Lausanne and Bern) is outside the Alps, while the southern and eastern parts are inside. As you would expect, most of the country's football clubs are based in the more populated north-west; but this book focuses on some of those coming from the mountainous areas.

The Schweizerischer Fussballverband (Swiss Football Association or SFV) came into being in 1895. Three years later, the country's first national championship took place; initially called Serie A, it was structured as a tournament between the winners of three regional leagues. Switzerland became one of seven founder members of FIFA in 1904, and the following year played its first international with a friendly against France in Paris. The Swiss Serie A operated until it was eventually replaced in 1931 by the Nationalliga A (National League A, sometimes abbreviated to NLA). In 2003, the football authorities rebranded the top division as the Swiss Super League.

Like many other countries, the Swiss football league structure has changed over the years, but at the time of writing it looked like this:

1. Swiss Super League
2. Challenge League
3. Promotion League
4. 1. Liga (sometimes called 1. Liga Klassik)
5. 2. Liga Interregional
6. 2. Liga (2ème Ligue)
7. 3. Liga (3ème Ligue)
8. 4. Liga (4ème Ligue)
9. 5. Liga (5ème Ligue)

The bottom four levels have both their German and French names provided because the next few chapters look at football in Bern and Valais, two of the four Swiss cantons (local states) that are officially multilingual. Altogether, there are 26 cantons, making up what is officially called the Swiss Confederation.

i. From the Cowshed to Highbury: FC Thun, 569m/1,867ft

Whereas the city of Bern, capital of the canton that shares its name, is located just outside the Alpine region, the town of Thun stands inside it. With a population of about 40,000 people, Thun is often regarded as the gateway to the Bernese Oberland, the mountainous area that includes the stunning massif of the Eiger, Mönch and Jungfrau. Pronounced 'Toon', the name of the place derives from an ancient word for 'fortified town'. Apart from picture-postcard views of the mountains and a lake called the Thunersee, Thun also boasts a football club with a fairytale story.

Formed in 1898, FC Thun participated in the lower leagues before eventually winning promotion to the Nationalliga A in 1954. Unfortunately, FC Thun only lasted one year in the top division, suffering relegation back to the second tier in 1955.

In 1964, Thun participated in the Coppa delle Alpi, only to lose both its matches to Foggia of Italy. Another relegation meant that FC Thun found itself in the third tier in 1970, followed by a further drop down to the fourth level in 1974.

After nine years languishing in the fourth tier, a revival started with promotion to the third level in 1983, then a move up to the second tier in 1997, culminating in the club regaining its top-flight status in 2002 under coach Hanspeter Latour.

The first time I heard of FC Thun was during a summer holiday in the Bernese Oberland resort of Grindelwald. Needing to recuperate from an exhausting hike up and down the Faulhorn mountain, I travelled to Thun after discovering that a match would take place in the town that afternoon.

The game I attended, on Saturday, 24 August 2002, was Thun's ninth overall and its fourth at home back in the Nationalliga A. On discovering that the opposition would be FC Basel I had a slight panic, worrying that the match would be a sell-out. However, after arriving in the town and asking around, a local person directed me to a pharmacy which sold tickets over the counter (without a prescription). Despite previously buying football tickets from a tobacconist store in Amsterdam and a bank in Rome, I had never thought of asking for them in a pharmacy!

FC Basel was at that time Switzerland's top club, having won a league and cup double the previous season under former Tottenham coach Christian Gross.

Home of FC Thun since the club's promotion in 1954, the timing of the Stadion Lachen's construction enabled it to be used as a training pitch for West Germany during that year's World Cup finals which were staged in Switzerland. The Stadion Lachen was one of those rarities, a stadium surrounded by a running track that still managed to retain an atmosphere, although perhaps I just got lucky that particular day. With all the seats in the small Subbuteo-style grandstand along one side already taken, the pharmacy sold me a *stehplatz* ('standing') ticket for the terracing around the rest of the pitch. I took up a position opposite the grandstand, near the halfway line. Although the stadium usually offers impressive views of the nearby mountains, that day they were unfortunately obscured by clouds.

Thun, in all red, lined up in a 4-3-3 formation; while Basel, in a change kit of all white, opted for what looked like a 4-3-1-2. Before kick-off, most of the crowd of 6,740 expected FC Basel to comfortably defeat Thun. The visiting fans, mainly crammed into one of the opposite corners behind an 'Inferno' ultra banner, were particularly optimistic, judging by their lively singing at the start. Some of the locals responded by chanting 'Hopp Thun! Hopp Thun!' ('Go Thun! Go Thun!') which had the same rhythm as 'cuckoo' and was duly clocked by a couple of Basel fans standing next to me who thought it highly amusing. Talking of humour, although the city of Thun's local government website mistranslates Stadion Lachen as 'Laughing Stadium', the joke would soon be on Basel.

After half an hour, Thun took a shock lead with a goal from Milaim Rama. Five minutes into the second half, Basel equalised with a goal from the Cameroonian striker Hervé Tum. Patrick Baumann restored Thun's lead after 65 minutes. Then in the last six minutes there was a rush of goals: a second from Rama after 84 minutes made it 3-1; Thun went further ahead through Adrian Moser on 86 minutes; before Tum got his second for Basel in the last minute to make a final score of 4-2. The atmosphere had been terrific and I had certainly landed on my (blistered) feet by choosing this match, one of the most enjoyable I have seen, which just goes to show that you can sometimes see great football games in the most unlikely of places.

Man of the match Milaim Rama had been born in 1976 in what was then Yugoslavia, but moved to Switzerland and became a Swiss citizen. He played for FC Interlaken at the other end of the Thunersee, before joining FC Thun in 1997 at the age of 21. Rama's goals played a major part in Thun's promotion to the top flight in 2002 and the team's consolidation the following campaign. After seven seasons at Thun, Rama moved to FC Augsburg in 2004, only to struggle in Bavaria. After just one campaign, Rama returned to Switzerland to play for FC Schaffhausen, then following a single season there he returned to Thun in 2006. Rama won seven caps for Switzerland and was a member of the country's Euro 2004 squad. He retired in 2012, aged 36.

Thun's victory over Basel caused such a sensation that it even earned a mention in a review of an art exhibition at the Kunstmuseum Thun (the local art gallery). On the day of the match, a retrospective opened at the gallery commemorating the centenary of the birth of Johann Peter Flück. Widely regarded as one of the most important Swiss painters of the mid-20th century, Flück was born in the canton and much of his output consisted of portraits and landscapes, inspired by people and places in the area.

The review in a local newspaper, *Jungfrau Zeitung*, mourned the clash between the opening of the art exhibition and the timing of the afternoon's match in Thun, explaining that it had originally been scheduled for the Sunday but been put back a day because of Basel's involvement in the Champions League. The writer added that visitors to the gallery were kept informed of the score in the Thun versus Basel game by using text messages, still a relatively new form of technology in those days: 'Not only the impressive pictures of the artist, who died in 1954 at the age of 52, were a topic here, but also – thanks to mobile phones and SMS – the interim results of the match in the Lachen Stadium.'

As mentioned by the exhibition reviewer, Basel competed in that season's Champions League; several months later, Christian Gross's team would finish second behind Valencia and knock Liverpool out of the tournament, achievements which emphasise how well Thun had done. Meanwhile, FC Thun finished the 2002/03 NLA campaign in third place.

For the following season, the NLA underwent rebranding as the Swiss Super League, with the second-tier Nationalliga B becoming the Challenge League.

Thun faced a challenge of its own in December 2004 when Hanspeter Latour, the coach who had led the club to the big time, moved to Zürich to join Grasshopper Club. Thun subsequently appointed Urs Schönenberger as Latour's replacement. Despite never having coached in the top tier, Schönenberger oversaw an incredible run that included seven successive wins and ended with Thun finishing second in the league.

Such a high finish in the Swiss Super League in 2004/05 put Thun into the second qualifying round of the following season's UEFA Champions League. The little club from the Bernese Oberland immediately plunged in at the deep end after being paired with Dynamo Kyiv in the qualifier. To put this in context, Thun had never been in a major European competition before, with just a couple of entries in the Intertoto Cup; whereas Dynamo Kyiv had a rich European pedigree, including three UEFA trophies: European Cup Winners' Cups in 1975 and 1986 and the Super Cup in 1975. The Ukrainians had also reached the Champions League group stage for the last eight years and got as far as the semi-final in 1999.

Despite going behind, Thun recovered to earn a remarkable 2-2 draw in the first leg away in Kyiv. With the Stadion Lachen not up to UEFA standards, Thun played all its home European games in Bern at the Stade de Suisse. A dramatic goal in the final minute of the second leg confirmed Thun's progression to the next round.

In the third qualifying round, Thun's players found themselves drawn against Swedish side Malmö, a club that had reached the 1979 European Cup Final. Thun won 1-0 away in Sweden, followed by a 3-0 victory in Bern to clinch qualification for the Champions League group stage. The attendance in Bern was 31,243, equivalent to more than three-quarters of Thun's entire population. On the subject of population size, Thun became the third-smallest town, at that time, to have a team reach the Champions League group stage.

While UEFA's men in suits gathered in Monaco to make the draw for the group stage, Thun's players had other concerns after a mixture of heavy rainfall and rivers bursting their banks caused severe flooding and left their Stadion Lachen under a metre of water.

The suits pulled out Sparta Prague, Ajax and Arsenal as Thun's opponents, with the first game involving the little Swiss club travelling to Highbury. At Thun's last domestic fixture before the trip to London, some fans, mindful of the importance of dairy farming in the Bernese Oberland, unfurled a banner with the slogan 'Vom Kuhstall ins Highbury' ('From the Cowshed to Highbury'). I had a rather easier journey, living at that time in Finsbury Park, only a 20-minute walk from Arsenal's famous stadium.

In the old days, Highbury could hold over 70,000 people, but by 2005 the terraces were long gone and the stadium had become all-seater with a capacity of just 38,500. UEFA's demands for larger advertising boards surrounding the pitch and increased media facilities meant that more places were lost, resulting in an attendance of 34,498. The Thun match was a complete sell-out, forcing me to use an agency to get a ticket, which turned out to be for a seat in the lower part of the West Stand. Although expensive, it would be worth every penny.

On the evening of Wednesday, 14 September 2005, I arrived at Highbury expecting, like most of the crowd, to see an Arsenal side coached by Arsène Wenger (formerly of AS Monaco) and containing the likes of Cesc Fàbregas, Robert Pires and Robin van Persie, thrash Thun. Although Thierry Henry was injured and normal goalkeeper Jens Lehmann suspended, Arsenal still had Dennis Bergkamp on the bench if needed. This was the era of the 'Invincibles', the Arsenal team that had recently gone through an entire Premier League season undefeated in 2003/04 and won the 2005 FA Cup. As the match programme that night said, 'It is unlikely that most of the spectators present this evening will have heard of any of the men wearing Thun's colours.' What chance could FC Thun possibly have?

That day's edition of *The Guardian* described the upcoming game as a 'stark mismatch', explaining that the

Thun players had been part-timers until 1996, adding, 'Their annual budget is £2m – three times less than Thierry Henry earns per year at Arsenal, the sixth-richest club on the planet. No Thun player has an annual salary of more than £50,000. Their stadium boasts 878 seats.'[10]

The two teams walked out of the tunnel opposite me, then formed a single straight line on the pitch, as the UEFA Champions League anthem rang out. For that season, Arsenal had ditched the famous bright red shirts with white sleeves and wore what the club described as 'redcurrant' ones instead, together with white shorts and more of the dark red on the socks. Similar to maroon, this had been Arsenal's original colour, chosen to commemorate the final season at Highbury before moving to the Emirates Stadium. Thun appeared in white shirts, bright red shorts and white socks, creating a slight colour clash.

Reflecting the high turnover during Thun's meteoric rise, only two of the players from my game in the Stadion Lachen against Basel three years earlier lined up against Arsenal: defender Selver Hodžić and midfielder Silvain Aegerter. As well as Swiss footballers and players from other European countries, the club's squad included South Americans, Africans and Australians.

Wenger deployed his team in a 4-4-2 formation, while Schönenberger opted for a 4-5-1 with the star player, Swiss international Mauro Lustrinelli, as the sole out-and-out striker. Born in 1976, Lustrinelli played for his local club Bellinzona before joining FC Wil and then Thun. In his first season (2004/05) Lustrinelli became Thun's top scorer with 20 goals, making a massive contribution to the team's second-placed finish. Lustrinelli then scored three times in

---

10 www.theguardian.com/football/2005/sep/14/thefiver.sport

the Champions League qualifiers, once against Dynamo Kyiv and twice versus Malmö.

After four minutes, Lustrinelli received a welcome to English football, being hacked down by Kolo Touré just inside the Arsenal half. It could have been a red card because there were no covering defenders, but Touré just received a yellow, probably because it was still a long way from goal and early in the game. Encouraged by winning a free kick, the contingent of about 1,000 travelling fans concentrated in a corner to my right began to chant 'Hopp Thun! Hopp Thun!' The free kick led to the first chance in the game, but sadly for the Swiss it went to Arsenal when Pires gained possession and burst forward on the left before hitting a shot narrowly wide.

Thun's first opportunity came around the ten-minute mark, when Adriano led a breakaway attack and slipped a pass forward to Lustrinelli. Manuel Almunia did well to rush out of goal and grab the ball without conceding a foul. However, Thun's 20-year-old Eldin Jakupović became by far the busier of the two keepers, with his efforts including a couple of punches to clear shots by van Persie and then Touré. A couple of minutes before half-time, he made a mess of a shot from José Antonio Reyes, allowing the ball to slip between his legs; although it crossed the line, it was only after Freddie Ljungberg lunged in and pushed Jakupović into the goal, so it was disallowed and a foul awarded instead. A few years later, Jakupović kept goal in the Premier League for Hull City.

The most dramatic moment of the first half occurred just before the interval, when the referee sent off van Persie after he jumped up with a leg raised and his boot caught Thun defender Alen Orman in the head. These days, such a challenge would be judged reckless and out of control prompting an automatic red card, but back in 2005 intentionality was more of a factor in punishing dangerous play, and with van Persie not looking at the Thun player some observers were surprised at the referee's decision. Orman was left with a bad gash on his cheek and forehead, which had to be patched up and bandaged. Ludicrously, the home fans proceeded to jeer Orman every time he touched the ball until the end of the match, even though he had been the victim in the incident and made no attempt to overreact or get van Persie sent off.

At half-time it remained goalless, and although Arsenal had dominated possession and created more chances, Thun fielded a well-organised defence and now benefitted from a one-man advantage.

Thun needed to remain solid at the beginning of the second half, but five minutes after the restart the Swiss team failed to defend an Arsenal corner, resulting in a free header for Gilberto which ended up in the back of the net. Everybody expected the floodgates to open, but a couple of minutes later Thun equalised through Nelson Ferreira. Andreas Gerber hit a looping cross into the penalty area from the right. Touré headed it clear but only as far as Ferreira, who had his back to goal 15 metres out but still managed to lob the ball over Almunia and under the bar. Most reports in England described it as a fluke, a mishit cross; however, replays show that after kicking the ball Ferreira immediately looked hopefully at Almunia as if he knew that the keeper had strayed off his line. Either way, it was Ferreira's revenge on the match programme for dismissing him as a 'lightweight midfielder'.

Having done so well to get back on level terms, Thun nearly threw it away twice through bad back-passes. The first came just minutes later when José Goncalves hit his short towards Jakupović; Reyes dashed towards the ball and the keeper's attempted clearance hit him and nearly rebounded into the net. Then with 20 minutes left, Ljubo Milicevic tried to head the ball back to Jakupović, but it fell short and Ljungberg's shot went narrowly wide.

Soon after that, Bergkamp came on as a substitute, energising the Arsenal team, although Thun's bank of five players ahead of the back four repeatedly frustrated Arsenal. Lustrinelli continued to be the sole outlet for Thun, but even he was substituted five minutes from time. Immediately after that change, an Arsenal free kick into the box provided Touré with an opportunity to get the winner, but although he escaped the attentions of the defenders his header went wide of the goal.

At the end of normal time, three additional minutes were signalled, and after the first of these Sol Campbell launched a long ball towards the Thun goal. A tangle in the box resulted in Bergkamp appearing to foul Milicevic. Both players hit the deck but the Dutchman recovered first and scored with a close-range finish to make it 2-1 to the hosts. The following day's edition of *The Independent* summed it up with the headline 'Bergkamp robs Thun to seal win for 10-man Arsenal'. Only 100 seconds remained, so it was a cruel blow for the Bernese Oberlanders, and the winning goal should possibly have been disallowed.

In the next group game, Thun beat Sparta Prague in Bern with a last-minute goal from Hodžić. The Swiss club then lost 2-0 at Ajax, followed by a 4-2 defeat at home to the Dutch side, with a couple of the goals conceded in stoppage time. Defeat also came in the fifth group game which Arsenal won 1-0 in Bern. With Arsenal and Ajax already through, this meant that Thun needed to avoid defeat in the last game in Prague to finish third and enter the UEFA Cup; however, defeat would see Sparta claim the place. A scoreless draw in the Czech Republic rounded off an amazing Champions League debut for the Bernese Oberlanders.

In the UEFA Cup, Thun met Hamburger SV in the round of 32. Bizarrely the club sacked Urs Schönenberger just three days before the first leg, after a run of ten games without a win that saw the team in the bottom half of the Swiss Super League. Those running the club obviously didn't bother to consider whether the six Champions League games were always likely to adversely impact on domestic form, as both a distraction and a burden on a small club with a limited squad. Despite the shock sacking of the coach, Thun won the first leg in Bern 1-0, before being eliminated after losing 2-0 in Germany.

Despite the disappointing conclusion to Thun's European adventure, the fact that Arsenal reached that season's Champions League Final only emphasises the Swiss team's incredible achievement.

Thun then entered decline and suffered relegation in 2008, spending two seasons in the Challenge League before returning to the Swiss Super League in 2010. That year also saw the start of construction work to build a new stadium. The Stadion Lachen had been atmospheric, but wasn't considered suitable for a club with big ambitions and fell short of UEFA standards. Although the old stadium is still used for various sports, such as American football, it no longer hosts major soccer matches.

The new Arena Thun was completed in July 2011, and a few weeks later I returned to Grindelwald for another hiking holiday; luckily the fixture list made it possible to fit in a game at the new stadium.

For the match, on Sunday, 14 August 2011, Lausanne-Sport, from the city of that name by Lake Geneva, provided the opposition. The original Lausanne Football and Cricket Club (reputedly the first football club formed on the continent) became defunct in 1899, and Lausanne-Sport shares no connections to it, having formed separately in 1896. Going into the game, the fifth fixture of the season, Thun stood joint top of the Swiss Super League and Lausanne-Sport second from bottom.

It was only the third competitive game at the Arena Thun. Although providing good views of the action, I found the new stadium to be a rather functional affair, with bland concourses and no distinctive features. The old Stadion Lachen had been nearer to the lake, while its replacement stood on the edge of town on slightly higher land at 569m/1,867ft. The playing surface provided a major difference; whereas the old stadium had a grass pitch which often cut up quite badly, the new stadium used a synthetic one. This group of Thun players had recorded notable results away from home on other teams' artificial pitches, which seems to have been a factor in the choice.

The deterioration of sterling against the Swiss Franc meant that my CHF 38 match ticket for a seat behind the goal was vastly more expensive than for the previous visit in 2002. With a capacity of 10,000, the attendance of 5,706 meant that the stadium was only just over half full and there were plenty of empty shiny new red and white seats.

Now coached by Bernard Challandes, Thun's players appeared in their usual kit of all red, lining up in a 4-2-3-1 formation; Lausanne-Sport wore blue, arranged in a 4-4-2.

Thun opened the scoring after just six minutes when Christian Schneuwly gained possession of the ball after careless Lausanne defending and passed to Lustrinelli on the right. The striker rounded Lausanne keeper Fabio Coltorti (formerly of Thun) and finished from a tight angle. Both sides then hit the woodwork in a matter of minutes. First, Lausanne's Steven Lang surged down the left and passed to the French player Gaël N'Lundulu (previously on the books at Portsmouth). N'Lundulu struck the ball with his left foot across the goal, but Thun keeper David Da Costa managed to push it against the post. Stephan Andrist, one of Thun's best players that day, then picked up a pass from Schneuwly and curled a shot from just outside the area on to the crossbar.

Thun's second goal came after 14 minutes. Dario Lezcano passed to Schneuwly, who exchanged a one-two with Lustrinelli before hitting home from just outside the goal area. The home side could have gone further ahead when Lustrinelli intercepted a weak header from a Lausanne defender, but the keeper managed to save his lob. Andrist then crossed from the left to Lustrinelli who stretched, but couldn't quite reach the ball.

On 25 minutes, Lausanne reduced the deficit when N'Lundulu received the ball on the right and crossed it past several players to Lang, who hit a shot into the far corner. Lustrinelli then had a couple of chances to extend Thun's lead. First, looking suspiciously offside, he ran on to a long ball, but hit his effort wide with only the keeper to beat; then Lezcano received a long ball down the right and slipped it inside to Lustrinelli, whose shot was saved.

It was 2-1 at half-time, but a minute after the restart Andrist got a third for Thun. Receiving a pass from Lustrinelli, he raced down the left, beating several defenders, before shooting from a very tight angle into the far corner of the goal with his right foot. Definitely the pick of the goals, it was rapturously received by the home fans at the south end of the ground where I was sitting.

Just when you thought Lausanne might give up, two minutes later N'Lundulu provided another assist, this time for Matt Moussilou to score. However, things got worse for Lausanne on 52 minutes when one of the goalscorers, midfielder Lang, was judged to have dived over a tackle from Stipe Matić. Lang had already been booked and received a second yellow for simulation. I later watched a replay of this incident several times, before concluding Lang had been tripped and that the sending off was harsh.

Just after the hour, Thun made it 4-2. Lezcano collected the ball outside the penalty area and delivered it to Andrist on the left. Andrist crossed to Lustrinelli, who slotted it past the keeper with his left foot. Although Lustrinelli looked at least two yards offside at the moment when the ball was crossed, the goal was still given.

The seventh goal of an eventful encounter came three minutes from the end of normal time. Lausanne lost possession to Schneuwly down the right and he crossed the ball for Andreas Wittwer to score from close range. There were no more goals, so it finished 5-2. Although it had been an action-packed game with plenty of goals, the contest had been marred by some poor decisions from the officials.

Lustrinelli was the only survivor of Thun's Champions League match at Highbury six years earlier. After that European campaign Lustrinelli had moved on, with spells at Sparta Prague in the Czech Republic (who he must have impressed in the Champions League), then back to Switzerland at Luzern, Bellinzona and Young Boys (YB). In the summer of 2011, shortly before the match against Lausanne, he rejoined Thun. Lustrinelli had a very eventful game, scoring twice, providing a couple of assists and had a few other chances. He later became the coach of Thun, and still performs that role at the time of writing.

My second Thun match of the holiday took place exactly a week later, on Sunday, 21 August 2011, away at YB in *Das Berner Derby*, the biggest local rivalry in the canton of Bern.

Going into the match, Thun topped the league, two points ahead of YB. After travelling by train from Grindelwald to Bern I arrived at the Stade de Suisse, the home of YB (which had also been Thun's temporary residence for its Champions League fixtures back in 2005).

Although I asked for the cheapest ticket, it still provided a good view of the dark green artificial pitch below. Interestingly, I found myself in an unsegregated area among the crowd of 26,834, surrounded by both YB and Thun fans. The next chapter mentions allegations of violent encounters involving some supporters of YB and Thun in later years, but that day there was nothing of the kind and fans of the two clubs mixed together without any trouble.

Playing away at one of Switzerland's top teams caused Challandes to arrange his side in a 5-3-2 formation, with two wing-backs allowing the team to morph into a 3-5-2 when attacking. YB looked more like a 4-4-2. Thun appeared in an all-white change kit, while YB wore yellow and black.

Coached by Christian Gross (who had been with Basel for the 2002 match at the Stadion Lachen) YB started the brighter of the two sides with chances for the midfielders Mario Raimondi and Pascal Doubaï. These two were then involved in another attack, Raimondi hitting a long ball down the left to Doubaï, who crossed for Raphael Nuzzolo to head just wide of the far post.

With 28 minutes gone, Lustrinelli ran on to a long pass, only to be fouled by Alain Nef just inside the penalty area. Lezcano smashed the penalty kick straight down the centre of the goal as the YB keeper, Marco Wölfli, dived to his right.

Trailing 1-0 to Thun at the break, YB applied lots of pressure in the second half, only for Thun's defenders to be repeatedly rescued by their keeper, Da Costa. A Young Boys corner from Scott Sutter was met with a header by Nef, but Da Costa blocked it on the line with his feet. Soon after that, a long clearance from the YB keeper reached Marco Schneuwly (brother of Thun's Christian) who headed it back for Nuzzolo to shoot, but again Da Costa saved. YB followed this up with a cross from the right towards striker Emmanuel Mayuka, who stretched to meet the ball with his left foot; this time Da Costa batted the ball away with his hand from just under the crossbar.

It seemed only a matter of time before YB would get a goal, with Thun visibly tiring. Then on 78 minutes Andrist came on for Lustrinelli. Andrist had been one of Thun's best players against Lausanne the previous weekend with a goal and an assist; however, he had surprisingly started on the bench in Bern. His arrival gave fresh legs to the visitors and it was Andrist who scored the second and decisive goal four minutes from time. Thun gained possession from the YB keeper's clearance, and three quick one-touch passes sent the ball to another substitute, Muhamed Demiri, in the centre circle. Demiri passed to Andrist down the right, who outpaced the YB defender and shot over the keeper and into the net.

There was no way back for YB after that second goal and the canton derby finished 2-0 to Thun. Da Costa's series of saves made it one of the most memorable goalkeeping displays I have seen. He was given six out of six by national newspaper *Blick* and was rightly made man of the match.

Thun remained top of the table after the game, but could not retain such impressive early season form and fell away, eventually finishing fifth.

Following the 2011/12 season, Thun entered the Europa League several times, but only managed to reach the group stage once, and even on that occasion the team finished last.

Three years after my visit, the club's stadium became known as Stockhorn Arena, after selling the naming rights in a sponsorship deal with Stockhornbahn, the company operating a cable car to the summit of a nearby mountain. Despite the stadium's new name, Thun didn't reach new heights; instead, the club faced insolvency. Things got so bad that in 2016 Jungfrau Railways offered Thun fans a round trip to Jungfraujoch at a special price with all proceeds going to the beleaguered football club. The highest railway station in Europe, Jungfraujoch has another footballing claim to fame which features in a later chapter.

In 2019, Thun became part of Pacific Media Group, one of the biggest multi-club ownership groups in world football, including the likes of Barnsley and Kaiserslautern in its portfolio.

After the 2019/20 season ended with Thun second from bottom of the Swiss Super League, the club was forced to enter a play-off to preserve its top-flight status. Unfortunately, that play-off ended in a defeat at the hands of FC Vaduz. Two more play-off defeats in 2020/21 and 2023/24 have ensured that the Bernese Oberland club remains in the second tier. At the winter break in the 2024/25 season, Thun occupied top place in the Challenge

League, but will have been hoping for automatic promotion rather than risk more play-off setbacks.

Despite the club losing some of its magic by being part of a foreign, multi-club ownership group, Thun's achievement in reaching the group stage of the Champions League in 2005 is one of Alpine football's greatest stories, and I feel fortunate to have witnessed part of it. The next chapter looks at some of the club's fans.

ii. Spirit of Spiez

About 13km/8 miles south of Thun along the shore of the Thunersee lies the town of Spiez. Home to 12,000 people, Spiez has a football team competing in the 2. Liga; however, for some followers of the game, particularly those from Germany, the most important place in Spiez is not the local football stadium but the Belvédère, a luxury hotel where the West German squad stayed during the 1954 World Cup.

During those finals, the West German coach, Sepp Herberger, decided that the team's star player, Fritz Walter, should share a room in the Belvédère with the lively Helmut Rahn to cheer him up and boost his self-confidence. This proved to be particularly important after the Germans lost their second group match 8-3 to Hungary. The room pairing began what became known as *Der Geist von Spiez* ('The Spirit of Spiez') with the players bonding in the hotel and taking their new-found optimism on to the training pitch at the Stadion Lachen in Thun and then all the way to the final in Bern. The World Cup Final, held on 4 July 1954, later became known as *Das Wunder von Bern* ('The Miracle of Bern') and to continue the story, we head north from the Alps to the German city of Magdeburg.

In 2009, I attended a match between 1. FC Magdeburg and Hamburger SV's second team in the German fourth division. The goalkeeping coach for Magdeburg that day was a certain Jo Stock.

Born in 1963 near Düsseldorf in the Rhineland, in what was then West Germany, Stock played in goal for a couple of local teams in Langenfeld. Later, as he approached his 40th birthday, Stock became a goalkeeping coach, performing that role for several clubs, starting in 2002 at SC Fortuna Köln. In 2007, Stock became the goalkeeping coach for Magdeburg, and featured in the official programme for the match I attended. While researching this book, I asked Stock if he remembered that particular game and he replied, 'Yes, of course. I did the goalkeeping warm-up for Christian Beer [Magdeburg's keeper] and during the match I was standing by the bench observing his performance. In the half-time break I gave him some advice for the second half.'

Stock is a man of many talents; as well as having coached in Germany, Africa and the Middle East, he plays multiple other sports, speaks several languages, sings, and also plays a variety of musical instruments. In 2022, he started performing concerts in Brazil and Germany with what he calls his 'Subcultural Rock 'n' Roll Entertainment One-Man-Band', Ramones on 45, playing unusual cover versions of songs by the former American punk band the Ramones. If that wasn't enough, Stock is also a professional actor, with a repertoire including television, theatre and film.

Of particular significance for this book, Stock appeared in *Das Wunder von Bern*, a 2003 German film about the 1954 World Cup, described by former Chelsea and Scotland winger Pat Nevin as 'the best football film ever'. Stock played the part of Toni Turek, West Germany's goalkeeper, who coincidentally had also been from the Düsseldorf area. Stock played the part of Turek in all the scenes, both on and off the pitch.

In the film, we see the West German squad arriving in Spiez and staying at the Belvédère, which like the adjacent Thunersee features on several occasions. It shows West Germany recovering from the thrashing by Hungary and qualifying from the group stage, then overcoming Yugoslavia in the quarter-final, followed by Austria in the semi to reach the final and a rematch with Hungary.

The final took place at the Stadion Wankdorf in Bern (since redeveloped as the Stade de Suisse). As expected, the Hungarians, who hadn't lost a game for four years, took a 2-0 lead. Just when there seemed to be no way back for West Germany, the 'miracle' began.

As any visitor to this part of Switzerland knows, it rains a lot; something that proved crucial to the final for two reasons. Firstly, while serving on the Russian front during the war, Walter had been taken prisoner. After contracting malaria in captivity, he found it difficult to play in hot conditions; to this day, cold wet weather is referred to in Germany as *Fritz Walter wetter* ('Fritz Walter weather'). Secondly, the founder of the Adidas sportswear company, Adi Dassler, supplied the Germans with removable studs, enabling the players to put on longer ones to cope with the muddy pitch. These two things, together with some Spirit of Spiez and a dose of luck (Hungary hit the woodwork twice) enabled West Germany to fight back and equalise.

Another key factor was Turek's goalkeeping. Herbert Zimmermann provided the German radio commentary for the final, and the film shows the moment when an emotional Zimmermann responds to a great save by Turek by calling him 'a football god', a comment he later had to apologise for to appease religious sensitivities. When I asked Jo Stock about playing the part of Turek in the film, he said, 'Shooting the scenes was big fun and a great time in my life.'

Six minutes from time, Rahn scored the winner; which is why the old restored clock that I saw outside the Stade de Suisse when watching FC Thun play away at Young Boys still says 'Ungarn 2, Deutschland 3' ('Hungary 2, Germany 3'). West Germany's 1954 World Cup triumph did much to restore national pride and has even been credited with helping kick-start the country's post-war economic miracle, explaining why a hotel in the Bernese Alps is still an important place of pilgrimage for German football fans.

Chapter 13

Switzerland: Fan Scenes

NO ACCOUNT of football in any part of the world is complete, in my view, without considering the sport's fans. With eight countries in the Alps and various types of supporter, it's a subject deserving several books; however, in this publication there's room for just one chapter, which I have decided to devote to ultras following FC Thun.

Ultras first appeared when young fans of some Italian teams broke away from the official supporters' organisations formally attached to their clubs in order to set up new independent groups and provide more fervent backing. The precise origins of ultras are disputed, with early candidates including the *Fellissimi Granata* ('Maroon Loyalists') who started following Torino in 1951. The label 'ultra' came nearly 20 years later, coined by the media to describe fans involved in crowd trouble. Whereas in English, the word 'fan' is short for 'fanatic', the Italian term 'ultra' means 'extreme', describing the most passionate supporters of their chosen team. The word can also mean 'beyond', with many ultras regarding themselves as renegades from wider civil society, alienated from 'the system' and beyond all forms of control.

You don't need to be an anthropologist to see that Italian ultras have drawn on different parts of their country's history and culture: rowdy behaviour in stadiums resembles crowds in ancient Roman amphitheatres; fondness for ritual and ceremony owes a debt to the Catholic Church; black clothing reflects Italian sense of fashion and style; while Italian operas provide tunes for many of the songs. On the negative side, living in the country that invented fascism possibly accounts for some ultras having far-right political affiliations; while drug dealing, counterfeit merchandising or ticket touting among a minority of ultras shows some similarity to organised crime groups like the Mafia. However, it should be pointed out that not all ultras, whether in Italy or elsewhere, have such extreme political views or are involved in illegal activities.

Rather than wear scarves or replica shirts, ultras prefer to demonstrate support for their team through a spectacular choreography of flags and flares. Ultras congregate in particular parts of the stadium, traditionally in the *curva* ('curve'), a term originating from the bend of the running track behind the goal. A *capo* ('boss') uses a loudhailer to lead rehearsed chants and songs, often aided by a drummer. Ultra groups frequently include members with different responsibilities, such as artistic types who create banners; choreographers who plan displays; organisers of trips to away games; people who deal with finances; as well as the previously mentioned drummers and chant leaders.

For most of the matches featuring in this book, the only ultras out in force followed teams from just outside the Alpine area, such as LASK from Linz at away games in Innsbruck and Salzburg. The ultras at the Stade des Alpes in Grenoble were one of the few exceptions, because in the Alps the smaller size of crowds tends to discourage the formation of significant fan groupings. Before looking at an example from Switzerland, a few observations about the evolution of English fan culture to try and understand why ultras are rare in England.

In the early days, English supporters adopted the Victorian tradition of community singing before sporting events, including hymns such as 'Abide with Me', while noisy wooden rattles provided the 'music' and rosettes the colour. Things changed during the 1960s. Firstly, the growth of pop music enabled songs like 'You'll Never Walk Alone' to be added to the repertoire, while other tunes from the music charts were given new football-related lyrics. Secondly, the decade saw increasing challenges to the old way of life and questioning of authority. Finally, travel and television enabled greater exposure to international influences.

Coming from the country that invented football, English fans are rightly proud of their traditions and have been mainly resistant to continental-style ultra culture which, until recently, simply wasn't needed. In fact, crowd atmosphere in English stadiums was the envy of many foreign fans, some of whom would travel to England especially to experience it.

However, the last 30 years in England has seen developments like all-seater stadiums; reserved places dispersing those who want to sing; loud announcements and pre-recorded music deliberately drowning out fans; expensive match tickets and a gentrification of the game. At some clubs, historic old venues have been demolished and replaced by soulless modern stadiums. Many grounds are increasingly full of new types of fans who don't support their team when it struggles, but stay quiet (or chat with their friends) and only cheer to celebrate success. Large numbers of empty seats at the start of the second half at certain venues suggest that some people are motivated more by socialising, drinking and eating (sometimes in expensive hospitality areas) than actually watching the football. The hyping of the Premier League brand has also attracted tourists, many of them preoccupied with taking selfies and buying 'merch' from the megastore. Recent years have seen the introduction of the video assistant referee (VAR), causing supporters to be reluctant to celebrate a goal until it has been confirmed. All these things have contributed to a marked decline in matchday atmosphere in 'elite-level' football.

In 2005, Crystal Palace's Holmesdale Fanatics got together in an attempt to literally drum up a decent atmosphere, becoming the first ultra grouping in the English Premier League. One observation from more traditional supporters who have seen ultras in action, whether on the continent or at Selhurst Park, is that their singing lacks spontaneity, with ordinary fans discouraged from initiating other ditties, lest it undermines the authority of the *capo*. Lack of improvisation limits the variety of songs, meaning that they can become, at worst, a repetitive background noise. The music and songs are from a set list, not helped by the chant leaders sometimes having their backs to the pitch, restricting their ability to react to incidents during a match. While not mentioning the term 'ultras' in his brilliantly observed book *The Soccer Tribe* published in 1981, Desmond Morris referred to something similar when he wrote, 'To British ears, these continental hooting and drumming routines are too random. They seem to go on and on, without sufficient relationship to what is happening on the pitch. The British Soccer Tribes prefer their noise displays to come and go with the dramas of the game.'

Bans on pyrotechnics in all English stadiums, as well as regulations prohibiting 'unauthorised' musical instruments and large banners at certain grounds, have also discouraged the importing of this variant of European fan culture.

Moving from the grey concrete of Croydon to the blue lakes of the Bernese Oberland, the importance of fan culture at FC Thun is shown by the club's official website, which explains the different supporter groupings at the club.

The first fan clubs came into being soon after Thun gained promotion to the top tier of Swiss football in 2002. One of them, Aebikurve, got its name from a group of supporters who for several years had gathered to drink at a stall called Aebersold, although it didn't officially become a supporters' club until 2004. Another group, formed after the promotion of 2002, went by the name Dopamin Thun. Both groups involved themselves in the usual supporter activities, such as supplying match tickets, generating support in the stadium and arranging travel to away games. As the members of Aebikurve and Dopamin Thun aged, newer and younger groups appeared on the scene.

In 2008, the Red White Boys fan group was formed while Thun still played at the Stadion Lachen. After the club moved to the Arena Thun in 2011, the Red White Boys became involved in establishing Block Süd Thun (literally 'South Block Thun'), named after the south end of the new stadium where its members congregate to try and create an ultra-style atmosphere. Three other groups then appeared, Varlets and Invictus in 2013 followed by Ultimativ in 2018. All three, plus some individual supporters, joined up with Block Süd Thun, which operates like an umbrella organisation covering several different fan groupings.

In 2020, Invictus decided to leave Block Süd Thun and constitute itself as the third supporters' club, alongside

Aebikurve and Dopamin Thun. Those two older fan clubs still exist, but have been less active since the move to the new stadium and the disruption it caused to their old routines. In general, Aebikurve and Dopamin Thun tend to be primarily concerned about the performance of the team on the pitch and the financial health of the club off it.

The focus of this chapter is on the younger fans of Block Süd Thun who are more into ultra culture, as shown by their colourful displays with banners and flares, as well as their campaigning on issues impacting on fans and engaging in a dialogue with officials at the football club about them. As FC Thun's website says, 'Block Süd is a critical observer of modern football and is in regular contact with FC Thun. Furthermore, choreographies and pyro shows are an integral part of the "ultra" subculture and are organised by the members of Block Süd.'

The only sign of ultra culture in the Stadion Lachen at my match in 2002 had come from the visiting Basel supporters, while at Highbury in 2005 I sat among the Arsenal fans so didn't get much of a look at the travelling Thun supporters. However, things were different when I attended the match between Thun and Lausanne-Sport in 2011. From my seat in sector H20 in the south stand of the Arena Thun, I saw to my right a *capo* with a loudhailer leading the chanting, next to a banner with the slogan 'Alle aus Derby' ('Everyone to the derby') encouraging fans to travel and support the team against YB in Bern the following weekend. A large banner close by said Block Süd alongside another that read 'Kampfen & Siegen' ('Fight and Win'). The *capo*, scaffolding and banners were all provided by Block Süd Thun.

The Thun ultras provided vocal but well-behaved backing for their team, so I was surprised to discover that a few years later the Stadt Thun ('Town of Thun' or local council) met to discuss the ultras and crowd trouble at matches.

Between 1990 and 1994, I served as an elected local councillor in the London Borough of Haringey. Most of the debates in the civic centre were extremely tedious, mainly centred on financial problems and procedural wrangling, with none of the discussions involving anything as interesting as football fan culture. Here's what put ultras on the agenda of the Stadt Thun.

On 5 August 2017, FC Basel visited Thun accompanied by a boisterous contingent of travelling fans who saw their team win 3-0. Thun's local council reported on what it called 'Ausschreitungen' ('riots') with FCB fans who had congregated in the north stand of the Stockhorn Area setting off flares in the stadium, forcing the match to be stopped. At Thun railway station, two police officers were slightly injured after being attacked by hooded Basel yobs. The council meeting's recommendations included introducing exit controls at the stadium following any incidents of crowd trouble and upgrading CCTV surveillance. The meeting also declared, as reported on the Stadt Thun website, 'Violent fans dress alike from head to toe. The flags and banners are misused in order to hide behind them and carry out illegal activities.'

Several dozen young Thun fans attended a debate in the council chamber, during which Alice Kropf, a politician from the SP (Social Democratic Party), described the Thun fans as *'Ultras, aber eben nicht Hooligans'* ('ultras, but not hooligans') and criticised the measures implemented as unnecessarily repressive, calling for them to be de-escalated. Other speakers opposed her proposal and called for the measures to be upheld, as reported by local media.

A keen football supporter, Kropf's website lists several campaigns which she has either joined or is sympathetic towards, and alongside the logos of organisations such as Greenpeace and Amnesty International is that of Block Süd Thun! In a section about her likes and dislikes, the former begins with 'Civil courage, feminist gangs, Prosecco, atmospheric choreos at football games, FC Thun ...'[11]

Around the same time, Kropf also participated in a panel discussion with a youth worker and a fan who had received a Rayonverbot (Swiss version of an ASBO) imposed by the police and courts banning a person from certain places, in this case his team's football stadium. The discussion highlighted positive sides of the ultras: how they can provide structure to young people through the regular scheduling of matches; encourage social skills such as working with other people in a team; teach youngsters to be creative when making things like banners; as well as being an outlet for youthful exuberance in places where there is often little else to do.

The panel raised the need for social workers or youth workers from the local authority to engage with the ultras; however, Stadt Thun had earlier declared in the local press, 'The municipal council lacks the belief that a dialogue with this small group is even possible. You shouldn't have any illusions here: ultras have neither a real interest in football nor in a constructive fan culture.'

Unfortunately, since the Basel disturbances, there have been other violent incidents connected to Thun, or as Kropf told me, 'The Thun fans are not always very good.' Following the visit of Grasshopper Club during the 2018/19 season, there were reports of a clash at Thun railway station

---

11 alicekropf.ch/ueber-mich/

between fans of the Zürich team and members of a local gang called Thun Group 36er, resulting in several injuries and some damage to property.

Stadt Thun has also commented on confrontations between Thun supporters and their local rivals, Young Boys, claiming on its website, 'Numerous supporters of the two opposing Super League clubs FC Thun and BSC YB live in the catchment area and also meet outside of matchdays. Such encounters often end in violent clashes in public spaces.'

In November 2019, while returning home from an away match at Neuchâtel Xamax, some Thun fans were accused of damaging property and attacking police by throwing stones in the village of Ins, just outside Neuchâtel in north-west Switzerland. A confrontation developed outside Ins railway station between about 50 Thun supporters and the police, who fired rubber bullets.

After Stadt Thun reported an overspend in its budget on security at Thun matches in four out of six years between 2013 and 2019, Kropf backed a resolution to the Stadt Thun, posted on the council's website, which read, 'The municipal council is asked to consider in cooperation with the cantonal police, involving FC Thun and, with scientific support, the principle of a dialogue-oriented approach to the management of football fans [on and off matchdays] with the aim of reducing police and administrative costs in the medium and longer term.'

Supporters of the resolution argued that the council's response to football fan misbehaviour was not only harsh, but also costly and ineffective. Looking for examples of a different approach, one of the places referred to was West Yorkshire where a senior officer of the local police was reported to have said that dialogue is the only tried and tested solution to the problem. At that time, members of West Yorkshire police were helping implement Enable UK, a community policing strategy which relied on police liaison teams talking to fans and relying on communication instead of confrontation. Among the first fixtures where the new strategy was piloted involved my very own Leeds United, a club plagued by a history of hooliganism. Stadt Thun heard that policing costs had been reduced significantly in West Yorkshire as a result of the new approach.

During the debate, advocates of the proposal argued for unarmed police to be organised in 'sports dialogue teams', whose job involved liaising with fans both on matchdays and at other times. The dialogue teams should consist of the same officers, in order to get to know the supporters, working alongside youth workers from the club and the council. Whereas the spotters (police who identify known troublemakers) had developed an adversarial relationship with some fans, the dialogue teams should aim to establish a better one. On matchdays, the dialogue teams should act as the main point of contact with supporters at the stadium, ready to de-escalate any incidents that may develop; with the regular police remaining in the background and only intervening when necessary. The resolution also called for an end to the policy of treating all fans as hooligans and applying 'collective punishment'; instead, only those actually proven to be culprits should be dealt with.

Kropf told me that rather than clashes tending to be between ultras attached to rival teams or different political views, in Thun, 'The main conflict is between the police and fans.'

At the start of the 2021/22 season, Thun's ultras signed a statement about the impact of the COVID-19 pandemic which was endorsed by a number of similar groupings.

The declaration shows the presence of ultras at other Swiss clubs, as well as a degree of cooperation between them. Among the groups joining Block Süd Thun in endorsing the statement were (in alphabetical order by club name): Szene Aarau (FC Aarau); Muttenzerkurve (FC Basel); Zürcher Südkurve and Sektor IV (both Grasshopper Club); Loz Boys (Lausanne-Sport); Teste Matte – I Bravi Ragazzi (FC Lugano); USL (FC Luzern); Fidelis, Neuch'boys and Tigers 95 (all from Neuchâtel Xamax); EBSG (FC St Gallen); Section Grenat 1988 (Servette FC); Lousy Scum, Walliza Boyz, Red Tigers, Ibi Sumus and Sedunum (all FC Sion); and Ostkurve Bern (YB).

Interestingly, for a book about football and the Alps, Block Süd Thun opposes FC Thun promoting itself as a Bernese Oberland club, referring to the mountainous hinterland in the canton of Bern. Instead, the ultras want the club to identify more with the town of Thun. When I looked back at my match programme from the Thun versus Basel fixture in 2002, I noticed that the Berner Oberland branding was attached to the club's badge and featured prominently on the front of the magazine, so it's hardly something new. Nevertheless, on its website, Block Süd Thun calls the Berner Oberland branding 'ultrapeinlichen' ('ultra embarassing').

Clubs sometimes conflict with their independent supporters' groups, so it's good to see that FC Thun's official website has included a direct link to that of Block Süd Thun. However, Thun's ultras may have a cordial relationship with their club, but things are not so good between them and the local council and the police, undermining a dialogue-based strategy. The municipal council claims that between 2015 and 2019, fan representatives only attended two out of 13 meetings open to them, questioning their commitment to discussion. Four years later in early 2023, Kropf told me about continual delays with establishing a conversational approach to football supporter management, explaining, 'There was a majority for it in the city council, but it hasn't been implemented yet – I'm still waiting. The project could not start, among other things, because no one from Thun police was willing to take part in the project.'

In February 2023, Thun met Young Boys at home in the quarter-finals of the Swiss Cup. Although it was the 85th canton derby, Thun's second-tier status meant that the two sides hadn't met for nearly three years, making it extra special. Unfortunately, crowd congestion at a sold-out Stockhorn Arena caused some fans to still be trying to enter the stadium several minutes after the start. It probably won't surprise you to hear that the fans suffering the delays were trying to access sectors G and H where the ultras congregate. Block Süd Thun had spent a lot of time preparing for the derby, and such problems at the big match are unlikely to have helped improve relations with the police. Things got even worse when Thun lost 5-0.

Thun's ultras also criticised some of the Swiss football authorities' proposals to change the way final league placings are decided; particularly opposing the introduction of play-offs. Many of the reforms, including an increase in the number of matches played, as well as splitting the league at the end of the regular season into championship and relegation groups, were eventually implemented from the start of the 2023/24 campaign. Under the new system, teams carry forward all the points accrued in the first part of the season and these are added to those earned in the second stage to decide the winners. The ultras claimed that these changes undermined the integrity and significance of matches during the main part of the season and were being introduced purely for commercial reasons. However, the idea of a play-off to decide the champions was abandoned; according to *World Soccer* in August 2023, this was because 'the Swiss Football League's members voted against the idea under pressure from the supporters'.[12] Such an outcome contradicts the claim of some Stadt Thun councillors that the town's ultras have no 'real interest in football' – they wouldn't have joined fans of other teams in campaigning so successfully against the end-of-season play-offs if that were the case.

In August 2023, Block Süd Thun was one of the 16 Swiss ultra groupings that urged their members to stay away for the first 15 minutes of matches, in protest at the ban on away fans at fixtures between FC St Gallen and FC Luzern following crowd trouble the previous season. At the time of writing, tensions between Thun's ultras on one side, and the police and local authorities on the other, show no sign of easing.

So, what should be made of Thun's ultras, or indeed other similar fan groups?

While Italian ideas of organising supporters and choreographed displays have been adopted by some fan groupings in and around the Alpine region, their versions of ultra culture are less intense and many of the negative features of some Italian ultras are less common, or sometimes completely absent. In the case of ultras following Alpine teams, I have personally not witnessed any signs of racist or extremist views or violent behaviour.

Interestingly, none of the 20 Swiss supporters' groups that signed the statement about lockdown used the word 'ultra' in their name; Block Süd Thun, for example, usually

---

12 *World Soccer*, August 2023, p83.

prefers to talk about a *Fanszene* ('fan scene') rather than ultras, possibly to avoid association with the excesses of the Italian movement or to create more of an independent identity.

In my experience, ultra groupings following clubs such as FC Thun, FC Basel, Grenoble Foot 38, BSC Young Boys or LASK Linz, have made real efforts to improve matchday atmospheres, and are to be welcomed. Although lively crowds survive at certain English stadiums, for others, ultra culture, with its drums, banners and choreographed routines, may be the way forward.

Chapter 14

Switzerland: Valais

OFTEN INCORRECTLY referred to as 'the Valais', the canton of Valais in south-west Switzerland possesses the country's highest mountains as well as some of its most extraordinary football venues. French is the main language in the west of Valais, with German predominant in the eastern part of the canton. The multilingual nature of Valais is reflected in the canton's football association which is called Association Valaisanne de Football/Walliser Fussballverband, containing both French and German names in its title. Responsible for overseeing local football, the AVF/WFV is based in the canton's capital, Sion.

This chapter looks at two famous football personalities from Valais, before focusing on the story of one of Europe's most remarkable stadiums.

i. Football's Officer Class

A geographical location at the centre of Europe, high standard of living, favourable taxation policy, a skilled and multi-lingual workforce and a reputation for neutrality have made Switzerland an attractive destination for international organisations. For these reasons, both of football's leading governing bodies are based in Switzerland, with FIFA formed in 1904 in France before moving to Zürich, and UEFA established in 1954 in Basel but now based in Nyon.

Despite its small population of less than 7,000, the town of Visp in the east of Valais has one big footballing claim to fame (although some would say infamy), namely that Sepp Blatter was born there in 1936. Blatter reportedly grew up in a poor family in Visp, before starting to work for FIFA.

Blatter became FIFA's director of development programmes in 1975, its general secretary in 1981, and finally president in 1998. After 17 years as the boss of world football, Blatter resigned in 2015 amid various accusations and financial controversies. At the time of writing, Blatter remains banned by FIFA from football-related activities.

Although Blatter's rule ended under a cloud, his achievements include making football less centred on Europe and South America by bringing the World Cup to Asia and Africa for the first time (Japan and South Korea in 2002, then South Africa in 2010). Even if Blatter may have been motivated by extending his power base throughout the world, those two tournaments remain historic achievements, helping spread the game. Under Blatter's leadership, FIFA decided to host the 2018 World Cup in Russia, and more controversially, the 2022 tournament in Qatar.

Visp is proud of its famous son, as shown by the school which he attended between 1943 and 1948 being renamed after him 50 years later. The tan-coloured building with large letters on its front saying Primarschulhaus Sepp Blatter (Sepp Blatter Primary School) can clearly be seen through the windows of trains heading south from the town. Elsewhere in Valais, a football tournament called the Sepp-Blatter-Turnier has often taken place at the Sepp-Blatter-Fußballplatz; while Blatter is a co-founder and honorary ambassador of the Bergdorf-Europameisterschaft (Mountain Village Euros), a tournament described in the next chapter.

Early in his career, Blatter had various jobs, including helping out during the winter at ski resorts in between university terms, then working as a waiter, journalist and PR man, before moving into sports administration. However, for this book the most impressive job on Blatter's CV was when he worked as a professional yodeller during his teenage years, singing at weddings and other ceremonies.

Yodelling is a form of singing involving quick changes in vocal range. No one knows exactly when, where or why yodelling started. Some claim it originated from Alpine farmers using high-pitched calls to herd livestock, while others argue that it developed as a form of communication between people on opposite sides of a valley. During the 19th century, special *Jodellieder* ('yodelling songs') were composed and it became popular as a folk custom. Today, there are nearly 800 yodelling clubs in Switzerland with about 12,000 members; however, the only time I have heard someone yodel in the Alps was actually in Austria at the Alphorn festival in the valley of Kleinwalsertal mentioned in chapter seven.

In November 2003, Newcastle United played FC Basel in the second leg of a UEFA Cup tie at St James' Park. When a Basel defender conceded an own goal, the home fans taunted the 1,000 travelling Swiss supporters by singing 'You're not yodelling any more', a chant that helped inspire the title of this book.

Only 9kms/5 miles east of Visp, the larger town of Brig is home to about 12,000 people. Incredibly, despite its proximity to Visp, Brig is the birthplace of another member of what in 2016 *The Guardian* called 'Switzerland's officer class of sports administrators'.

After already providing two FIFA presidents (Ernst Thommen, born in Basel outside of the Alpine area who briefly became acting president in 1961, as well as Blatter), Giovanni Vincenzo Infantino – more commonly known as Gianni – became the latest member of this Swiss 'officer class'.

The son of Italian immigrants who had moved to Switzerland, Infantino was born in Brig in 1970. After qualifying as a lawyer and advising various European football leagues, Infantino took up a role at the International Centre for Sports Studies at the University of Neuchâtel in western Switzerland. Infantino joined UEFA in 2000, working in the field of legal and licensing matters, before becoming deputy general secretary in 2007, followed by general secretary a couple of years later.

A few months after Blatter's resignation, Infantino succeeded him, becoming FIFA's ninth president in early 2016. The following year, Infantino staged a match in Brig to celebrate his presidency. Ronaldo Luís Nazário de Lima and Diego Maradona were among more than 50 football legends appearing in three teams: a Switzerland XI, an Italian XI, and a World XI. Infantino played for all three sides in what was described as 'Gianni's Game', held at local club FC Brig-Glis.

During Infantino's presidency, he has built up considerable power and authority, helping FIFA earn record revenues, with the likelihood of more to come.

Infantino has big plans for the World Cup, none of them good. He has talked about holding the World Cup every two years instead of four. What is certain is that the number of matches in the finals will rise from 64 in Qatar to 104 at the 2026 tournament spread across three North American countries. In March 2025, Infantino announced that the following year's final in New Jersey will feature a half-time music show, with acts selected by Coldplay. Leaving aside the question as to whether the World Cup Final needs to imitate the Super Bowl, there are more practical objections. Normal NFL half-times last the same length as football intervals, but are extended to half an hour for the Super Bowl. FIFA claims that the music acts, as well as the erection and dismantling of temporary stages, will be contained within the usual 15-minute slot; however, if they overrun expect a furious response from the finalists, concerned about the effect of delays on players' physical and mental readiness. If footballers aren't warmed up, it could be a case of cold players rather than just Coldplay.

Infantino has also expanded the FIFA Club World Cup from seven teams to 32 in 2025. Such changes may prove to be lucrative in terms of broadcasting revenue, but only at the expense of causing further fixture congestion, with the added danger of too much football exhausting not only players' bodies but the interest of fans.

Having facilitated the introduction of VAR at the World Cup finals in 2018, Infantino later claimed that delays while refereeing decisions were checked added to fans' excitement rather than their frustration. His predecessor, Blatter, had been against VAR being used in Russia because of its lack of consistency; the question is which of them made a clear and obvious error?

ii. The Impossible Stadium: FC Isérables, 1,030m/3,379ft

While investigating which football club to visit in the valley of the River Rhône, I came across a team called FC Saxon-Fully that played in an apricot-coloured kit and featured the fruits on its badge. Keen to know if there were any apricot orchards to look out for when heading to a match in early September, I asked the Martigny tourist office, who advised me to contact Alain Mermoud, director of VS Fruits, an agricultural company. After messaging the businessman, his speedy reply explained that unfortunately the apricots would already have been harvested by the time of my arrival. Intriguingly, Alain Mermoud ended his email by saying, 'I hope you mention Isérables in your book and its impossible football pitch.' I had never heard of a place called Isérables, nor of any 'impossible football pitch', but subsequent enquiries led to me abandoning my search for apricot footballers and discovering instead a fascinating sporting story that is largely unknown outside Valais.

Located to the south of the River Rhône about 15km/9 miles south-west of Sion, the Valaisian settlement of Isérables is perched high up on the side of the valley. About 1,000 people live in the vertiginous village, with French their local language.

In the past, the position of Isérables high on the mountainside led to its isolation, helped by a ladder. Every morning, the first villagers to descend into the valley to work in the fields would position a ladder to enable them to climb down over some particularly tricky rocks. Then, at the end of the working day, the last person to return would pull the ladder up after them in order to prevent any unwanted night-time incursions.

Such seclusion made Isérables a suitable hideaway for the likes of the famous smuggler and forger Joseph-Samuel Farinet, who stayed there a couple of times back in the 1870s. Given his involvement in counterfeit money, it is rather ironic that these days he's remembered by a micro-currency called the Farinet which circulates in Valais alongside the Swiss Franc. Farinet also inspired the name of a vineyard in Saillon, on the opposite side of the Rhône valley; named Les Amis de Farinet, it claims to be the smallest in the world and has been owned since 1999 by the Dalai Lama.

Long ago, a mule trail provided the main route up to Isérables, but in 1942 a cable car from Riddes to the village was constructed; followed in the 1960s by a road which winds around the steep slope until it eventually reaches the settlement.

Although it sounds like a misspelling of a popular West End musical, the name Isérables actually comes from a species of tree that grows nearby (*érables* is French for 'maple trees'). The maple leaf has become a popular symbol of the village and appears on the badge of the local football club, FC Isérables.

The villagers call themselves *Bedjuis* ('Bedouin'), claiming to be descended from Saracens who settled in the Alps after their defeat at the Battle of Tours in AD 732, bringing a halt to the Muslim advance into western Europe. Reflecting this identity, FC Isérables presents itself as *le club bédjui* ('the Bedouin club').

At the time of FC Isérables' formation in 1966, the 5. Liga (or 5ème Ligue in French) didn't exist, so FC Isérables started life competing in the 4ème Ligue, then the lowest level of the Swiss football league pyramid. The president of the club at the time of its foundation was Pierre-César Crettaz, while Laurent Monnet coached the team.

Being located on such a steep slope meant Isérables lacked suitable flat land for a pitch, forcing the village's footballers to train and play 'home' games at a whole host of places down in the Rhône valley, such as Martigny,

Sion, Leytron, Saillon and the other end of the cable car at Riddes.

During its early years, FC Isérables played in red and black, but later abandoned red because it was a popular choice and clashed with opposing teams, frequently requiring a different jersey for away matches. After the club had tried purple, it then settled on its present colour of green. One of the club's founders, Gérard Favre, told me how the change came about, saying, 'In 1976 I was appointed president of the club and we celebrated ten years of existence. My first proposal was to green the club and give it a new image. So, I suggested going green. The year 1976 was a big one for the greens of AS Saint-Étienne with Robert Herbin as coach and his emblematic scorers Dominique Rocheteau and Hervé Revelli – that's where the idea came from.'

People of a certain age may remember the European exploits of French side AS Saint-Étienne half a century ago. After losing the European Cup Final to FC Bayern München in 1976, Saint-Étienne suffered elimination from the quarter-finals of the same competition the following season, courtesy of Liverpool 'supersub' David Fairclough. Years after watching highlights of the Anfield game on television, I bought a retro Saint-Étienne shirt, so I dug it out of the cupboard and took it with me to Isérables and told representatives of the club that I would be wearing it to help them recognise me.

Since 1970, several studies had looked at whether it might be possible to build a football ground in Isérables before one proposal was finally selected. It involved finding a suitable part of the mountainside, digging out some of the rock and earth above the level of the proposed pitch and moving it just below to create a shelf big enough for a level playing surface. The reuse of the earth and rock in this way had the added advantage of providing a solution to the problem of what to do with large amounts of displaced material in a village with limited road access at an altitude of 1,030m/3,379ft.

An engineer called Guillaume Favre designed the stadium, and the owner of the land, the Commune of Isérables (the local government), managed the project. As local newspaper *Nouvelliste et Feuille d'Avis du Valais* reported at the time, the project represented *'une gigantesque entreprise technique et financière'* ('a gigantic technical and financial enterprise').

To pay for the stadium, villagers and the local government launched an appeal for sponsorship from banks, industry, businesses, local organisations and individuals. Finally, on 20 April 1976, the first blow of the pick-axe on the side of the mountain heralded the beginnings of one of Europe's most remarkable football stadiums.

Bulldozers were used to excavate 100,000m³ of earth and rock. The work was hard and dangerous, with much of it carried out by Swiss army engineers. Nearly 70 local people also helped, including one of the footballers, Michel-Gérard Crettenand, who lost the end of a finger in an accident.

During the construction work, FC Isérables experienced its most successful season; still playing 'home' games down in the valley, the team not only won promotion to the 3ème Ligue in 1980, but remained unbeaten throughout the campaign. Unfortunately, FC Isérables' stay at the higher level only lasted for one year before relegation back down to the 4ème Ligue in 1981.

After six years, the huge building project was completed at a cost of around CHF 1,500,000, with FC Isérables paying CHF 425,000 to the Commune and contributing to the work. Allowing for inflation in Switzerland, the cost of the stadium is equivalent to about CHF 2,700,000 in today's money, or £2,310,000.

The new pitch hosted its first game on 16 July 1982 when FC Isérables played a team from Vouvry. Although officially called Stade des Combes (Stadium of the Valley), the incredible achievement of building a football ground on the 31° slope of a mountainside led to the venue being described as *'terrain de foot de l'impossible'* ('impossible football pitch') and *'Stade de l'impossible'* ('impossible stadium').

To put Stade des Combes into perspective, its altitude of 1,030m/3,379ft means that it is higher than England's tallest mountain, Scafell Pike. It is also worth pointing out that whereas the mountain village stadium at FC Gspon, described later in this book, is smaller and designed for eight-a-side matches, the playing surface at Isérables is a full-size pitch; in fact, it is the third-highest 11-a-side venue that I have visited (after Austrian clubs SV Kleinwalsertal and FC Bad Gastein).

Despite its improved playing facilities, FC Isérables slipped down to the 5ème Ligue in 1999. The team's stay at the lowest level of the official Swiss league structure lasted for six years until promotion back to the 4ème Ligue in 2005.

Having played on its impossible pitch for 30 years, FC Isérables found it impossible to play at all in 2012, after failing to muster a team. However, the motto of the club is *'Pa capona'* ('Don't give up') and after a three-year hiatus, the club resumed competition in 2015, once again participating in the 5ème Ligue.

The rebirth of FC Isérables proved to be timely, because the following year marked the 50th anniversary of the founding of the club. As part of the celebrations, the club helped organise a 'Snow-Soccer' tournament which took place at Lac de Tracouet, on another mountainside above the Rhône, at an altitude of 2,171m/7,123ft. Although nicknamed *Lac Noir* ('Black Lake') because of its appearance in the summer, it was definitely white during the winter when the footballers played on its snow-covered surface.

A kick-off time of 10.30am on Sunday, 3 September 2023 for my chosen game at FC Isérables required an early start from the holiday apartment in Stalden-Saas. After taking the train to Riddes, I headed for the nearby cable car station. It took six minutes for the cable car to climb up to Isèrables, passing over houses, small vineyards and sections of the old mule trail.

From the station, it was a short walk to the Stade des Combes, past charming houses and old barns on stone feet. The barns are still used, with straw poking out complete with agricultural aromas. Approaching the football ground, I noticed the almost vertical drop at one end of the stadium of about 24m/79ft down to the road below, suitably named Chemin du Stade ('Stadium Path'). The embankments of the stadium, originally bare earth and rock, now have trees growing on them, following a mass planting by young villagers.

On entering the stadium, the panoramic view of Bernese Alps such as Grand Chavalard, Grand Château and La Seya on the other side of the Rhône valley was stunning. Despite their name, not all Bernese Alps are in the canton of Bern: some are in Valais and Vaud. Although not tall enough to be snow-capped in September, these mountains merged together to form a huge wall of grey rock that contrasted with the green trees bordering the pitch in the foreground and the blue sky above.

My choice of the Saint-Étienne shirt turned out to be a good idea, as I was instantly recognised by Alexandre Crettenand, president of FC Isérables, who then introduced me to Gérard Favre. At the time of the match, Gérard was 76 years old and clearly still as devoted as ever to his local club and football generally. As a custodian of FC Isérables' history, Gérard had been incredibly helpful before my visit by telling me the amazing story of his club. As soon as we met, he took me on a tour of the stadium.

The Stade des Combes consists of a natural grass pitch, surrounded on one side and one of the ends by high fencing to try and stop balls flying off into the gorge. Gérard explained that a strip of land six metres deep was lost on the fenced side following a landslide in 1989. The fenced end of the stadium towers above the road, while the other end backs on to a steep rock face covered with vegetation below some houses. The unfenced side is the only part with level access, so it contains the entrance to the stadium and the club's facilities, including a bar and cafe area with tables and chairs for customers, as well as the main building.

The ground floor of the main building contained the dressing rooms, and we briefly popped inside the home team's which consisted of a rectangular room with a tiled floor and white walls displaying the slogan 'Vert l'impossible' ('Green impossible') in large green letters, above foldaway benches and hangers for the players' clothes. Also on the ground floor was the clubhouse, which contained natural wooden beams and furnishings decorated with FC Isérables' trophies and memorabilia plus football shirts, hats and pennants from other clubs. I donated a Leeds United scarf, which was immediately put on display.

After this, we took the stairs up to the first floor, which contained a function room capable of accommodating up to

60 people. A balcony at this level provided the best vantage point from which to see the game, so we opted to stand here just as the players came out on to the pitch from the dressing rooms immediately below us. Many of the crowd of about 75 people were relatives or friends of the players, and most watched either from this balcony, or by the bar and cafe area. Throughout the game, children and pet dogs played happily in the background.

The game was the second fixture of the season in the Championnat 5e Ligue – Groupe 2 (known for short in French as 5ème Ligue and in German as 5. Liga) at the ninth tier of Swiss football. The *Bedjuis* players had won their first game of the season, but the opposition, FC Vionnaz 2, had lost.

The second team of a club established in 1957, FC Vionnaz 2 comes from the town of that name in the north-west of the canton, further down the Rhône valley towards Lake Geneva, but still within the Alpine area. The club's first team competed two tiers higher in the 3ème Ligue.

FC Vionnaz 2 appeared in yellow shirts and black shorts, while FC Isérables appeared in all green. Bells around the necks of goats grazing in nearby meadows rang out as the game kicked off.

To tell the story of this match, I will focus on one particular player, Thibault Vouillamoz.

Only 17 years old at the time of the match, Vouillamoz, wearing number 8, started on the left side of the Isérables attack. After 20 minutes, he controlled a long diagonal ball from a colleague, beat the defender, but then shot wide. Eight minutes later, he hit another shot wide of the goal, this time from a more central position.

Undeterred, Vouillamoz demonstrated his ability half an hour in. After receiving a long ball down the left-hand side, he beat the defender then used the time available to him to slowly pick his spot and calmly curl a right-footed shot around the keeper and into the far corner. Vouillamoz immediately turned around, milking the applause from the cheering fans on the balcony.

A couple of minutes later, Vouillamoz made an impact at the other end of the pitch when Isérables' defence failed to get in any challenges, allowing the visitors to have an attempt on goal which the greens' number 8 cleared. After that, Vouillamoz drifted across from the left, taking up various positions along the front line.

Interestingly, both teams supplied a linesman; the one from Isérables dismissed any suspicion of possible bias when he flagged that the ball was out, so halting a promising attack by the greens. The incident occurred directly below our balcony, and the ball looked as if it had not crossed the line, which the home fans quickly pointed out.

That Vionnaz remained very much in the game was shown three minutes into the second half when André Baptista Viegas de Sa (the visitors' best player) shot from the edge of the penalty area, forcing the Isérables keeper, Killian Crettenand, to make a good save.

On 50 minutes, Vouillamoz attacked down the right, beat his man and hit a cross-cum-shot, which turned out to be neither one nor the other. Five minutes later, Vouillamoz had a moment to forget when an Isérables shot was parried, but after being presented with an open goal and the keeper lying prone, the number 8 skied the ball over from close range.

Five minutes later, the glaring miss momentarily looked like it could prove costly when a Vionnaz counter-attack down the right culminated in Baptista Viegas de Sa getting in a shot which Crettenand saved well.

By now it was nearly midday and over 20°C, so the players had a drinks and cooling break. After a spell when Vouillamoz's impact on the game had been limited, he burst into life for the last quarter of an hour, getting in a good position before being flagged offside, then shooting over following another long ball. With 12 minutes remaining, Vouillamoz scored his second goal, lobbing the ball over the opposing keeper.

After conceding that second goal, Vionnaz became desperate, with the team's Dylan Jakob booked for diving in an attempt to get a penalty. Vouillamoz's final contribution came three minutes from time when he crossed for Baldwin Maverick Garcia to knock in the third. With two goals and an assist, Vouillamoz had undoubtedly been the man of the match.

By the time the final whistle confirmed the home side's 3-0 victory, only two balls had flown over the high perimeter fencing, which surprised me as the game had been played in a rather direct style with quite a lot of long balls. According to Gérard Favre, an average of three balls per game go over the fence at Stade des Combes, although most are later retrieved.

FC Isérables' starting 11 had included five players with the popular local surname Crettenand: Killian Crettenand in goal; Ryan Crettenand at right-back; Sylvain Crettenand at left-back; Arnaud Crettenand in midfield; and (most confusingly) a second Killian Crettenand on the left wing. However, it is another Crettenand, Kevin, who watched the game from the sidelines that I shall now turn to.

As a footballer, Kevin played a vital role in relaunching the FC Isérables team in 2015, and after the game against Vionnaz, Gérard introduced me to him. Kevin told me that a combination of injuries during his playing days and being in his late 30s had led to him retiring from playing at the end of the previous season, 2022/23. He explained that his heart wanted to continue the 'adventure in green' but unfortunately his body said 'stop'. These days, Kevin sits on the committee that runs the club, in addition to spending time coaching the juniors.

After joining several groups of families and friends enjoying a tasty lunch of sausage, bread and salad served on tables in the stadium cafe, I left the ground and walked back up the road towards the cable car station. On the way, one of the FC Isérables players waved as he passed in a car; a small incident that sums up this friendly and genuinely community club, where the younger players appreciate the dedication of the older generation whose vision enabled the 'impossible stadium' to become possible, giving them the chance to play football in their village.

Going into the last match of the season on Sunday, 2 June 2024, FC Isérables stood second in the table, one point behind the leading team, FC Massongex 2 from the north-west of Valais. However, the final fixture was a home one against the leaders, meaning that a win would clinch the title and promotion to the 4ème Ligue. A brace of goals from Baldwin Maverick Garcia and another two from Thibault Vouillamoz secured an emphatic 4-0 victory and promotion.

Chapter 15

Switzerland: Mountain Village Football

i. Hiking up to Europe's Highest Football Stadium

In 1983, directors of FC Tobias Mund, from the village of Mund on a hillside above the Rhône, invited football clubs from Valais to attend a meeting to consider the formation of a championship for mountain village teams. Seven clubs responded positively: FC Bürchen, FC Eggerberg, FC Flamingos, FC Gspon, FC Nadelhorn, FC Saas-Almagel and FC Visperterminen. The subsequent meeting resolved to establish the Bergdorf Meisterschaft (Mountain Village Championship or BDM).

Severe winters in the mountains mean that the BDM season runs from early May until the end of June, the teams then have a mid-summer break, and football resumes around the end of August and concludes in early October.

BDM matches are played with several changes to normal football rules. Limited space on mountainsides means that games take place on smaller pitches, with new ones measuring 60m to 80m long and 35m to 45m wide; goals are proportionately smaller; the size of pitches means the games are eight-a-side (seven outfield players plus a goalkeeper); there is no offside; and teams can field a maximum of two 'foreigners' (players from outside the canton of Valais) at any one time. Matches also consist of two halves, each lasting 40 minutes, but seniors' and women's matches are five minutes shorter for each half. The canton's football association, Association Valaisanne de Football/Walliser Fussballverband or AVF/WFV, told me that the BDM is a completely amateur competition outside of the national regulations and does not therefore occupy a formal place on the Swiss league pyramid.

Since the BDM's formation, new mountain clubs have joined the eight original members. In recent years, the BDM has included two men's divisions, eight teams in Group A with the bottom side relegated to the similar-sized Group B. A third division, Group C, operated for a time, although not since the COVID-19 pandemic. The BDM also organises women's, veterans' and youth leagues, as well as knockout cups.

In 2008, mountain village football went international when the first Bergdorf-Europameisterschaft (European Mountain Village Championship) took place. Often referred to as the Bergdorf-EM or Mountain Village Euros, the tournament is held every four years in tandem with the main Euros. Each country is represented by a club team, and a side from Spain triumphed in that first Bergdorf-EM which was held in Gspon. Spain retained its title at the 2012 tournament at Kleinarl in Austria. A Russian team won in 2016 at Morzine in the French Alps, while Italians were successful in the next finals, which were actually played in 2022 because of the pandemic and held in Zermatt. In 2024, the Bergdorf-EM took place in the Italian village of Macugnaga, with Sweden emerging victorious. Interestingly, Swiss teams have never won the tournament.

Involved in the BDM from the very beginning, and host to the first Bergdorf-EM competition, FC Gspon also has the highest permanent football stadium in Europe. It had long been an ambition of mine to reach the stadium by hiking up the mountainside, and in 2023 I finally had the chance to achieve that aim.

The village of Stalden-Saas (known as Stalden for short) is located by a gorge at the junction of the Mattertal and Saastal valleys. Stalden is an important transport interchange for local trains and postbuses, making it ideal for exploring the eastern part of Valais; however, it is the village's proximity to Gspon that explains why I chose it as a base for my visit in September 2023.

Positioned high up on a shelf on the mountainside above Stalden, Gspon is car free and the only ways of reaching the village and its stadium are by cable car or on foot. I arrived in Stalden in the afternoon, but although FC Gspon had a home match that evening, there wasn't enough time to hike up and arrive before kick-off. Consequently, I decided to travel to the game by cable car, and hike up on another occasion.

Five days later, I set off on my hike up to Gspon, only to discover that the construction of a new road down in the valley had turned the lower slopes into a building site, with some roads and paths blocked. Consequently, I decided to cheat by taking the cable car as far as Staldenried, a village about a quarter of the way up the mountainside, then hike the rest of the way from there.

The bright red cable cars were quite large, with each gondola capable of holding up to a dozen people. My cable car passed over the gorge and its roadworks, then sailed over houses and roads surrounded by small vineyards growing on hillside terraces. It took seven minutes to reach Staldenried at a height of 1,155m/3,789ft, meaning that I needed to hike 768m/2,520ft to reach the stadium.

Ten minutes after leaving the cable car at Staldenried, I encountered two women herding sheep down the valley. About half of their flock were Walliser Schwarznasenschaf (Valais Blacknose), with distinctive dark faces, large horns and shaggy white woollen coats. Specially suited to grazing in harsh conditions on rocky mountainsides, the breed is native to the canton and highly prized. Although small in scale, this example of transhumance provided a sure sign of the end of summer.

After about an hour hiking up through the woods, the path reached the tiny settlement of Bildje. The scent of wild thyme by the side of the path mixed with the pungent smell of bacon from one of the households cooking rösti for lunch.

The next stage turned out to be the most punishing, with the path zigzagging up the steep and forested slopes. For a couple of minutes, a golden eagle came into view, using its massive wingspan to soar in the air currents above the valley, with the snow-capped peaks of Balfrin providing a dramatic backdrop to the south.

An hour later, the zigzag path ended at the edge of an Alpine meadow. After 20 more minutes, I reached the southern outskirts of Gspon and briefly popped into the village's 17th-century church. Gspon is the highest settlement in the region to be inhabited throughout the year, rather than just in the summer, and I strolled past a number of wooden chalets that house some of the nearly 600 people who live in the village.

A short climb up a slope at the northern end of the village finally brought me to the Ottmar Hitzfeld Gspon Arena, the home of FC Gspon. Some reports claim that the little stadium is 2,000m high, while others provide a figure of 6,600ft; however, I reckon its real altitude is 1,923m/6,309ft. Even that lower figure means that the stadium is well over a mile above sea level, twice the height of the tallest mountain in England, Scafell Pike, and higher than any other permanent football venue in Europe.

Although the signpost in Staldenried said it would take just over two hours to hike up to Gspon, it actually took me an additional half an hour. To avoid anyone getting into difficulty, this hike should only be attempted by people with hill-walking experience, sufficient fitness, and equipped with suitable waterproof clothing, sturdy footwear plus sufficient water supplies. If in doubt, take the cable car all the way up.

ii. Can You Hear the Balfrin Sing? FC Gspon, 1,923m/6,309ft

FC Gspon was set up in 1974 by five enthusiasts from Staldenried; however, all the flat land large enough for a football pitch in Staldenried had either been built over or used for agriculture; the only remaining level bit of land stood at the end of the cable car, further up the mountainside at Gspon. Even that land is not big enough for a full-sized pitch, so the games at Gspon, like other BDM fixtures, are eight-a-side rather than 11.

During winter, FC Gspon's pitch is covered by deep snow and becomes part of a ski run. In the spring, players and other helpers clear the snow, then erect goalposts and fencing to enable the football season to get under way.

FC Gspon entered the limelight in 1989 when a training session was held at its high-altitude pitch by Timo Konietzka, famous for being the scorer of the first goal in the West German Bundesliga. Konietzka's historic goal came for Borussia Dortmund against Werder Bremen on 24 August 1963, a minute after the start of the match. Konietzka later enjoyed a career playing and coaching in both West Germany and Switzerland. Among other notable visitors is Sepp Blatter, who came to Gspon's mountain stadium in 2000, two years after starting his reign as FIFA president.

The original Gspon pitch consisted of earth and gravel. Later, the pitch was improved by having woodchips and sand spread over it.

The biggest club in Valais, FC Sion, responded positively to an invitation to play in the first game on the new surface in 1994.

The biggest drawback at such high altitude is losing the ball; despite tall perimeter fencing, several get booted out of the stadium during most games. After the match, players have to descend the mountainside to retrieve as many balls as they can find, with some of them having rolled or fallen hundreds of feet down the slopes. The players then have to climb back up with any balls they recover. One estimate is that FC Gspon has lost over 1,000 footballs since the stadium's construction.

It is a cliche to say that football clubs are the heart of a community, but in Gspon and Staldenried it is undoubtedly true, with many of the people who live in either settlement active in the club in one way or another. A women's team was added in 2008, and FC Gspon occasionally entered a second team in Group C of the BDM when there were enough teams to run that division.

In 2009, the little stadium underwent renovation, with the installation of a modern artificial playing surface, complete with a clubhouse for post-match refreshments. It was then that the stadium acquired the title Ottmar Hitzfeld Gspon Arena, named after the German coach then in charge of the Swiss national side. One of a select group of coaches to have won the Champions League with two different clubs (Borussia Dortmund in 1997 and FC Bayern München in 2001), Hitzfeld was the guest of honour at the first game in the renovated stadium on 31 October 2009.

Despite winning the BDM Group A title in successive seasons as recently as 2017 and 2018, FC Gspon only avoided relegation by the pandemic halting fixtures in 2021 with the team at the bottom of the table. At the end of the 2022 season, the team again struggled, finishing seventh just one place above the drop.

On the day of my arrival in Stalden on Friday, 1 September 2023, Gspon had a home match in the BDM. The 8pm kick-off enabled spectators to catch a cable car down to Staldenried after the game, but it was not possible to return all the way to Stalden. Hiking down from Staldenried to Stalden in the dark was not a sensible option, which meant having to stay overnight in Gspon. Consequently, I decided to book accommodation at the Alpenblick, the local mountain inn.

Variously called a Berghotel, Berghaus, Berggasthaus, or Auberge de montagne, these mountain inns were built to provide accommodation for mountaineers and hikers at high altitude. Although there are dozens of mountain inns in Switzerland, they don't exist in any other Alpine country. Before the trip, I had slept overnight in five of them, but only to be able to hike in the Alps; this time I was staying in one to see football.

Built in 1965, the Alpenblick has always been a mountain inn and certainly lives up to its name, which translates from German into English as 'mountain view', providing visitors with a superb Alpine panorama. The upper floors have a dozen bedrooms, while the downstairs contains a bar serving excellent Feldschlösschen Swiss beer and a restaurant where I tucked into a tasty pork schnitzel and chips.

The evening's opposition, FC Spycher, came from Visperterminen, a settlement several times bigger than Gspon. When I walked from Gspon to Visperterminen a few days later, it took a couple of hours, and the relative proximity of FC Gspon and FC Spycher means that the two clubs are deemed to be *Derby-Rivalen* ('derby rivals'). That hike ended at the Spycher stadium, located next to the village's postbus terminus and cable car station. Like Gspon's pitch, it is an eight-a-side artificial surface, but at the lower altitude of 'only' 1,385m/4,544ft.

Visperterminen's name is a bit of a mouthful, so most locals refer to it as Terbiner; however, the village's main claim to fame is being located above the highest vineyard in Europe. With a sunny and dry climate, Valais is the main winemaking area in Switzerland, producing about a third of the total yield in the country. Grapes grow on the clay and sandy soil of the Heida Vineyard up to an altitude of 1,150m/3,773ft, helping to fill 400,000 wine bottles every year.

My game was the tenth out of 14 rounds of fixtures in the BDM Group A season. Before kick-off, SV Ausserberg led the way with 23 points; Spycher stood sixth in the table, having earned only six points, three of which had come in an 8-0 thrashing of Gspon earlier that season in the game at Visperterminen. Gspon languished at the foot of the table with only three points, all of which were gained in the opening round back in May, the team having lost every subsequent game.

The Ottmar Hitzfeld Gspon Arena consists of a pitch surrounded on three sides by tall green fencing, while the other side has two dugouts for the coaches and substitutes positioned in front of a bank where most spectators watch from temporary benches or sit on the grassy slope. The small clubhouse is located in one corner, while a larger building at the opposite end contains the players' dressing rooms. Skiers stay in this building during the winter, as indicated by the sign 'Gruppenunterkunft Gspon' ('Group Accommodation Gspon') on the wall.

Historically, some English football stadiums had ends referencing local features, such as Highbury's Clock End, Chelsea's Shed or Nottingham Forest's Trent End. In a similar vein, I shall call the south goal at Gspon the 'Balfrin End', because of the snow-capped series of peaks which dominate the southern part of the Alpine panorama; while the opposite goal is the 'Bietschhorn End', named by me after the triangular mountain looking like a piece of Toblerone chocolate standing prominently to the north. I accept that 'Can you hear the Balfrin sing?' or 'You'll never take the Bietschhorn' are unlikely to catch on as terrace chants, but they'll do for helping me describe matches at Gspon.

The view from the grassy slope was spectacular; apart from the mountains already mentioned, you could also see the Weisshorn in the distance. For once, the Weisshorn seemed aptly named, looking whiter than on my previous trips to Valais, thanks to the recent snow.

A few months earlier, the website of the Barcelona-based newspaper *Mundo Deportivo* had named Gspon's little ground as one of the world's three 'most stunning soccer stadiums' and after visiting it I have to agree. For the record, *Mundo Deportivo*'s other two stadiums included one on a Norwegian island and the other floating on a bay in Singapore.

In the first half, Gspon in an all-red kit attacked the Balfrin End, while Spycher in green played towards the Bietschhorn. It was immediately noticeable that while the referee was dressed in neutral colours, each team supplied a linesman wearing club colours under a bib.

Most of the crowd of 21 people watched from the grassy bank as the match kicked off a few minutes early; it later became clear that this was to enable it to finish in time for spectators to catch the cable car down to Staldenried. Not in a hurry to go anywhere were animals in nearby fields whose bells rang out from time to time, although in this instance the sound came from sheep; there were no cows in Gspon that weekend.

Soon after the game started, the sun went down over the mountains and the five floodlights along the opposite side were switched on. Although it had been 26°C down in Stalden, the temperature began to drop quite sharply up in the mountains until it felt distinctly chilly, vindicating my decision to bring plenty of thermal clothing.

Like all the eight-a-side mountain village matches I would see, the game was fast and furious, rather like basketball with one side attacking followed by the action rapidly switching to the other end, helped by the small size of the pitch and the quickness of its playing surface. The players constantly switched positions, making tactical observations rather difficult, although according to a later report both teams were arranged in a 3-2-2 formation.

The artificial pitch was rather unforgiving, with several loud cries as players acquired grazed and bloody legs from tackles or slips; however, a bucket of water with a magic sponge by the dugouts provided immediate soothing.

In the early stages, Gspon had some of the best chances, but failed to capitalise on them. Invariably, this means the opposition will score, and the inevitable happened after 25 minutes when Spycher striker Flavio Studer shot from a tight angle on the left into the net past goalkeeper Hannes Biner. The same player then scored eight minutes later, again shooting from the left, but this time further out.

After a few more minutes, the referee blew for half-time and the players of both teams headed to their dressing rooms behind the north goal, while the fans poured into the clubhouse at the other end to grab beers in the ten minutes provided by the break. When the match resumed, half the fans opted to stay in the clubhouse and watch through the windows.

The only part of the stadium spectators can't watch from is the side opposite the dugouts, which is above a fairly steep slope down the mountainside. Tall net fences try to prevent balls being lost, but early in the second half they served another function when one of the footballers slid off the pitch and under the fence! For one awful moment it looked like he might have fallen down the mountain, adding a whole new meaning to offside; however, other players pulled him back to safety. Talking of things disappearing down the mountain, five balls went over the fence during the match; hopefully some of them would be recovered later.

Early in the second half, a couple of things happened that are apparently quite common in mountain village football, but unheard of in the mainstream game; firstly,

Gspon's goalie swapped shirts and position with an outfield player; then one of the linesmen came on as a sub.

Gspon, now attacking the Bietschhorn End, played a lot better at the start of the second half, but once again failed to make the most of goalscoring opportunities. You can guess what happened next. With 66 minutes gone, Spycher took a throw-in and the ball reached Studer, enabling the 20-year-old to complete his hat-trick with another shot from a tight angle, although this time on the right. Three minutes later, one of Spycher's defenders, Mattia Burgener, shot from the halfway line and the ball went past several players, including Gspon's keeper (who may have been unsighted) and into the goal.

After 80 minutes, the final whistle confirmed Spycher's 4-0 victory. Some of the crowd went into the clubhouse for more drinks while others dashed for the cable car. Meanwhile, I headed back to my room in the Alpenblick, feeling pleased with myself for having fulfilled a long-standing ambition to see a football match at this incredible venue.

A few days later, the local weather forecast predicted a storm for Sunday, 10 September, which might stop the cable car operating; consequently, I decided not to attend Gspon's next home game against FC Inter Wiler scheduled for that afternoon. Luckily, the forecast changed, saying that the storm would come a bit later, so I revised my plans and headed back up from Stalden to Gspon. This time there was no need to stay in the Alpenblick, because a 4pm kick-off allowed plenty of time to return to my apartment after the game.

As I took the cable car up from Stalden, one of Gspon's coaches boarded at Staldenried and joined me for the last part of the journey. He maintained a serious expression on his face throughout the ride; perhaps aware of what might be about to happen.

After arriving in Gspon, I noticed several black cows grazing in a field between the cable car station and the pitch; presumably they had moved from another pasture during the week since the previous game. The arrival of the cows confirmed the Ottmar Hitzfeld Gspon Arena to be the only stadium in this book to qualify as truly Alpine in the strict geographical and agricultural sense of the term. Some of the cows were sitting, and although it's a myth that they sit in anticipation of bad weather, there were certainly clouds gathering over the Bernese Oberland to the north and heading this way; but would I be about to witness a meteorological storm or a sporting one?

With a name and badge similar to the more famous Internazionale of Milan, the visitors came from the village of Wiler located on the north side of the Rhône valley at a height of about 1,500m/4,921ft. Before kick-off, Inter Wiler stood in mid-table, while Gspon occupied last place on goal difference. Once again, Gspon appeared in an all-red kit and adopted a 3-2-2 formation, while FC Inter Wiler wore white and played 3-3-1, with a lone striker.

This time a larger crowd of about 50 people gathered on the benches and the grass bank to watch the game, with some sitting under parasols in the shade; a dozen of them had come to support the visitors.

In the first half, Gspon attacked the Bietschhorn End, but it was at the other end where the first goal went in after only five minutes. Inter Wiler's Tobias Ritler was given far too much time and space before firing a firm right-footed effort into the goal. Gspon then had a decent chance, only to blast the ball wide. Thirteen minutes proved to be unlucky for the hosts, because it was then that Michael

Ebiner hit a powerful shot on the turn down the centre of the goal to put Inter Wiler 2-0 ahead. A few minutes later, Gspon had a corner, only for Inter Wiler to break away and score through a firm Jonathan Ritler shot. Seconds later, Andy Furrer gave Gspon a glimmer of hope, scoring from just outside the area on the right, greeted with loud cheers from most of the fans.

The scorching hot weather then prompted a drinks and cooling break, but any hopes that Gspon could use that to regroup and mount a comeback were dashed soon after the restart when a long cross from the right was tapped in at close range by Raphael Ebiner to put Inter Wiler 4-1 ahead. Arguably the man of the match, 29-year-old Ebiner acted as a focal point up front, bringing others into the game.

Just before the interval, an Inter Wiler attack down the left ended with Sven Ritler grabbing his team's fifth. As with the previous weekend's game, the fans headed towards the clubhouse during the interval, only this time smoke drifted from it while a barbecue was being prepared.

Last weekend, a Spycher player scored a hat-trick at Gspon; this time it was the turn of Inter Wiler's Lars Ritler to do the same. The best of his trio was a shot from a tight angle on the left after 45 minutes; followed by further goals either side of a second drinks and cooling break. Lars Ritler's hat-trick made it 8-1 to Inter Wiler, but sadly for Gspon there were more goals to come. The home side managed to hit a post, only for Gspon's defence to be torn open again, enabling Sven Ritler to score his second and Inter Wiler's ninth, shooting into the goal from a central position. Although it was 9-1, the referee nevertheless allowed a full quota of stoppage time, and in the fifth of those additional minutes Jonathan Ritler scored his second goal following an attack down the right with practically the last kick of the game.

It ended 10-1 to the visitors, the first time I had seen a team score ten in a single game. Looking on the bright side for Gspon, only three balls disappeared down the mountain.

Despite losing the next match 7-1 away at FC Zermatt, Gspon sensationally defeated third-placed SV Gamsen in the penultimate round of fixtures 4-3, thanks to a winning goal from Andy Furrer 11 minutes from time. Those three points proved to be enough to preserve the team's place in Group A for another season. FC Spycher finished fourth, FC Inter Wiler sixth, with SV Ausserberg winning the title.

In 2024, FC Thun once again finished the BDM season second from bottom, avoiding relegation by just three points.

FourFourTwo magazine's website has listed attending a match at the Ottmar Hitzfeld Gspon Arena second out of 53 things that every football fan should do before they die. Having been lucky enough to visit Europe's highest stadium, I think it's definitely worth adding to your bucket list.

iii. (Not Quite) As Old as the Hills

The morning after Gspon versus Spycher, I was just about to leave Hotel Alpenblick and hike back down to Stalden when I noticed people wearing football shirts heading towards the stadium. Intrigued, I followed them and found players warming up on the pitch. Totally unaware of any match that day, I assumed it was just a training session. It therefore came as a surprise to see a notice on the door of the clubhouse saying 'Fußball Veteranenturnier 2023

Gspon' ('Football Veterans Tournament 2023 Gspon'), with notes in German explaining the format of a competition that would be starting in just a few minutes.

Organised by the Veteranen Vereinigung des SFV Section Oberwallis (Veterans' Association of the SFV Section Upper Valais) and the Oberwalliser Fussball Veteranen (Upper Valais Football Veterans), the tournament involved four teams, each with eight players. Joining Gspon were three teams from down in the Rhône valley: FC Siders, FC Steg and FC Visp, each of whom paid CHF 500 to participate.

The format of the tournament involved each team playing the other three sides once, with matches lasting just 15 minutes, no half-time break and an interval of only five minutes between each game.

Three types of tournaments have been held annually in Valais for the past 15 years by the canton's football veterans' organisations (with an enforced break because of the pandemic): an indoor competition in Visp; an event on grass taking place at various venues; while the high-altitude contest in Gspon is the only one held on the pitch of a mountain village club. FC Gspon acts as the point of contact between the BDM and the SFV veterans, establishing an important link between mountain village football and the clubs affiliated with the AFV/WFV.

Veterans' football has become increasingly popular in many countries during recent times, with more players keen to stay involved in the game and wanting to play against others who are also not as quick as they used to be. There are different variants of veterans' football, with some having slightly different rules to the mainstream game, such as bans on sliding tackles and not allowing the ball to go over head height. However, those two changes were not applied to the tournament at Gspon, and apart from the timing of the matches, the rules seemed identical to BDM games. Despite the title of this section of the book, the players were not nearly as ancient as the Pennine Alps, with the youngest participants just over 35 and the oldest approaching pensionable age.

The tournament kicked off at 10.30am, with recorded music emerging from the clubhouse, reflecting the age of the contestants by featuring the likes of Tina Turner, Queen, ABBA and the Monkees. With only five spectators present, the music seemed to be for the players' benefit.

In the first match, Gspon faced Steg. Football started to develop in Steg when the Lonza AG pharmaceuticals company moved to this small settlement in 1898 and attracted foreign workers. A club called FC Lonza existed from that time until dissolving at the onset of the First World War. The present club, FC Steg, was established after the end of the conflict and these days plays in the 3. Liga.

Gspon appeared in an all-blue change kit while the Steg team played in their usual kit of green shirts and black shorts. Steg hit the bar, but weak defending couldn't prevent Gspon taking the lead before going on to secure a 2-0 win.

In the second fixture, Visp – wearing black – came up against Siders, in red and yellow. Founded in 1914, FC Visp is based in the town of that name at the bottom of the valley. In 2014, the club's centenary celebrations were attended by Sepp Blatter, then FIFA president, happy to be seen with his local team which these days competes in the 3. Liga.

The boundary between French-speaking and German-speaking parts of Switzerland is often called the *Röstigraben* ('Rösti trench') named after the potato dish popular with Swiss-Germans. The *Röstigraben* runs right through the town of Sierre/Siders, explaining why it has a bilingual name. Interestingly, the team appeared in the veterans' tournament under the German name of FC Siders, even though the 2. Liga club is normally known by the French title of FC Sierre, while all the players spoke to each other in French throughout the morning.

Although still veterans, the Visp players looked to be considerably younger and stronger than those from Siders, hitting first the post and then the crossbar, before taking a 1-0 lead. However, Siders, featuring a couple of players over 60, played the more skilful football and scored two close-range tap-ins, including one in the final minute, to steal a 2-1 victory.

Next up, Gspon met Visp, with the visiting team having only a five-minute rest between the two matches. Despite that disadvantage, Visp once again took the lead then conceded late, this time with the final kick, resulting in a 1-1 draw.

In the fourth fixture, Siders took an early lead, but Steg nearly equalised by hitting the post twice and forcing a great save by Siders' goalkeeper, who was surprisingly wearing glasses. The Steg players' hopes effectively ended after conceding a second following a corner, although they did grab a consolation goal towards the end of a 2-1 defeat.

The next game proved to be the most crucial, as well as the most interesting. Gspon faced Siders, leading the competition and only needing a draw to win it. However, the decisive moment in the whole tournament came when a Gspon player launched a speculative effort from distance and the bespectacled goalkeeper for Siders, who until then had played well, carelessly let the ball through his hands. Although the same keeper pulled off a good save later on,

Gspon proceeded to run Siders ragged and score three more to secure a 4-0 win.

Siders looked to have run out of puff, with the advanced age of some of the team's players possibly counting against them; if so, this was probably for two further reasons. Firstly, the tournament took place at an altitude of 1,923m/6,309ft, much higher than the town of Sierre/Siders down in the Rhône valley at a mere 520m/1,706ft; meaning that the Gspon players were more familiar with the thinner air. Secondly, the Siders players had the disadvantage of only five minutes' recovery time after their previous game, while the hosts benefitted from 25 minutes' rest.

The final game saw Visp beat Steg 1-0, with the only goal scored by a header immediately after a team-mate's shot had hit the crossbar.

Winning the veterans' tournament emphasised Gspon's former playing strength, compared to the weakness of the village's younger generation of footballers.

So, what did I make of mountain village football? Overall, I found the two BDM games and the veterans' tournament to have been highly entertaining, played in a great spirit, with few fouls and no dissent. Sometimes players acquired bloody knees by sliding on the artificial surface, but there was no feigning injury or time-wasting, with play resumed after a quick wipe of the magic sponge. The footballers played for their own enjoyment rather than for financial reward, relishing the chance to appear at Europe's highest stadium and in such a beautiful location. All three events were free to watch, completing the contrast with over-hyped and money-dominated 'elite-level' football.

Chapter 16

Champions from the Foothills

MY RESEARCH has identified six players born within the perimeter of the Alpine Convention who have won football's top two honours: the FIFA World Cup and the European Cup/UEFA Champions League. This includes those who played on the winning side in finals of both competitions or were on the bench (including unused substitutes), but not squad members who may have featured in other matches during the tournaments (even if they received a medal) or those on the coaching staff. Given that only around 13 million people live in the Alpine region, six is a commendably high number. By comparison, England, the country that invented football, has a population of about 57 million, but can only offer Bobby Charlton and Nobby Stiles. (Ian Callaghan won the European Cup with Liverpool in the 1970s and was a member of England's 1966 World Cup squad, receiving winners' medals from both competitions, but didn't make the starting team or bench for the final against West Germany.)

The careers of these six 'champions from the foothills' will be summarised with particular reference to the times when I saw them play.

Despite a relatively small area and population, the Bavarian Alps have produced no fewer than four players who have won both the World Cup and the European Cup/ Champions League.

To hear about the first of these champions, I need to go back to the day before the game at Garmisch-Partenkirchen when we were in Munich so that my wife Josie could see her team Chelsea in the 2012 Champions League Final at the Allianz Arena. Unfortunately, we only managed to obtain one ticket, which meant that I had to be content with watching a game featuring footballing legends at the old Olympic Stadium earlier in the day.

Part of UEFA's Champions Festival to celebrate European club football's biggest game coming to Munich, FC Bayern München All-Stars faced a World All-Stars side. Turning out for the former was Bayern legend Paul Breitner, by then a grey-haired 60-year-old. During the game, the referee awarded the Bayern team a penalty at the same end of the same stadium where Breitner took a spot kick in the 1974 World Cup Final against the Netherlands.

Two minutes into that final, the Dutch had taken the lead from a penalty, but after 25 minutes West Germany had the chance to equalise, also from the spot. Breitner hit a right-footed shot into the corner of the goal to the right of Dutch keeper Jan Jongbloed. West Germany went on to win 2-1, securing the country's second World Cup.

Coincidentally, another Dutch goalkeeper faced Breitner at the match in 2012: Edwin van der Sar. Breitner hit another right-footed shot to the keeper's right, but this time his penalty was too close to van der Sar, who saved easily. Contrasting the miss with the rather more important 1974 kick, the following day's *Bild* newspaper report headlined 'Legenden-Spiel! Breitner scheitert mit Holland-Elfer' ('Legends' Game! Breitner fails with Holland penalty'.)

Born in 1951, Breitner started playing football at the age of six. His first club, SV Kolbermoor, is based in the town of that name where he was born in Oberbayern.

Up against Atlético Madrid in the 1974 European Cup Final, Bayern trailed 1-0 in extra time, only to snatch a last-gasp equaliser, causing the final to go to a replay for the only time in the competition's history. Two days later, Breitner's team won 4-0 to become the first German side to take home European club football's top trophy.

After winning a haul of other honours with Bayern, Breitner joined Real Madrid, where he won a couple of Spanish league titles. Usually deployed at left-back, Breitner is remembered as one of Germany's greatest players.

For our second Bavarian champion we have to go to Weiler im Allgäu, which in 1965 provided the birthplace of Karl-Heinz Riedle.

After playing youth football for lower-league sides, Riedle joined FC Augsburg and Blau-Weiß 90 Berlin before rising to prominence at Werder Bremen, where he won the Bundesliga in his first season. In 1990, Riedle played four times for West Germany at the World Cup finals in Italy, including an appearance as a substitute in the semi-final victory over England where he scored in the penalty shoot-out. Although Riedle stayed on the bench for the final, he collected his winners' medal after the defeat of Maradona's Argentina in Rome. Altogether, he earned over 40 caps for Germany, the last of them in 1994.

After helping win Germany's third World Cup, Riedle stayed in Rome with a transfer to Lazio. Three years later he returned to Germany, joining Borussia Dortmund. Riedle won two more Bundesliga titles in Dortmund and scored twice in the 1997 Champions League Final to help his team beat Juventus 3-1. After that triumph, Riedle signed for Liverpool.

The only times I saw Riedle play came in a couple of pre-season matches at Lansdowne Road in Dublin during the summer of 1998. Staged over a weekend, Liverpool faced local side St Patrick's Athletic and then my club, Leeds United. My main memory of Riedle from the tournament was when he scored with a shot from inside a congested penalty area during a 3-2 victory over the Irish team. A year later, eclipsed by the young Michael Owen, Riedle left Liverpool to wind down his career at Fulham.

Riedle now has his own soccer academy, and since 1996 has organised the Karl-Heinz Riedle Football Camp. Held in the Allgäu town of Oberstaufen, the camp offers boys and girls between the ages of six and 15 the chance to improve their football skills and technique under the guidance of professional trainers.

My last sighting of Riedle came in his role as an ambassador for UEFA at the 2024 Champions League Final at Wembley between Real Madrid and Borussia Dortmund. Just before kick-off, the famous trophy was brought into the stadium, with Riedle holding one of its big ears on behalf of his old club, while the other handle was firmly in the grasp of Real Madrid's representative, Zinedine Zidane.

Germany's fourth World Cup triumph came in 2014, defeating Argentina once again, this time in Brazil. Amazingly, that success meant that despite having a population of less than 18,000, Kolbermoor produced a second world champion, with Bastian Schweinsteiger having been born in the little town in 1984. Also appearing in the Rio final was Thomas Müller, born in 1989 in

Weilheim in Oberbayern, a town about halfway between Munich and the mountains. After playing as a child for local club TSV Pähl, Müller joined the youth system at FC Bayern and has stayed at the club ever since.

I have been fortunate enough to see Schweinsteiger and Müller play alongside each other for Bayern on several occasions, but the most important of these was undoubtedly the 2013 Champions League Final. About that game, Müller is quoted in Raphael Honigstein's book *Das Reboot* as saying, 'There, the pressure on us, on me and Bastian in particular, was inhuman. We had lost two Champions League finals already, we had never quite done it with Germany in the big competitions. We were playing against another German team at Wembley. If we had lost that game too, we would have been *kaputt*. Dead. It was brutal, horrible, playing that game.'

At Wembley, Schweinsteiger, nominally a midfielder, played very deep and apart from dead-ball situations hardly got on the ball. Müller, the busier of the two, spent most of the match deployed in the 'hole' behind the central striker. With just over quarter of an hour remaining and the score level at 1-1, Müller nearly restored Bayern's lead with a shot from a narrow angle, only for his attempt to be cleared off the line. Although Schweinsteiger played further forward in the second half, he had little more influence until three minutes from the end; Müller dummied the ball allowing Schweinsteiger to shoot on goal, but although his effort was on target, the keeper made a save. Just when it looked like the final would go to extra time, Arjen Robben grabbed the winner for Bayern in the last minute.

The year after Wembley, Schweinsteiger and Müller won their World Cup in Rio. Schweinsteiger then left Bayern, winding down his career at Manchester United and later in the USA. At the time of writing, Müller still plays for Bayern and during the 2021/22 season he wore the club's third kit inspired by the Alps. With glacial white and blue colours, the shirt displayed a panoramic mountain view. Müller enthused about the kit, telling ESPN, 'Being a born and bred Bavarian, I particularly like this look. I love the mountains, I love my home.'

Germany suffered elimination in the group stages at the World Cups of 2018 and 2022, so there have been no further world and European champions from the Bavarian Alps.

For the next champion from the foothills, we must go to the town of Cossato, in the province of Biella, part of the Italian region of Piedmont. In 1982, Cossato provided the birthplace for Alberto Gilardino. After playing for local teams, Gilardino joined Piacenza, Verona and then Parma, where his goalscoring exploits earned him a transfer to AC Milan and the award of Serie A Footballer of the Year in 2005.

Having made his international debut a couple of years earlier, Gilardino was selected for Italy's 2006 World Cup squad. At the tournament in Germany, Gilardino played in five of Italy's matches, scoring in a group game against the USA and providing an assist for the semi-final win against the hosts. However, he remained on the bench for the final when Italy defeated France in a penalty shoot-out following a 1-1 draw.

At the end of the next season, Gilardino won the 2007 Champions League with Milan, coming off the bench two minutes from the end of normal time in the final against Liverpool. Although Dirk Kuyt scored within a minute of Gilardino's arrival, the *Rossoneri* hung on to win 2-1.

The following year, Gilardino joined Fiorentina, and a few months later in February 2009 I had my only sighting of him in an international friendly between Italy and Brazil at the Emirates Stadium in London. Aged 26 at the time, Gilardino played in the first half as the sole out-and-out striker in a 4-1-4-1 formation, but he made little impact and became one of several Italians replaced at the interval. Brazil won the game 2-0, to the satisfaction of most of those sitting around me in the upper tier behind one of the goals.

After four years, Gilardino left Fiorentina and went on to play for several clubs, including a spell in China, before retiring in 2018 and moving into coaching.

The most recent champion from the foothills comes from the French Alps. Born in 1986 in Chambéry, about 50km/31 miles to the north of Grenoble, Olivier Giroud grew up in Froges, a small town a few miles outside the city. All his family came from the area, including a grandfather who milked cows high up on Alpine pastures to make cheese for selling in the family shop.

A keen skier from infancy, Giroud had to give up that winter sport when he became a professional footballer to avoid the risk of injury. After being spotted by scouts from Grenoble Foot 38 at the age of 12, Giroud played for the club's youth sides, eventually working his way up to the first team. Needing more match practice, Grenoble loaned Giroud to third-tier Istres FC by the Mediterranean in 2007. After returning to GF 38, Giroud signed for Tours FC, then in Ligue 2. In 2010, Giroud joined Montpellier, scoring 25 goals to help the club win its first and only Ligue 1 title in the 2011/12 season. Giroud then joined Arsenal where he won more silverware including three FA Cups, before getting a fourth after crossing London to sign for Chelsea.

My main memory of Giroud is from a Europa League match I attended during 2018/19, when he scored the opening two goals in Chelsea's 4-0 victory over Greek side PAOK; the first a beautifully curled shot, the second a smashed volley.

In the 2021 Champions League Final, Giroud was an unused substitute as Chelsea defeated Manchester City 1-0. Soon after that triumph, he moved to AC Milan, winning Serie A in his first season.

Giroud earned his first cap for France in 2011. At the 2018 World Cup in Russia, he failed to get on the scoresheet despite playing in all seven of his country's matches; however, that didn't prevent France defeating Croatia in the final 4-2. At the 2022 finals in Qatar, Giroud got four goals, becoming France's all-time top scorer after overtaking Thierry Henry. Unfortunately for France, Giroud didn't score in the final which his country eventually lost in a penalty shoot-out to Argentina after he had been substituted.

In the summer of 2024, Giroud retired from international football and joined Los Angeles FC (the same MLS outfit that has invested in Wacker Innsbruck). At the time of writing, Giroud is the only footballer born in the French Alps to have won both the World Cup and the Champions League.

Chapter 17

Football and Altitude

ON THE morning of 8 June 2007, the largest glacier in the Alps, the Grosser Aletschgletscher (Great Aletsch Glacier) on the border between the Swiss cantons of Bern and Valais, became the highest place to host a football game in Europe. At an altitude of 3,454m/11,332ft, the event organisers laid out a green artificial pitch on the snow and ice, large enough for seven-a-side teams. The record-breaking match was planned as a promotional event for the following year's UEFA Euro 2008 tournament, jointly hosted by Switzerland and Austria. About 200 people, many of them journalists, broadcasters or other media personnel, watched the spectacle. Cold temperatures and high altitude meant that the game consisted of two short halves, each lasting only five minutes. Surprisingly, all the outfield players bravely wore shirts and shorts without thermal leggings.

Transporting the pitch, goalposts, players and spectators up the glacier had been made possible by the location's proximity to Jungfraujoch, the highest railway station in the whole continent and billed as the 'Top of Europe'. Completed in 1912, the Jungfrau railway is an incredible engineering achievement. Using cog wheels, the train climbs up the mountain behind the notorious North Face of the Eiger, with the station at the top providing spectacular views of the glaciers below.

The temporary pitch was positioned on a patch of flat land near a path I had walked along a few years earlier when completing a 45-minute hike from Jungfraujoch to the Mönchsjochhütte, the highest staffed mountain hut in Switzerland. Hikers are usually advised to stay off glaciers, and sometimes this path through the snow is closed because of avalanches, crevasses or snowstorms. Although the route was considered safe at the start of my hike with sunny weather and clear views, snow then started to fall, reducing visibility to near zero. Being in a white-out is not an experience I want to repeat.

On 1 October 2024, another match took place on the Grosser Aletschgletscher at the same location. This time a couple of women's sides competed: Team Switzerland and Team European Ambassadors, with the latter representing footballing legends. The game had been organised as a publicity stunt to coincide with tickets going on sale for the UEFA Women's Euro 2025 football tournament. Switzerland hosted the finals at seven stadiums, three of which are within the Alpine region: Thun, Sion and Lucerne.

Widely reported as having been in the Bernese Oberland, according to my reckoning both Grosser Aletschgletscher games took place a few metres over the border in Valais. That same canton has also submitted another claim to have hosted the highest football match in Europe.

People arriving in the ski resort of Saas Fee are greeted with a stunning view of the Feegletscher (Fee Glacier). From Saas Fee, visitors can take two cable cars and the

Metro Alpin underground funicular railway to reach Mittelallalin near the top of the glacier. Most tourists come to Mittelallalin to dine in a revolving restaurant and take in the stunning mountain panorama from its viewing platform; however, on 12 March 2016, footballers came to the glacier station to play a match.

Two amateur eight-a-side teams, FC Gspon representing Switzerland and ASD Piedimulera flying the flag for Italy, participated in a promotional event for the Bergdorf-EM (European Mountain Village Championship), scheduled to be held a few months later in the French Alps. A crowd of about 100 people watched the match, held on a small pitch, marked off with net fencing and dubbed for the occasion as the 'Gletscher-Arena'. The contest consisted of two halves, each lasting 15 minutes. For the record, the Swiss team won the encounter 3-0.

Local magazine *Allalin News* reported that the game 'goes down in the annals as the highest football game in Europe. On the Mittelallalin at 3,500m.'

Such a height would indeed set a new record for the continent's highest football match. In 2023, I visited Mittelallalin and saw where the game had been played seven years earlier on a relatively flat area near the cable car station, under the summit cone of a mountain called the Allalinhorn; a photograph included in the central pages of this book shows the location. I thought it advisable to check the accuracy of the altitude of the 2016 game, because 3,500m sounds like an approximation rather than a precise figure.

My investigations concluded that the Mittelallalin game took place at 3,451m/11,322ft; consequently, the Grosser Aletschgletscher beats the Feegletscher by 3m/10ft, keeping its record intact. However, the narrow margin leaves an element of doubt, and the Mittelallalin event might also claim to have been more like a real match than the two events at Jungfraujoch.

While the highest match in Europe is a matter of dispute, there is no doubt about the highest goal.

In 2009, three years after his retirement, Zinedine Zidane successfully climbed Mont Blanc, the highest peak in the Alps, accompanied by a sports journalist and some mountain guides. On the summit at a height of 4,806m/15,766ft, Zidane simulated scoring, by kicking a football towards a small goal that his guides had temporarily erected. Fortunately, the former French international hit the back of the net, otherwise it could have been a long way down to retrieve the ball. The goal was a publicity stunt, filmed to raise awareness of leukodystrophies diseases.[13]

Another former footballer living the high life is the one-time Premier League striker Darius Henderson. Eleven years after I saw Henderson convert a penalty for Watford against Leeds in the 2006 Championship play-off final in Cardiff, he retired from the game. Henderson then took up mountaineering, emulating Zidane by summiting Mont Blanc. In 2024, Henderson went one better, becoming the first former professional footballer to climb Mount Everest, the highest mountain on Earth.

Zidane and Henderson were well aware of the influence of altitude when climbing mountains, leading on nicely to a look at some of the ways altitude impacts on football.

In recent times, sports science in football has developed into an industry, funded by the vast amount of money pouring into the game at 'elite level', with clubs, national teams, coaches and star players desperate to gain any

---

13 See tinyurl.com/Yodel09 for the full story.

edge over opponents. One of the consequences of all this is a greater understanding about the effect of altitude on sporting performance. In fact, so much has appeared on the subject in recent years that only some of the key findings can be mentioned here.

Lower air pressure at higher altitude means that air is thinner, with oxygen molecules spread further apart. For example, if we take the lowest football stadium to feature in this book (AS Monaco at 21m/69ft) about 20.9 per cent of the atmosphere there is oxygen; however, at the highest stadium in this book (FC Gspon at 1,923m/6,309ft) that proportion falls to about 16.4 per cent. Consequently, there is a smaller amount of oxygen in every breath you take at higher altitude, and those not acclimatised to the conditions can suffer from less oxygen in the blood which in turn leads to reduced fuel and energy for muscles, impeding physical performance.

If unacclimatised people can suffer altitude sickness, the minor symptoms of which include headaches, dizziness and nausea. Severe cases of altitude sickness can include oedemas with life-threatening build-ups of fluid in the lungs or brain. Severe symptoms rarely develop below 2,500m/8,200ft, so hardly impact on football in the Alps.

Following a game in 2007, when Brazilian footballers playing against a Bolivian team in the Andes had to use bottled oxygen because of thin air, FIFA introduced a ban on matches above 2,500m/8,200ft. With no permanent stadiums in Europe reaching that height, the ban only applied to South America, and following widespread international criticism it was withdrawn after a year.

Whereas the Bolivian footballers coped with the high altitude, those from Brazil did not, because, unlike the hosts, they were not acclimatised. For players, acclimatisation essentially involves staying at high-altitude training camps for a period before a tournament. The purpose of such camps is to give players time to adjust to the new environment, particularly by producing more red blood cells to enable sufficient levels of oxygen to reach muscles and other body tissues. To provide maximum encouragement to the production of red blood cells, training camps chosen for acclimatisation are usually located even higher than where the team will be playing its matches.

At the 2010 World Cup in South Africa, six of the venues were at over 1,200m/3,937ft. Before the tournament, Jiri Dvorak, FIFA's chief medical officer, told the BBC that such altitudes were 'not an issue which will significantly impact on the players' health or performance'. However, two countries, the Netherlands and Denmark, both later complained that their team's performance had suffered because of the higher altitude in South Africa. Belgian sports scientist George Nassis then claimed that although the conditions at that World Cup had only limited impact on players' technical skills, the altitude did impede their physical performance. Massis found that the total distance covered by participating teams was, on average, over three per cent lower when playing in stadiums above 1,200m/3,937ft compared to matches in the same tournament that took place near sea level.

Until fairly recently, acclimatisation was often thought to only be necessary before playing at heights similar to those in the Andes. However, after studying the World Cup in South Africa, Nassis wrote a paper entitled 'Effect of Altitude on Football Performance: Analysis of the 2010 FIFA World Cup Data', recommending that footballers should have several days of acclimatisation before playing at altitudes of over 1,200m/3,937ft, a lower starting level than previously recommended.[14] (This height would include games played at Gspon.)

Apart from impacting on footballers' physical performance, higher altitude can influence the game in other ways, particularly the movement of the ball when kicked, because lower air density reduces the aerodynamic drag on a football in flight. For approximately every 300m/984ft increase in altitude, air density reduces by about three per cent. Using the same examples, this means that the air density at Gspon is nearly a fifth less than in Monaco.

A 2010 study, 'Aerodynamics of FIFA World Cup footballs and effects of altitude', estimated that at altitudes of between 1,000m/3,281ft to 2,000m/6,562ft, the average speed of a football when kicked with a similar degree of force can be up to ten per cent faster than at a game near sea level. This means that the speed of a football kicked in Gspon could be ten per cent faster than one booted just as hard at Monaco's Stade Louis II.

As well as influencing the speed of the ball, reduced air resistance and drag at altitude also means that the ball tends to curve and bend less in flight, as well as travelling further after being kicked with the same force. If the player aims upwards, the ball may also lift more when kicked at higher altitude. Consequently, a footballer's technical skills need to be able to deal with all these variations, which can be particularly testing for goalkeepers.

It's not only sports scientists, coaches and players who are interested in this subject, but sports equipment manufacturers too. Designs of footballs, with different numbers and shapes of panels, can produce balls with a

---

14 Visit tinyurl.com/Yodel10 for the article.

variety of aerodynamic properties. Some footballs were designed with the World Cup in South Africa specifically in mind.

The most recent large-scale study of the effect of altitude was carried out by two researchers from Ghent University, Dr Nils van Damme and Professor Stijn Baert, who examined more than 2,000 matches between 2008 and 2016, all of which were fixtures in either the UEFA Champions League or Europa League. Dr van Damme and Professor Baert then published a paper in 2019 containing their findings.

After taking into account factors such as the comparative wealth and strength of clubs as well as the usual advantages of playing at home, Dr van Damme and Professor Baert concluded that teams regularly performing at higher altitude are more likely to win when competing at home against teams used to playing nearer to sea level, because the former are more familiar with lower oxygen levels. However, there is no discernible advantage when a high-altitude team travels to play on an opponent's pitch which is nearer to sea level. The academics argued that when the home team's stadium is at a higher altitude, every additional 100m/328ft in height increases the home side's probability of winning the match by 1.1 percentage points, and is worth on average a goal difference of 0.05 (or a 20th of a goal).

The academics identified general trends rather than suggest that the outcome of individual matches is predetermined by altitude. Although chapter 15 speculated that FC Siders may have faded in the veterans' tournament because they were unused to playing at the highest stadium in Europe, this book contains notable examples that defy such expectations. Playing home matches at a higher altitude certainly didn't give the players of FC Gspon any noticeable advantage when playing FC Inter Wiler; despite their pitch being 423m/1,388ft higher, they still lost 10-1! We should also remember Lamine Camara scoring with a shot from inside his own half, measured at an astonishing 58.37m from the opposing goal. The long flight of the ball cannot in this instance be attributed to reduced air density at high altitude, because the goal took place at Monaco's Stade Louis II, the lowest venue in this book and the stadium with the highest air density.

Chapter 18

Conclusion

ACCORDING TO some geological calculations, mountains in the Alps continue to increase in height by about one millimetre per year because of the movement of tectonic plates; this means that since the arrival of football in the region in the 1870s, the peaks have risen by around 15cm/6 inches. That has to be one of football's more unusual statistics, but it's far from being the only thing that has happened during the 150 years that have elapsed since the beautiful game came to the Alps.

The region has contributed a great deal to the sport, including several footballers born in the Alps who have won both the FIFA World Cup and the European Cup/ UEFA Champions League. My research has identified six such double champions, which is a remarkably high number given the relatively small population of the Alps. By comparison, England is represented only by Bobby Charlton and Nobby Stiles.

The biggest achievement of a club from the Alps came in 2004 when AS Monaco appeared in the final of the Champions League, although the greatest story is undoubtedly tiny FC Thun reaching the group stage of the same competition two seasons later. In more recent years, supporters of that team have provided a fascinating case study of friction between fans and the authorities in a small provincial town.

Assessing the strength of Alpine teams today has been helped by the introduction of one big league table to replace the old group stages in UEFA's Champions League, Europa League and Conference League. In the first season under the new system, three teams from the Alps participated: AS Monaco and Red Bull Salzburg in the Champions League, plus Swiss side FC Lugano in the Conference League.

After beating mighty FC Barcelona on matchday one of the Champions League, Monaco finished 17th in the league stage, entering the play-offs, where the Monégasques narrowly lost 4-3 to Benfica. Red Bull Salzburg lost seven of eight games to end third from bottom of the 36-team table and be eliminated. In the Conference League, FC Lugano achieved a creditable sixth place and qualified for the knockout stages.

Overall, the performances of the three teams have been mixed, but around the time of this book's publication, it will be possible to see one of these clubs on the world stage in the FIFA Club World Cup. At the time of writing, Red Bull Salzburg seems to be heading for a difficult time in the US; however, regardless of how the tournament goes, the Alps having a first club to appear in the Club World Cup is still a notable achievement.

Talking of FIFA, the Swiss canton of Valais provided the birthplaces of Sepp Blatter and Gianni Infantino, and whatever you think of these two presidents, their impact on world football has been considerable. Valais has also hosted the highest football matches ever played in Europe on the Aletsch Glacier and the Fee Glacier, while the same canton is home to the highest permanent football stadium in the continent at FC Gspon.

For some football teams in the Alps, mere survival is an achievement in itself, with five of the Alpine clubs mentioned in this book suffering severe financial problems at one time or another. Although the same could be said of football outside of 'elite level' in other parts of the world, including the UK, the mountainous terrain of the Alps presents particular difficulties. Swiss club FC Isérables building its 'impossible stadium' on a 31° slope, and SV Kleinwalsertal training youngsters in a valley totally cut off from the rest of Austria by mountains, are two notable examples of Alpine football rising to the challenge.

Visiting the clubs and stadiums that feature in this book has been a lot of fun, taking me to some beautiful locations and uncovering many memorable stories. I hope readers enjoy this account and feel encouraged to head to the mountains and see matches of their own. When it comes to football in the Alps, you can never peak too soon.

Appendix: List of Matches Involving Alpine Teams

1. 24 August 2002: FC Thun vs FC Basel, Nationalliga A, Stadion Lachen
2. 26 May 2004: AS Monaco vs FC Porto, UEFA Champions League Final, Arena AufSchalke
3. 14 September 2005: Arsenal vs FC Thun, UEFA Champions League, Highbury
4. 18 August 2007: FC Wacker Innsbruck vs LASK, Austrian Bundesliga, Tivoli-Neu Stadion
5. 14 August 2011: FC Thun vs FC Lausanne-Sport, Swiss Super League, Arena Thun
6. 21 August 2011: BSC Young Boys vs FC Thun, Swiss Super League, Stade de Suisse
7. 20 May 2012: 1. FC Garmisch-Partenkirchen vs SV Eberfing, Kreisliga 1 Zugspitze, Stadion am Groben
8. 25 August 2013: FC Bad Gastein vs UFC Radstadt, 1. Klasse Süd, Alpenstadion
9. 16 August 2014: VfB Admira Wacker vs Red Bull Salzburg, Austrian Bundesliga, BSFZ-Arena
10. 24 August 2014: FC Bad Gastein vs SK Taxenbach, 1. Klasse Süd, Alpenstadion
11. 1 September 2019: FC Südtirol vs Carpi FC, Serie C, Stadio Druso

12. 29 April 2023: Grenoble Foot 38 vs Chamois Niortais FC, Ligue 2, Stade des Alpes
13. 30 April 2023: FC Pays Voironnais vs ASL St Cassien, Départemental 1, Stade Plan Menu Est
14. 1 September 2023: FC Gspon vs FC Spycher, Bergdorfmeisterschaft Gruppe A, Ottmar Hitzfeld Gspon Arena
15. 2 September 2023: Fußball Veteranenturnier, Ottmar Hitzfeld Gspon Arena
16. 3 September 2023: FC Isérables vs FC Vionnaz 2, 5. Liga, Stade des Combes
17. 9 September 2023: ASD Virtus Villadossola vs ASD Agrana Sportivo, Prima Categoria Girone A, Stadio Silvestro Curotti
18. 10 September 2023: FC Gspon vs FC Inter Wiler, Bergdorfmeisterschaft Gruppe A, Ottmar Hitzfeld Gspon Arena
19. 22 October 2023: AS Monaco vs FC Metz, Ligue 1, Stade Louis II
20. 13 April 2024: FC BW Feldkirch vs SV Frastanz, Vorarlbergliga, Waldstadion
21. 14 April 2024: FC Triesen vs FC Ems, Meisterschaft Frauen 2. Liga Gruppe 1, Sportanlage Blumenau
22. 18 May 2024: NK Škofja Loka vs NK Šobec Lesce, 3. SNL, Nogometno Igrišče Puštal
23. 13 September 2024: SV Kleinwalsertal 1 (F-Junioren) vs FC Oberstdorf (F-Junioren), Walser-Arena
24. 20 September 2024: TSV Fischen 1 (E-Junioren) vs TV Hindelang 1 (E-Junioren), U11 (E-Jun.) OA/KE Gruppe 2, Weidachsportanlage
25. 23 November 2024: FC Red Bull Salzburg vs LASK, Austrian Bundesliga, Red Bull Arena

Bibliography

Books and journals:

Connolly, C., *Stamping Grounds: Exploring Liechtenstein and its World Cup Dream* (London: Abacus, 2005)

Corinti, A., *La Coppa delle Alpi* (Alfredo Corinti, 2015)

Cresswell, P., and Evans, S., *The Rough Guide to European Football* (London: Rough Guide, 2000)

D'Acampo, G., *Gino's Italian Express* (London: Hodder and Stoughton, 2019)

Giroud, O., *Always Believe* (Worthing: Pitch, 2021)

Greaves, P., *In the Bavarian Highlands: Edward Elgar's German Holidays in the 1890s* (Herts: Elgar Editions, 2000)

Hesse-Lichtenburger, U., *Tor! The Story of German Football* (London: WSC Books, 2002)

Honigstein, R., *Das Reboot: How German Football Reinvented Itself and Conquered the World* (London: Yellow Jersey Press, 2015)

Inglis, S., *The Football Grounds of Europe* (London: Collins Willow, 1990)

Koch, A., 'Spiel und Sport am Jesuitenkolleg Stella Matutina in Feldkirch', published in Schwank, W., (ed.), *Begegnung. Schriftenreihe zur Geschichte der Beziehung zwischen Christentum und Sport*, Volume 4 (Aachen, 2003)

Lee, C., *Origin Stories: The Pioneers Who Took Football to the World* (Worthing: Pitch, 2021)

Lijnders, P., *Intensity: Inside Liverpool FC* (Reach Sport, 2022)

Marruci, L., Daddi, T., and Iraldo, F., *Sustainable Football: Environmental Management in Practice* (Abingdon: Routledge, 2023)

Morris, D., *The Soccer Tribe* (London: Jonathan Cape, 1981)

Powell, Mrs R., *Edward Elgar: Memories of a Variation* (London: Oxford University Press, 1937)

Rhomberg, C., and Margreiter, S., *Vorarlberger Fußballgeschichte* (Hohenems: Vorarlberger Fußballverband, 2021)

Simonis, D., *Italy* (London: Lonely Planet, 2010)

Tejwani, K., *Wings of Change: How the World's Biggest Energy Drinks Manufacturer Made a Mark in Football* (Worthing: Pitch, 2020)

Van Damme, N. and Baert, S., 2019. *Home Advantage in European International Soccer: Which Dimension of Distance Matters?*, IZA Discussion Papers 12143, Institute of Labor Economics (IZA)

Newspapers and magazines:

Allalin News

Bild

Blick

Dolomiten

L'Équipe

The Independent

Match programme, Arsenal vs FC Thun, 14 September 2005

Match programme, FC Bad Gastein vs SK Taxenbach, 24 August 2014

Match programme, FC Südtirol vs Carpi FC, 1
September 2019
Nouvelliste et Feuille d'Avis du Valais
Der Standard
World Soccer

Websites and social media:
alicekropf.ch
alpconv.org
alpin.de
asmonaco.com
bbc.co.uk
bdm.ch
bernerzeitung.ch
borgenproject.org
bwfeldkirch-at
espn.co.uk
fcems.ch
fcgap.de
fcpaysvoironnais.fr
fcthun.ch
fctriesen.li
fc-wacker-innsbruck.at
footballinfrance.wordpress.com
fourfourtwo.com
france3-regions.francetvinfo.fr
hotel-obermuehle.de
ici-grenoble.org
jungfrauzeitung.ch
lafc.com
lfv.li
meinbezirk.at
nkskofjaloka.si

oefb.at
redbullsalzburg.at
researchgate.net
scotsman.com
skofjaloka.si
sportverein-kleinwalsertal.at
ssk-werfen.at
suedtirol.info
swissinfo.ch
tagblatt.ch
theguardian.com
thesun.co.uk
thun.ch
thunertagblatt.ch
uefa.com
wsc.co.uk

Radio, television and films:

Das Wunder von Bern (The Miracle of Bern), directed by
    Sönke Wortmann (Bavaria Film International, 2003)
Cold-Water Challenge FC Bad Gastein, 2014 YouTube
The Sound of Music, directed by Robert Wise (20th
    Century Fox, 1965)
Where Eagles Dare, directed by Brian Hutton (Metro-
    Goldwyn-Mayer, 1968)